Analyzing
Contemporary Social Issues
A Workbook with
Student CHIP Software
Second Edition

Gregg Lee Carter
Bryant College

Allyn and Bacon
Boston London Toronto Sydney Tokyo Singapore

ISBN 0-205-32102-X

Printed in the United States of America

10 9 8 7 6 5 4 3 2   03 02 01

CONTENTS

Analyzing Contemporary Social Issues

In recent years, those of us believing that an appreciation of how data and theory fit together is crucial to every sociology course—indeed, that it is part and parcel of thinking sociologically and thinking critically—have had much to celebrate. Sociology texts and anthologies have become rich in data, and many authors try hard to demonstrate the interplay between sociological insight and the relevant empirical observations. Part of this trend has been the appearance of workbooks and related materials that get students involved in the analysis of sociological data as early as their very first introductory sociology course. *Analyzing Contemporary Social Issues (2nd Edition)* is now an established part of the trend and includes these features:

First, it provides students with a primer for critiquing sociological writing. At first glance, this primer may seem biased toward quantitative thinking. A deeper look, however, reveals that it will carry students not only through quantitative arguments, but through qualitative ones as well; not only through sociology, but through any empirical discipline (from history to physics). In short, critical thinking is critical thinking. Its essentials are universal and are structured to assess proposed answers to the question "Why?" and to suggest alternatives. (Why does the world look the way it does and why do things unfold the way they do? Why do earthquakes happen? Why do people get cancer? Why are some people poor? To what extent do the proposed explanations seem plausible?)

Second, it provides a primer on elementary data analysis and its connection to the problem of establishing causality. As with the chapter on critical reading, students should read through the data analysis primer slowly and carefully, and they should do all of the exercises.

Third, it provides data of the highest quality—including, the National Opinion Research Center's best known data sets (the 1972–1998 General Social Surveys); U.S. and international census and vital statistics reports; FBI crime summaries; the National Center for Education Statistics' "High School and Beyond" study. The data are used in computer exercises organized around the major subfields of standard social-problems courses. Each set of exercises is introduced by a brief summary reviewing some major concerns of the particular subfield and, when appropriate, clarifying related concepts and terminology.

In sum, *Analyzing Contemporary Social Issues* contains dozens of computer exercises that allow students to use serious data to explore and test the insights of sociology. The exercises cover the major subfields of the sociological study of social problems (e.g., inequalities in gender and race) and can accompany most textbooks for the study of social problems, as well as those for courses on social stratification, race and ethnicity, and gender. They will hold special interest for empirically oriented instructors and students. The exercises will appeal to instructors trying to bridge the gap between what they do as researchers and what they teach in the classroom.

Important Features of the Second Edition

Many instructors and students who used the first edition of this workbook were generous in offering suggestions for its improvement. Among the suggestions that have been incorporated into the new edition are the following:

➢ The DOS version of Student CHIP has been replaced with the Windows version. The CD also contains the latest Mac version of CHIP.

➢ The DOS version of Student CHIP assumed that the values of the independent variable were placed on the rows. The Windows version frees the user from this assumption, and I have set up tables using the standard protocol of putting the independent variable on the columns. The logic of this protocol is explained in the introductory chapter *Elementary Data Analysis Needed to Study Social Issues*.

➢ The Windows version of Student CHIP comes with many more graphics options for displaying relationships. Because some students are better able to "see" the relationship between variables when the data are presented graphically, these options are put to good use, and the new edition has students examine relationships not only in tables but graphically too.

➢ Because minorities and other groups that do not represent large proportions of national survey samples are often too small to allow any significant conclusions when a single year of the General Social Survey is used (especially when "control" variables are introduced, e.g., African-American women with college educations); the new edition combines the two most recent General Social Surveys (1996 and 1998) to produce a very large initial sample size of over 5,700 respondents.

➢ The chapter on critical reading has been re-shaped from its original concern of trying to get students to read and think critically in general, to the more focused concern of trying to get students to read and think critically about contemporary social issues in particular.

➢ Because sociological analysis can sometimes seem quite abstract and distant from our everyday interactions (we tend to deal with people on a name basis rather than as "Case-IDs"), the new edition of this workbook maintains the practice used in the first edition of labeling all cases whenever aggregate levels are used; thus, students can locate particular nations on a particular plot line or see where the aggregate unit fits in a cross-tabulation (putting it in an exact cell, e.g., being able to put Sudan in the "low gnp" column and "low literacy" row to see its exact location in the table).

➢ Because the power of interactive data analysis is never fully realized if students are doing only those analyses they are told to do, the new edition of this workbook includes a set of *Exploratory* exercises that allow students to create their own hypotheses and their own interpretations (whether grounded in their readings, their professors' lectures, or their own intuitions). The exercises appear at the end of 5 of the 11 chapters and are organized around a 12-step protocol that begins by asking the student to state a hypothesis about the relationship between two variables; it then asks the student to choose and defend either (a) an antecedent variable that might reveal the original relationship to be spurious, or (b) an intervening variable that might act as a causal mechanism connecting their independent and dependent variables. Some instructors will recognize the protocol and its use of control variables as an outgrowth of the famous "elaboration model" developed at Columbia Uni-

versity during the 1950s. The model is so named because its goal is to elaborate on the relationship found between two variables; the elaboration process involves adding control variables (antecedent or intervening), with the ultimate aim of being able to accurately interpret why the X–Y relationship exists. It lays the groundwork for understanding causal analysis in the social sciences. Students who become adept with the elaboration model will have the foundation they need to understand much more sophisticated statistical approaches such as multiple regression and structural equation models. However, even if the student never takes another social science course, learning the elaboration model will provide him or her a valuable set of intellectual tools for dealing with the world critically.

➢ To give students even further leeway in doing exploratory analyses, the CHIP data sets from the first edition of the workbook have been included in the subdirectory (folder) labeled *History*. Instructors wanting to assign individual work now have more options in assuring that individual projects are just that.

➢ Because the most important part of the exercises in *Analyzing Contemporary Social Issues* is the "white space" where students give their interpretations of the particular tables and plots at hand, I have provided several examples of how this should be done in the first chapter ("The Sociological Study of Contemporary Social Issues and Problems").* I have also included a basic "footer" to each table that includes a "prediction" for what the student expects to find and a "finding" to allow the student to state what was actually found. Over the years, I have discovered that when students prepare such a footer the quality of their answers improves significantly.

➢ Relatedly, to improve the "white-space" performance of students, I have added a new section on "The Art of Reading Partial Tables" at the end of the introductory chapter entitled

---

* **Note to the Instructor:** The chapters in this workbook may be used in any order; however, because Chapter 1 provides students with several concrete examples of how they should write up their findings, it is highly recommended that it be assigned before any others.

Elementary Data Analysis Tools Needed to Study Social Issues. Many of the advanced exercises in this workbook require that students be able to recognize what has happened to the original relationship after the introduction of a control variable; for example, did the relationship maintain itself? is a multivariable model evident? is there an obvious interaction effect? All discussion is kept at an intuitive level and no statistics beyond simple percentages are used; in short, the emphasis is on analysis, reasoning, and the ability to recognize patterns in one's findings—and not on high-level statistical analysis techniques.

➢ Many professors want their students to have more in-depth reading on the particular topic at hand than is offered in the introductory comments to each chapter of this workbook; to this end, the new edition has been closely coupled to *Perspectives on Current Social Problems*, (Boston: Allyn & Bacon, 1997), an edited anthology that provides this in-depth reading. Each chapter ends with a brief section entitled "Suggestions for Further Study," which contains recommended readings from this anthology, as well as relevant websites.

➢ To broaden its scope and to increase its relevancy, new chapters have been added to the workbook on education ("Chapter 10: Education Issues") and on the environment ("Chapter 11: Environmental Issues").

➢ Finally, *Analyzing Contemporary Social Issues* has its own World Wide Web address. You may visit it to obtain updates of CHIP data sets—for example, those developed from the 2000 General Social Survey. A special note to instructors: if you do not find the update that you are looking for, I will custom prepare it for you, or, for that matter, any other CHIP data file you might need (say, for example, you would like to combine selected variables from two files, because neither contains the right combination of variables you desire):

http://www.abacon.com/carter

Acknowledgments

Although many individuals—all of whom I am grateful to—provided suggestions for this new edition, the following were particularly helpful and deserve special thanks: Louis Anderson (Kankakee Community College), Diane Balduzy (Massachusetts College of Liberal Arts), Sharlene Hesse-Biber (Boston College), Charles Jones (University of Toronto), Margot Kempers and her Urban Sociology students (Fitchburg State College), Cornelius Riordan (Providence College) and Ellen Rosengarten (Sinclair Community College). I would also like to thank Bryant College librarians Colleen Anderson, Gretchen McLaughlin, and Paul Roske for their help in tracking down reference materials. My assistants, Michael Vieira and Elaine Lavallee, performed many valuable services in preparing my pre-publication manuscript. Ruth Bogart of Zeta Data (the producer of Student CHIP) is an excellent programmer and always open to new ways of improving her software. Finally, I appreciate the encouragement and advice of my editors at Allyn and Bacon, Karen Hanson and Sarah Kelbaugh.

I welcome your comments and suggestions on any aspect of *Analyzing Contemporary Social Issues*:

Gregg Lee Carter
Social Science Department
Bryant College
Smithfield, RI 02917-1284

gcarter@bryant.edu
http://www.bryant.edu/~gcarter

About Student CHIP

The following passages give a detailed description of Student CHIP. However, the program is easy to use, and in the early-going instructors and students need probably do no more than skim over these details before getting to the meat of CHIP—that is, doing crosstabulations.

Although CHIP calculates chi square and significance tests on *percentage differences* in crosstabs (sigma), most instructors can safely avoid any but the most cursory discussions of statistical significance (see my discussion in **Elementary Data Analysis Needed to Study Social Issues** later in this workbook). For data sets using the General Social Survey, the number of cases is very large and percentage differences of 9 or 10 are well above conventional standards for statistical significance (the ".05" level). For data sets using fewer cases, we would generally want percentage differences to be larger than 10 before getting too enthusiastic about the substantive or statistical significance of the relationship. Those professors wanting a formal statistical test of significance can have their students use CHIP's chi square option.

Student CHIP is a microcomputer program for the statistical analysis of contingency tables (crosstabulations). While it is designed for use by novices in social science data analysis, Student CHIP includes some advanced statistical features, such as direct standardization, which are of interest to advanced users.

Requirements and Installation

Windows: Double-click on the folder labeled CHIPWin. This folder includes the files needed to install Student CHIP on a computer running Windows 95 or 98 or Windows NT.

Double-click on the file labeled *Setup*, which will begin the installation program that places the necessary files on your computer's hard drive. During the installation procedure, you may select the directory into which the CHIP files are copied. By default, the files will be installed into a folder called *StudentCHIP*.

After installation is complete, the Windows *Start* menu will include the Student CHIP application. Choose Start→Programs→StudentCHIP to begin the program. If you prefer, you can start the application by double-clicking on the CHIP icon (a picture of a table) in the folder in which you installed Student CHIP.

Macintosh: This version can be installed on any Mac with MacOS 6.0 or higher. Drag the folder labeled *CHIPMac* onto your hard drive. Open that folder and double-click on the CHIP icon (a picture of a table) to launch the program. If you prefer, you can run the application directly from the CDROM. To do so, first open the *CHIPMac* folder, then double-click on the CHIP icon.

Using Student CHIP for Windows

File Menu

You will begin all CHIP sessions by clicking on **File**. From this menu, you can work directly with data files on your disk. Student CHIP can read two types of files: CHIP-format files, with data stored as cell frequencies, and raw data files in ASCII format. When you open an existing file, Student CHIP will determine which of the two file types you are using.

The **File** menu offers the following options that you will use in this workbook (see the "Instructions" file on your CD for details on other commands not used here, e.g., on how to "Read Raw Data Files"):

> **Open** lets you retrieve a saved file from the disk. Student CHIP will display a list of files available in your current directory. Simply move the highlighting bar to the file name of your choice, and choose OK or press <Enter>. Follow Windows conventions for changing the directory.

> After you have opened a data file, Student CHIP will display the descriptive title of the data set and the number of cases.

> **Print** provides a screen dump of your current

screen.

Start log prompts you for the name of a file in which you can save your session. You can print out this log at a later time, you clip and paste from it to bring tables into your word-processing documents.

End log turns off logging.

Exit exits from Student CHIP and returns you to the desktop.

Edit Menu

The **Edit** menu offers the standard Cut, Copy, and Paste operations. When you have a table displayed on the screen, you can highlight its contents, copy that material to the clipboard, and paste it into another document, such as an Excel spreadsheet or a word processing document.

Command Menu

The **Command** menu offers the following options:

Info prints the names of the variables, the number of categories in each variable (e.g., *Sex* will have two categories), the current "causal order," and the data description (if one is provided).

Marginals gives you the percentage distributions for all of the variables in the data set.

CrossTab creates a crosstabulation of two variables. CrossTab is the workhorse for data analysis once you have entered or retrieved a data set and have modified it to your satisfaction.

First, consider the bivariate case (when you have only two variables) with no control variables. As a hypothetical example, you might be looking at the relationship between *Region* and *Religion*.

After you choose **Crosstab**, Student CHIP asks you to choose your two variables. Do this by selecting the first variable, then the second, from the list boxes that appear. You must decide which variable goes in the rows and, which in the columns. Generally, you will want your independent variable to ap-

pear in the columns and your dependent variable in the rows. Therefore, choose the dependent variable first, so it will in the rows, and the independent variable second, so that it will appear in the columns.

Table Menu: CrossTab Options

After you have chosen the variables, the options in the **Table** menu will be available:

Frequency prints a crosstabulation in terms of frequencies—that is, the number of cases in the categories and cells.

Percent Across displays tables based on percentages across of the total or subtable.

Percent Down displays tables based on percentages down of the total or subtable.

Percent Diff calculates percentage differences. That is, it compares column categories in terms of their percentages for categories of the row variable. Or, if you change the default **Preference** noted above, you can use row variables instead of column variables (remember, choose "Base on percent across" in the Percent Diff Options box of the Preferences option.) Thus, for *Region* and *Partyid* you could compare regions to see whether they differ in the percentages Democratic, Independent, and Republican. Student CHIP is flexible here. It asks you for the categories in your "+" group and your "−" group. To assign a variable to a positive or negative group, click on the variable name, then click on the button labeled "Positive" or "Negative." You can put as many or as few categories in each group as you wish. For example, with four regions, you could compare:

(*south*) v. (*northeast* + *west* + *central*)

or   (*south*) v. (*west*)

or   (*west*) v. (*south*)

or   (*west* + *northeast*) v. (*south* + *central*)

or   (*west* + *northeast*) v. (*central*)

etc.

Percent Diff also prints *d/sigma d* for statistical inference. The program calculates the value of one standard error for *d* and divides *d* by one *sigma*. If *d/sigma d* has absolute value larger than 1.96, the difference is statistically significant at the .05 level and the difference will be highlighted. To find *sigma d*, divide *d* by *d/sigma d*.

Control enables you to perform multivariable analyses.

Beyond two, CHIP views additional variables as conditions or special cases of the relationship defined at the beginning of **Crosstab**. Thus, if you have a table with *Race, Sex, Region, Education,* and *Income,* and you choose *Income* and *Region* as your row and column variables, Student CHIP thinks of *Race, Sex,* and *Education* as defining subgroups in which the relationship can turn up. That is, it will let you look at the *Income/Region* relationship among black males with high education, among black males with low education, black females with high education, and so on. Of course, you may change at any time your bivariable pair by choosing **Crosstab** from the **Command** menu.

After you choose **Control**, Student CHIP will ask you to select among the available control variables. You can highlight more than one variable at a time. Highlight the variables you want to use as controls, then click the *Select* button. Then you can choose among *Frequency, Percent,* or *Plot*. CHIP will present you with all possible control conditions (combinations of categories of your control variables) one at a time. You can decide whether you want to have any given subgroup displayed or whether you want to choose another option. Your control variable(s) will be in effect until you choose the option **Release control** to return to the bivariate case.

Plot lets you plot a graph of percentages. You can choose the style of your graph: line, bar, stacked bar, or pie. Each graph has two buttons at the bottom: **Print** and **Copy**. Press the **Print** button to send your graph to an attached printer, and **Copy** to copy it to the clipboard. You can then paste the graph into a text document or spreadsheet.

Preferences lets you choose whether a graph is based on percentages across or percentages down. Percent Down is the default. If you

prefer to see a graph based on percentages across, choose the Plot Preferences option, then click the button labeled "Base graph on PctAcross" on the form that appears. To see percent differences computed on the basis of percent across, click the radio button "Base on percent across" in the Percent Diff Options box. You can also use the Preferences form to choose whether you prefer to display all categories of the dependent variable in a line graph, or just one selected category. Please note that *Doing Sociology with Student CHIP* requires no changes of the default preferences.

Chi-square calculates the Pearson chi-square statistic and gives its level of statistical significance. This option also calculates the sample size needed to attain a .05 level of significance.

Modify Menu

The **Modify** menu offers the following options:

Combine allows you to put into a single, pooled group two or more categories. For example, if you have *republicans, democrats,* and *independents,* you might combine *republicans* and *democrats* and call them *partisans,* so your variable *Partyid* would now include the two categories *independents* and *partisans.*

Omit allows you to delete a category from a variable. From then on, that category does not exist as far as Student CHIP is concerned. For example, with *republicans, independents,* and *democrats,* you might omit *independents* and limit your analysis to differences between partisans of the two major parties.

The options of the **Modify** menu affect only the working data set; they do not automatically change any of the files on your disk. To make changes permanent, use the **Save As** option from the **File** menu.

Help Menu

Choose **Help Contents** from the **Help** menu for a list of topics for which help is available. You can also press the **F1** key for help on a specific data entry form or input selection box. Clicking on **File**, then **Exit**, returns you to the main menu.

The Macintosh Version of Student CHIP

Most of the commands noted above also apply to the Mac version of the program. Key differences include: (a) only "line plot" is available for **Plot** options; (b) there are no **Preferences**, which means that you cannot change your X/Y locations to allow for row independent variables; this also means that if you put the independent variable on the row that you cannot use **Percent Diff** or do **Plots** for the exercises in this workbook. However, the standard social science convention of putting the values of the independent variable on the columns is used here, and you will not encounter any problems as long as you do the exercises as they are designed (that is, always using the line plot; and always putting the values of the independent variable along the columns). If you are using the Mac version of this program, please consult the *Instruct* file for further information.

Reading and Thinking Critically About Contemporary Social Issues[*]

This workbook, in general, and this essay, in particular, are designed to assist students in becoming informed citizens by teaching them to become critical thinkers. Students need to become critical consumers of the arguments that social scientists and journalists construct concerning vital issues of the day. Ability to participate in informed discussion and to support appropriate action is dependent on the ability to critically read the many written accounts—editorials, essays, news accounts, polling data, even scholarly articles—that describe and explain the social problems we face. This workbook and this essay will offer you the opportunity to become more informed about some of those issues, but still more importantly, to become better able to inform yourself about those issues which matter to you at any time in the future.

The student of social problems faces three barriers to complete understanding. The first is the impossibility of even being able to list everything that anyone has ever regarded as a social problem. The list is endless. As a consequence, each of us can only master some small portion of the whole. The second barrier prevents our complete mastery of even that small part. This barrier arises from the fact that every social problem is subject to examination by a multitude of experts and interested parties. Each field of expertise or interest group conveys its own distinctive account. None of us can hope to comprehend them all. Nor if we could, would we be likely to find a way to reconcile their variety into a meaningful whole. Beyond the difficulty of differing expertise arises a third barrier. People bring to their study of social problems highly diverse values, assumptions, and beliefs. In part this diversity arises from differences in their social positions. Study of many continuing social problems has revealed a frequent pattern. A problem that is not readily resolved generally provides some benefit to some

portion of the population even as it imposes hardships on other portions. Those seeking reform to reduce or eliminate the hardships they perceive are often at odds with others seeking to protect the benefits they fear would be sacrificed to reform. Because of their divergent value commitments (usually reflecting differences in self-interest), people differ dramatically in their notions as to what constitutes a problem. At its most extreme, and this is not all that uncommon, what one person sees as a problem is viewed by another as the solution.

The combined effects of these three barriers to understanding—too many problems to comprehend, too many expert opinions to analyze, and too many conflicting values and interests to reconcile—make a comprehensive and definitive treatment of social problems impossible. The alternative, which this workbook employs, is to develop a critical method of analysis that can be applied to various social problems. This chapter provides a basic framework that can be applied to all readings on contemporary social issues and problems.

The Societal Context of Social Problems

We should begin with a sense of what is essential to sociological understandings of social problems. Of primary importance is the societal context. Although there is no universally accepted definition of this term, it may be said to involve the following aspects. First, the empirical reality of the problem, the objective facts. Second, the social reality of the problem, what people perceive to be true. Third, the issue of negative evaluation: the facts, or the perception, must be judged to be harmful. Finally, the harm must be viewed as capable of being rectified through some collective action. To call something a social problem is to say that it need not be endured. Something could be done to make the situation better.

[*]Adapted from Louis E. Anderson and Gregg Lee Carter, "An Introduction to Reading and Thinking Critically About Social Problems," pp. 3–13 in Gregg Lee Carter (ed), *Perspectives on Current Social Problems* (Boston: Allyn & Bacon, 1997).

To a significant extent social problems are socially constructed. Our grasp of the empirical facts may be more or less personal, though it is hard to imagine that it could ever be entirely so. But the perception of what is true is continually subjected to the attempts of interested parties to manipulate the information we receive, or to establish the framework within which we will interpret it. These efforts overlap with those directed at reinforcing or creating the moral standards that we will apply in judging the degree of harm being done by what we perceive to be happening. And clearly, we must find others who agree if we are to pursue collective strategies for change. The fact that social scientists and journalists have begun to write about undesirable conditions that they believe can be improved is a strong indication that these conditions have become a social problem. No one sequence determines the recognition of a social problem, but in some way a sizable number of people must become convinced of the need for action. People become interested in social problems for a variety of reasons. Some have been victims or have had to deal with the victimization of a loved one in what they regard as an avoidable tragedy and want to do something to prevent its repetition. Some are drawn by their religious commitments to oppose behavior inconsistent with their beliefs. Some people seek public support for policies that protect their own special interests. Journalists and social scientists have a professional interest in informing others about any matter of social consequence that their research uncovers. The voices of many concerned people in support of their causes provide the societal context for the study of social problems.

Once identified, problems will not lie quietly and unchanging so that we can study them. Instead they remain a part of the ever-changing social scene. Many times their objective facts alter before we can fully confirm their existence. The weight of public opinion shifts, becoming more strongly in favor or against them. Our society's previous unsuccessful efforts to respond to social problems alters our willingness and ability to gather support for stronger responses or to reverse direction, because of the negative consequences of our attempted solutions. Sometimes a problem just seems to disappear from view, even though no objective improvement has occurred. It appears as though the public has simply tired of hearing about it, or journalists have found nothing new to say about it, or politicians have been so unsuccessful in claiming that they have an effective policy that the problem slides down below the level of conscious consideration for a time.

Other problems seem to be always with us: never solved and yet never something we can just ignore. Whatever the history of any one problem, it must struggle for acknowledgment against the din raised by all its competitors for our attention. Little wonder that proponents for any cause are tempted to overstate its seriousness or the magnitude of the harm involved. Little wonder too that critics are quickly found to contradict supporters' claims. The social problems arena seems often to resemble CNN's *Cross Fire* in the amount of energy devoted to shouting down any view other than one's own.

If individual citizens are to gain improved understanding of the controversies that swirl around such debates, they need some framework to organize their study. They need the means to transcend their own personal circumstances. At the same time, they need to be able to comprehend how the larger social context impinges upon their own lives.

The notion that our encounter with social problems exists at two levels of social reality has a long history. In *The Sociological Imagination*, C. Wright Mills offered us the labels "private troubles" and "public issues" to capture the difference and to acknowledge the connections between our personal experiences of misfortune and the social circumstances of the unfortunate. We can partially illustrate his conceptualization by considering two accounts of educational failure. One account tells of a student who is not quite bright enough and who does not work quite hard enough to complete his studies. His status as a "dropout" seems to be a story of personal failure. The second account focuses on the ever higher percentage of American students achieving high school graduation, and the ever higher grade point averages they have received while obtaining those diplomas. It juxtaposes these facts with international comparisons of student knowledge and skills that show American students to lag far behind equivalent students from other countries. In this account, the personal success or failure of an individual student appears a less crucial issue than the question of whether the educational system itself is performing adequately.

As you study any essay or book on a contemporary social issue or problem, you will need to recognize where the author has located the problem. Is it at the micro level of interpersonal relations? Or is it at the macro level of institutional arrangements? Does the account acknowledge any connection between the two?

Sociologists are inclined to believe that the best accounts effectively contextualize the personal/micro level by explaining their societal/macro location. Accordingly, they would prefer that the first story expand to consider how social location affects the likelihood that one becomes a "dropout." They would like to know whether dropouts are more common now or in the past, in urban schools or rural ones, among males or females, among wealthy students or poor ones. In the answers to these and similar inquiries, we gain a sense of whether the individual has beaten the odds or succumbed to them. The second account, which suggests the existence of system failure, may need to expand its consideration to include what the American high school graduates have been able to do with their less demanding diplomas. Have their job prospects diminished? Are their lives more circumscribed? In the answer to these and similar questions we would seek to assess the personal impact of these societal differences.

A Critical Reasoning Framework

The next step in our efforts to understand social problems is to have some framework for recognizing how authors go about presenting them to us. What follows is a much condensed account of a thinking frame that has proven very useful for this purpose. Its creator, Paul J. Baker, has shared it with colleagues for many years. The diagram in Box 1 summarizes the elements that we view as making up a complete social problem argument. Most social problems statements take the form of

a logical argument as they attempt to convince the reader of the author's position regarding the issue at hand.

Complete social problems arguments will include all five of the elements identified in this Box. This is not to say that all five will be equally fully developed. Nor does it mean that all statements about social problems consist of complete arguments. But we can assess whether any specific argument provides an adequate logical and empirical basis for its conclusion by examining these five elements and their logical consistency.

The beginning of any social problems argument consists in advancing a definition of the problem. To the extent that the definition employs widely shared standards and common understandings its ability to be convincing is enhanced. To the extent that it attempts to advance a specialized or partisan definition, it may limit its acceptance.

The most central role of evidence may be to show that some problem does exist and to document its extent and patterns of change. But evidence is also employed to show that the problem behaves in ways consistent with the author's causal argument. Whether evidence is drawn from personal experience or secondary sources, whether it is reasonably objective or obviously partisan, whether it is carefully documented or unverifiable all influence our judgment of its adequacy.

Causal statements establish who or what, in the author's view, is the source of the problem. Sometimes they only tell us who to blame. They are more useful when they establish what features of our social life have led to our current difficulties. Accurate knowledge of causes may suggest the changes that will most effectively move us toward solutions.

The value assumptions or the special interests of the author may be vague or may be clear, but in any case it is important to detect them. They are likely to color all of the other elements, so our knowledge of them can be crucial to rightly understanding what we read.

These four elements we identify as the argument's premises. In complete arguments the conclusion is logically derived from those premises. In the case of a social problems argument that conclusion is a statement of how the social problem might be solved or why a solution is unattainable. Adequate social problems arguments provide a logically connected set of premises which lead us to accept the plausibility of their statement of solution or non-solution.

A solution statement often consists of a public policy recommendation. The author claims that we should implement or revise or eliminate some public policy as the solution to our current problem. In evaluating any such solution statement, it is appropriate to ask these three questions: Is it practical? Would it be effective? Is it right? Good public policy probably requires that we can answer all three questions affirmatively. Different arguments may give greater weight to some of these considerations than others.

Some arguments focus almost exclusively on the moral issues involved. They may even ignore questions of practicality and efficacy as matters that must ultimately yield to the power of righteousness. They would rather be right than successful because they believe that there is no success except through doing what is right. As a result, logic and evidence play subordinate roles.

Other arguments are most concerned to develop answers that everyone involved can agree to and that will therefore actually be implemented. This concern for what is practical may compromise issues of efficacy and morality, though the participation of people with strong convictions or conflicting interests may be among the important factors determining what is practical at any given time.

Those arguments which place efficacy before morality and practicality are particularly likely to appear among social scientific accounts. While they are faultlessly logical and their evidence is scrupulously documented and appropriate, they run the risk of appearing unwilling to confront the principled opposition of the moralists, and unaware of the practical obstacles which stand in the way of implementing even the best ideas.

Data-oriented scholarly and journalistic articles on particular social problems do not always address all the elements in Box 1. An empirical approach may fit into the framework for the analysis of social problems arguments in any of several ways.

An empirical statement may concentrate on showing that social conditions have changed in ways that justify defining the existing situation as a social problem. Less commonly it may show that what once was a problem has now disappeared. Thus the primary focus of the account is on issues of definition.

Other empirical statements may emphasize evidence demonstrating that changes in the argument's proposed causal factors do, indeed, produce the predicted effects on the social problem. The primary goal of such accounts is to establish that the evidence is consistent with the author's claims as to why the problem has become worse. Such statements are largely elaborating on the second element of our model. They are statements of cause and effect. These are the most frequent types of accounts in this workbook. Moreover, the exercises are organized to encourage you to think in terms of cause and effect statements, and to assess the degree to which our best available data are in harmony with such statements.

An empirical statement may address the element of evidence. Some writings on social problems are primarily concerned with how we may most accurately measure the existence or severity of the problem. For example, how do we get an accurate grasp of the extent to which there is homelessness (or drug addiction or alcoholism—and so on).

Still other empirical statements may differentiate the characteristics of those who hold distinctive value positions regarding a given social problem. Writings based on public opinion surveys often take this track, showing—for example—how one's location in society influences one's attitude toward abortion (e.g., young, single women look upon the issue differently than older, married women). This approach is used often in *Analyzing Contemporary Social Issues* because much of our best data comes from opinion surveys such as the General Social Survey (described in the next chapter "Elementary Data Analysis Tools Needed to Study Social Issues").

Finally, empirical statements may address the evidence regarding the effectiveness of proposed solutions. Such statements may not be identical to those seeking to explain the causes of the problem. Their dependent variable is still changes in the problem, but they are less concerned with what brought the problem into existence than with what can alter conditions for the better. Research on the effects of capital punishment illustrate this type.

This summary should remind you that an empirical account is not necessarily a complete argument, but neither is it limited to providing only one element of such arguments. Creative social scientists and journalists make use of empirical accounts to advance our understanding of social problems in all of the ways we have discussed.

Box 1. A Critical Reasoning Framework Designed for the Analysis of Social-Problems Arguments

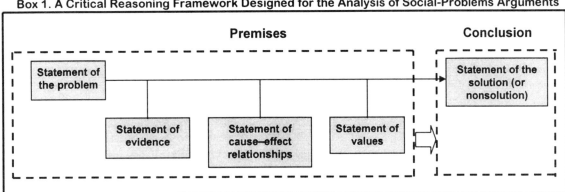

A Primer on Critical Reading

The balance of this article sets forth the intellectual steps for critiquing writing based on research. Together these steps form a foundation for reading and thinking critically; they have nearly universal applicability. You can use them not only in sociology, but in all courses that have empirical content (virtually all the natural, social, and business sciences), whether or not the subject matter is quantitative. Moreover, once incorporated into your thinking, these steps can help you critique studies reported in the popular media and the arguments presented to you in everyday discourse.

The fundamental strategy for explanation in all empirical disciplines, including sociology, is the following: *To explain is to account for change in one phenomenon (variable, thing) with changes in another phenomenon or set of phenomena (variables, things)*. If you reflect for a moment, it should become apparent that this strategy is also fundamental in everyday explanations of life's events. For example, why are you sad at some times and happy at others? Most likely, your mood changes in reaction to changes in the events, people, and situations in which you are involved. For example, it would not be unexpected that you would be unhappy if after practicing all week for the big dance contest on Saturday night you couldn't participate because you got a nasty blister on the bottom of your foot on Friday. In sum, changes in your physical well-being (the blister) created changes in your plans (dropping out of the dance contest) which, in turn, changed your mood (from excited anticipation to unhappiness). When one thing is explained by another, we say that the first is *dependent* on the second. The second is *independent*. Accordingly, your blister would be an *independent variable* that explained your dropping out of the dance contest (a *dependent variable*). Whether a variable is independent or dependent hinges upon the slice of reality under investigation. Thus, as we continue along the pathway of causation, dropping out of the contest becomes the independent variable that explained the change in your mood.

Because the world is complex, we can quickly begin discussing many variables simultaneously.

As such, it is often helpful to diagram the causal connections among variables. In its simplest form, such a diagram reads from left to right, with arrows imparting the causal order. For example, we would diagram the variables at hand as follows:

Blister→Dropping out of Contest→Unhappiness

Social scientists use the term *model* to describe an interrelated set of variables that represent a slice of reality.

The most important models are those which are *explanatory* (recall that *to explain* is to account for change in one variable with changes in another variable or set of variables). Much of the research in sociology, as in all the sciences, is organized around developing and testing explanatory models. However, even when this is not a primary aim, virtually all nonfiction writing is organized around some sort of model of the world and how it operates. As a critical reader, you must develop the ability to discern the model at hand.

The first step in critiquing an article or argument is thus to identify the model. This involves identifying the dependent and independent variables and ascertaining the relationship between them. Let us illustrate using the following newspaper article:

Poverty More Than Race Increases Risk of Cancer, Panel Concludes

Bethesda, MD (AP). A federal advisory panel yesterday focused new attention on poverty—far more than race—as one of the most powerful and under-estimated risk factors for cancer in America.

Both inadequate access to health care and unhealthy habits among the poor contribute to the problem, the President's Cancer Panel was told. "Poor people are more focused on day-to-day survival—and I'm afraid that health care more often takes a back seat," Health and Human Services Secretary Louis Sullivan told the panel.

Added Dr. Samuel Broder, director of the National Cancer Institute: "It is difficult for an individual to say, 'I'll go for a mammogram today' when you are worried about how to pay for dinner."

He linked the higher cancer rates for poor people to what he called "poverty-driven lifestyles" that may include unhealthy diets, greater use of alcohol and tobacco, occupational risks, and less access to medical care.

People living below the federal poverty level have a death rate from cancer that is twice as high as that for the rest of the population. Black men, who out-number whites in poverty three-to-one, have a 25 percent higher risk of contracting cancer.

Dr. Harold Freeman, a surgeon at Harlem Hospital in New York and the first black person to lead the panel, said, "Race in itself is not the cause of death. It is a circumstance in which people live, basically defined by poverty."

(*Providence Journal*, July 10, 1991, p. 4)

Step 1: What Is the Model?

In identifying the model, you must first determine the key dependent variable(s). A **dependent variable** is the phenomenon or event that the researcher or author is trying to explain. It's what is being caused. When sociologists think about individuals (as opposed to a collection of persons, such as a group or the residents of a city), the most important dependent variables they seek to explain involve behaviors and attitudes. (Why do some people drink heavily, while others abstain totally? Why do some whites hate blacks, while other whites are indifferent to skin color?) In the newspaper article quoted above, the key dependent variable is *cancer* (or the odds of dying from cancer).

Next, you must identify the key independent variable(s). An **independent variable** is the thing that explains, in part, the dependent variable. It is a reason for, or a cause of, the dependent variable. When trying to explain individual behaviors and attitudes, sociologists are drawn strongly to independent variables that indicate the groups and social networks to which people belong. In the article above, the key independent variable is *poverty* (purportedly much more important than *race*, which once was considered another key determinant of cancer risk). If race is linked with poverty, we would characterize race as **an antecedent variable**. That is, we would regard race as a variable that precedes poverty in time and that affects the odds of being poor. Poverty is linked to cancer via the **intervening variables** (variables that are simultaneously independent and dependent) of *unhealthy diets, use of alcohol and tobacco, occupational risks,* and *access to medical care.* In sum, poverty partly determines this latter set of variables, which, in turn, partly determine the odds of dying from cancer.

Next, you must be able to recognize the **form of the relationship** between the independent and the dependent variables. The easiest functional forms to conceptualize and to identify are the straight-line or *linear.* If two variables are linearly related and that relationship is *positive,* then increases in one are associated with increases in the other. If two variables are linearly related and the direction of the relationship is *negative,* then increases in one are associated with decreases in the other. In the above article, poverty is positively associated with unhealthy diets, the use of alcohol and tobacco, and occupational risks, whereas it is negatively related to access to medical care.

Especially when our subject of empirical inquiry is people and their behavior, thoughts, and feelings, explanation (i.e., accounting for variation in a dependent variable with variation in one or more independent variables) is not the same thing as **understanding.** Understanding is deeper; it is that "Aha, I see" experience within us. As a critical reader, you must understand why the independent variables are important. This understanding depends upon your ability to empathize with the people under study. In other words, you must not only identify each key independent variable, but also recognize the interpretation showing why it has the effect that it does. This interpretation may or may not be explicit. In the Associated Press article, Dr. Broder's interpretive comments give us a deeper understanding of the relationship between poverty and access to health care when he states: "It is difficult for an individual to say 'I'll go for a mammogram today' when you are worried about how to pay for dinner." His words suggest that a key aspect of the poverty effect derives from its power to limit the options that poor people have and perceive themselves as having.

A picture is worth a thousand words, and the model becomes clearer when we **diagram** it. The rules for sketching models are as follows:

> Begin the sketch on the left and follow the causal flow to the right until you have entered the final dependent variable; that is, the independent variable(s) on the left, the intervening variable(s) in the middle, and the dependent variable(s) on the right:

$$X_1 \longrightarrow X_2 \longrightarrow X_3$$

> Use single-headed, straight arrows to denote causal relationships:

$$X \longrightarrow Y$$

> Use a double-headed, curved arrow to denote an association between two variables that exists but is not causal (see the forthcoming discussion on the "criteria for establishing causality"):

> If there is a feedback effect or two-way causation, e.g., X affects Y, which, in turn, affects X, then use a second arrow:

$$X \rlap{\longrightarrow}{\longleftarrow} Y$$

> If a causal relationship is hypothesized but is not confirmed by the data, denote it with a cross-hatched, straight arrow; alternatively, you may use a broken arrow:

$$X \dashrightarrow Y \quad \text{or} \quad X \longrightarrow\!\!\!/\!\!\!/\!\!\!/ Y$$

> Note the functional form of the relationship between two variables by placing an appropriate symbol above a straight arrow and to the left of a curved double-headed arrow; the most common forms will be the linear, either positive (denoted "+") or negative ("−"):

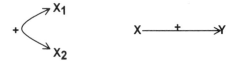

Although there is no rule for symbolizing nonlinear relationships, one simple strategy is to use a symbol that looks like the curve (e.g., a **U** for a parabolic association):

$$X \xrightarrow{\;\;U\;\;} Y$$

(the X,Y relationship is U-shaped)

> Nominal variables (those whose values do not have magnitude, i.e., cannot be ranked "greater than" or "less than,") need to be set at a given value. For example, if using the variable sex, you must specify either "male" or "female":

Sex———$+$———> Income
(M)

(Males are more likely to have high incomes)

> If a nominal variable has only two categories, e.g., Sex (male/female) or Race (white/black), then either category may be used in the sketch; the following sketch is equivalent to the preceding one:

Sex———$-$———> Income
(F)

(Females are less likely to have high incomes)

If we follow the above rules, our model sketch comes out like this:

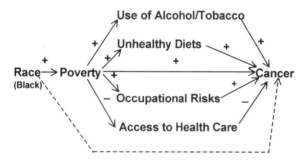

There are other ways we could have sketched this model. For example, it is not clear from the article whether race and poverty are simply associated or whether race is a determinant of poverty. If we think that the argument was for an association only between these two variables, then our sketch would look like this:

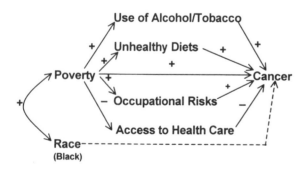

Step 2: How is each variable measured?

Variables are concepts. Theories clarify the causal links among concepts. To apply or test a theory, it is necessary to specify these concepts in terms of their manifestations in the concrete world. This process is called **measurement**. Scientific articles are very good at alerting us to the difference between conceptual variables and their measurements. Articles in the popular media and everyday arguments are not so good at this. Regardless, as a critical reader you must have the ability to distinguish a concept from its measurement, realizing that they are not the same thing. Measurement answers in concrete empirical terms the question: "By X, what do you mean?" ("By 'educational quality' of a college, what do you mean? Do you mean the grade point average of the student body? Do you mean the percentage of faculty members with doctoral degrees?"). Models tested with different measurements will yield different results, though the results will not differ by much if both measurements are fairly **valid**—that is, if they are truly indicative of the phenomena under study. And what if a researcher finds that a particular X and a particular Y are *not* related as hypothesized? Then one must ask, Did the research turn out this way because the model is wrong (i.e., does not truly represent reality)? Or is it that the model is perhaps right but simply was tested incorrectly (e.g., with poor measurements)?

In the newspaper article quoted above, measurement issues are given short shrift (and this should raise the eyebrows of the critical reader). *Poverty* is measured as living below the federal poverty line; although this line is not given here, it is readily available from the U.S. Bureau of the Census (in 1999, the poverty line for a family of 4 was a cash income of $16,600; this line is updated each year to reflect changes in the Consumer Price Index). *Cancer* is measured as a group death rate from the disease (e.g., number of blacks dying from cancer per 100,000 blacks); we must assume that all cancers are involved. We do not know the data source, but we could obtain it by contacting the presidential panel at the National Cancer Institute in Bethesda, Maryland. No measurements are given for any other variable. Thus, we cannot specifically answer the question "By X, what do you mean?" for unhealthy diets, occupational risks, or access to health care. Similarly, we are not really sure what constitutes a dangerous level of alcohol or tobacco use.

Step 3: How well do the data fit the model?

Critical thinkers realize that data rarely, if ever, fit a model perfectly. In sociology a perfect fit is even rarer because our measurements tend to be crude and because human affairs are so complex that any one data set is unlikely to contain the full range of needed independent variables. Thus, the fit between models and data is a matter of degree.

One standard that many scientists use to judge how well data fit models is **statistical significance**. A pattern in the data (say, a positive correlation between X and Y) is considered statistically significant if it is unlikely that it could have occurred by chance alone. For example, about a half million females and about a half million males live in Rhode Island. If it were simply a matter of chance who ended up in prison, then we would expect about half of the state's prison population to be male and about half female. But that is not the case. The prison population of Rhode Island (as in every state) is overwhelmingly male (94%). Thus, the data contain a strong pattern that is unlikely to be due to chance and that would support this model: Sex $\xrightarrow{+}$ Crime.
     (Male)

Researchers typically report whether their findings are statistically significant. At this point in your intellectual career, you should conclude that the data fit the model well if statistically significant associations are reported. At the same time, however, you should be developing an internal set of standards and an intuitive sense of how well the findings fit the model. For example, in the above newspaper article few data are reported (and none for the intervening variables and cancer rates), but those that are given convincingly support the following: (1) poverty is linked to dying of cancer ("People living below the federal poverty level have a death rate from cancer that is twice as high as that for the rest of the population"), and (2) race is linked to poverty and cancer ("Black men, who outnumber whites in poverty three-to-one, have a 25 percent higher risk of contracting cancer"). Imagine, however, that the article had reported that those below the poverty

line had a 27.2 percent chance of suffering cancer, while those above the line had a 26.4 percent chance. Even though this difference might be statistically significant given a population of tens of millions of people both below and above the poverty line (all things equal, the larger the sample size, the greater the likelihood of finding statistical significance), substantively and intuitively we would not be persuaded that the Poverty→Cancer model has much explanatory worth. Indeed, we would be prompted to seek out other potential predictors of cancer with which to construct more powerful models. Finally, you should be developing internal standards and an intuitive sense of how well data fit models because some scholarly essays and many journalistic articles do not contain quantitative information and therefore will not use tests of statistical significance.

Step 4: Propose an alternative model based on your assessments in Steps 1–3.

By definition, a model represents only a thin slice of reality. It can always be made more or less complex (say, by adding or deleting additional independent variables). Up to this point, in Steps 1–3, all the critical readers of an article should have made similar assessments (the various components of the model either are there or are not; the measurements are either presented or are not; the data are significant in total, in part, or not at all). At Step 4 you can make your unique contributions as a reader and a critic. If you are fairly well convinced by the model, its measurements, and the findings, then your contributions in Step 4 will be minimal (adding another independent variable, for example, along with your rationale). On the other hand, if you find the model unconvincing, either on theoretical grounds or because the data simply do not fit it very well (especially if you think the measurements of the variables seem adequate), then your Step 4 contribution may result in a complete reworking. In the newspaper article at hand, the theoretical model rings true to me. Further, the data presented—though scant—fit the model well. Thus, my "alternative model" is a tinkering of the original model, not a major overhaul. It would seem to me that getting cancer would increase the odds of working less or quitting one's job altogether; it would also seem likely that a person's expenses would rise, as any insurance one had — private or public — would be unlikely to cover all medical costs. Thus, it seems reasonable to argue that cancer feeds back into poverty; in short, not only does poverty lead to cancer, but cancer leads to poverty. My alternative model can be sketched as follows:

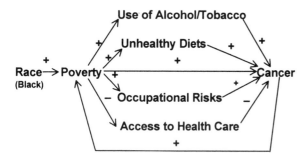

No matter what the model, you can always pro-

pose an alternative and produce a justification that appeals to intuition or collective common sense. (May your professor be generous in assessing your first efforts as a social theorist!)

Below, in summary form, are the steps we have been examining. A full appreciation of these steps takes practice. You must apply them again and again. However, even your initial use will sharpen your mind and reward you with insight.

A final comment: This brief primer on critical reading and thinking does not, of course, cover the full spectrum of analytic approaches to studying the world, in general, or the components of society, in particular. Rather, it lays a foundation upon which you can construct subtler and more sophisticated techniques of observation and analysis (whether the analysis involves reading, writing, researching, or just thinking). Indeed, such subtlety and sophistication will be apparent in much of the sociological writing you will read now and in the future.

Box 2. Steps Toward Critical Reading (and Thinking)

1. What is the model?

   a. What is (are) the dependent variable(s)? (the phenomenon or the phenomena being explained)

   b. What are the independent variables? (the reasons for, or causes of, the dependent variable)

   c. How are the independent and the dependent variables functionally related? (e.g., as the independent variable increases, does the dependent variable increase too, or does it decrease?)

   d. Interpret the relationship between each independent and dependent variable. (What's happening in the world such that we would expect to find these two variables related?)

2. How is each variable measured?

3. How well do the data fit the model?

4. Propose an alternative model based on your assessments in Steps 1–3

Elementary Data Analysis Tools Needed to Study Social Issues

Dig a well before you are thirsty.
— Chinese proverb

Many students are limited in their quantitative abilities, and instructors cannot go into much detail without transforming the course into a class on research methods or statistics. However, all college students—regardless of major—should have a grasp of the following elementary concepts of data analysis and should be able to put them to practical use:

- Measures of central tendency
- Measures of dispersion
- Basic tabular analysis
- Scatterplots and the correlation coefficient
- The criteria for establishing causality

These basic concepts of data analysis are intrinsic to understanding many of even the simplest research efforts in sociology and to applying the protocol for reading critically (see the end of the preceding chapter) to the reporting of such efforts. I will illustrate these basic concepts using the information contained in Box 3. The data are for all 18- and 19-year-olds participating in the 1998 General Social Survey (GSS). The GSS was conducted almost every year between 1972 and 1994 by the National Opinion Research Center (NORC) at the University of Chicago.[1] Since 1994, it has been conducted every two years on a random sample of approximately 2,900 adult Americans. Respondents are asked a host of questions on their family backgrounds, personal histories, behaviors, and attitudes toward a variety of issues. Because NORC uses rigorous scientific sampling strategies and has a high response rate for the GSS, it is safe to assume that the data are of a very high quality.

Box 3. Selected Characteristics of All 18- and 19-Year-Old Respondents for the 1998 GSS*

CaseID	Father's Education (Yrs. Schooling)	Mother's Education (Yrs. Schooling)	Family Income ($)	Sex	Race	Health Status	Zodiac Sign
1	17	16	111,000	F	White	Excellent	Virgo
2	4	2	37,500	M	Nonwhite	Excellent	Gemini
3	12	12	45,000	F	White	Excellent	Leo
4	17	16	67,500	M	Nonwhite	Excellent	Leo
5	12	13	500	F	Nonwhite	Good	Taurus
6	12	14	67,500	F	White	Excellent	Virgo
7	17	12	45,000	M	White	Good	Capricorn
8	16	12	82,000	F	White	Good	Libra
9	11	9	9,000	F	White	Fair	Aquarius
10	12	12	67,500	F	White	Good	Pisces
11	14	12	67,500	M	Nonwhite	Good	Libra
12	16	12	67,500	F	White	Excellent	Libra
13	18	16	111,000	M	White	Fair	Cancer
14	16	13	500	M	White	Good	Aries
15	12	14	100,000	M	White	Excellent	Scorpio
16	16	12	45,000	M	White	Excellent	Capricorn
17	12	12	37,500	M	White	Fair	Capricorn
18	12	12	32,500	M	Nonwhite	Good	Libra
19	12	12	27,500	M	Nonwhite	Good	Taurus
20	14	18	111,000	M	White	Excellent	Gemini

*Respondents with missing information on any of these variables not included.

Measures of Central Tendency

One of the most important purposes of statistical analysis is to summarize and simplify information. One useful summary is the "typical value" of a variable. Three ways to calculate the "typical value" are the **mean**, the **median**, and the **mode**.

You probably learned to calculate the mean—or the arithmetic average—of a distribution in the fourth grade: you simply sum the values and divide by the number of cases. Which would be easier to keep track of in your mind, the 20 values of Father's Education listed in Box 3 or their rounded mean of 13.6 (that is, 20 divided into the sum of all of the Father's Education values, or 272/20)? Prove to yourself that you remember how to calculate the mean by finding it for Mother's Education.[2]

If Father's Education for CaseIDs 1, 4, and 7 were 47 instead of 17, then what would the mean for this variable be?[3] Although none of these 20 individuals had a father with exactly 13.6 years of education, this mean is in the "ballpark," that is, these individuals had fathers with educations within a few years (+ or −) of 14 or so. With the change in the values for Father's Education for CaseIDs 1, 4, and 7, however, the new mean of 18.1 is in no way a "typical value." The problem, of course, is that we now have "extreme values" (3 fathers with 47 years of schooling in the presence of most of the others being between 12 and 16 years). Whenever we encounter a variable with extreme values, the preferred measurement of the "typical value" is the median. The median is defined as the middle value of a distribution after all the values have been ranked (either from low to high, or from high to low; if there is an even number of cases, then the median is the average of the two middle values). For Father's Education, the original median of "13" is unaffected when we change the values of Father's Education for CaseIDs 1, 4, and 7 (it does not matter whether the values are "17" or "47")—just as any median for any set of values is unaffected by the presence or absence of extreme values. To prove to yourself that you can calculate a median, find it for Family Income.[4] Further, prove to yourself that you can do it for an odd number of cases; calculate the value of Family Income only for those who report being in "Excellent" health (CaseIDs 1–4, 6, 12, 15, 16, and 20).[5]

How does one calculate the "typical value" for a variable such as Health Status in Box 3—that is, for a variable with relatively few values? In this case, we designate the typical value as the one that appears most often. This typical value is called the *mode*, and for the variable "Health Status" the mode here is "Excellent." Show yourself that you can compute a mode: what is it for the Zodiac Sign variable?[6]

Measures of Dispersion

Generally speaking, a mean cannot be fully appreciated unless we have an idea of how spread out or dispersed the data are. For example, the mean for the following distribution is 50: [0, 50, 100], as is the mean for the distribution [49, 50, 51]. However, in the first case, the mean does not do a very good job of telling us the "typical value," whereas in the second case it does. In the first distribution, the data are dispersed widely; in the second distribution, they are dispersed narrowly.

Dispersion can be indicated with a numeric summary, such as the **range** or the standard deviation, or it can be captured graphically with a device such as a **histogram**. The range is computed by subtracting the lowest value from the highest. For example, the range for Mother's Education in Box 3 is 16 (18–2). Prove to yourself that you can compute a range; do it for Father's Education.[7]

Obviously, the range is a very crude measurement of dispersion and does not give us much feel for the data. Most importantly, it gives no idea of the shape of the distribution. For example, the following two families have equal ranges of education but present dramatically different configurations: The Skrang family includes Jim (8 years of schooling), Tim (7), Slim (7), and Sue (16); the Skrug family includes Wilbur (16), Phil (16), Mary (15), and Tom (7). In short, even though the range of education is the same for both families (9 years) the range statistic misses the fact that the Skrangs are bunched at the low end of education, while the Skrugs are clustered at the high end. These differences are highlighted more dramatically in the histograms in Box 4. A histogram is simply a bar graph in which the bars are contiguous and indicate the frequency or the relative frequency (percentage) of the values of a variable. For small numbers of cases, such as the Skrang/Skrug family data or the GSS data in Box 3, configurations in the data are readily observed. However, for larger numbers, the pattern of dispersion is not always eye-catching and recognizable. In such a situation, histograms and similar graphical techniques can provide the solution.

Prove to yourself that you can construct a histogram to see how data for a variable are dispersed. Construct one for Health Status.[8]

Scatterplots and the Correlation Coefficient

Measures of central tendency and dispersion tell us much about particular variables, but they do not get to the heart of what concerns most scientists—explaining the world. To do this, we must examine at least two variables simultaneously. (Recall the definition given earlier: *To explain is to account for change in one variable with change in another variable or set of variables.*) A second method for assessing whether a change in X is associated with a change in Y is a **scatterplot** (also called a scattergram). You learned how to plot data in your first math class in junior or senior high school. To refresh your memory, examine the scatterplot of the GSS levels of education of the respondent's mother and father as presented in Box 5. For each case, note how we proceed along the horizontal or X axis until we meet the value for Father's Education and then proceed upward until we reach the value for the Mother's Education. We could mark this point with any common symbol, such as an asterisk (*), a dot (.), or an x; or, we could be more informative and mark it with the CaseID number.

Box 4. Graphical Displays of Dispersion Using Bar Graphs (Histograms)

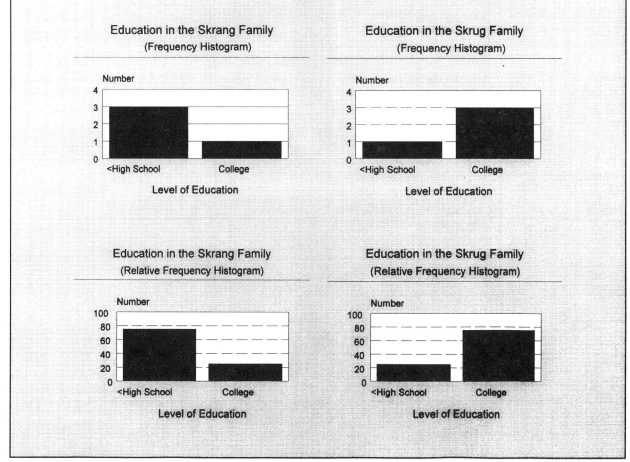

Box 5. Scatterplot of Mother's Education and Father's Education

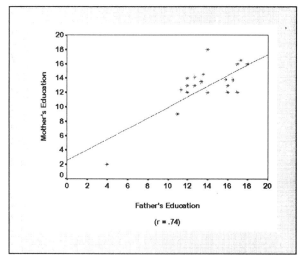

Father's Education

(r = .74)

The scatterplot confirms what you may have suspected: The educational backgrounds of a respondent's mother and father are very similar—or, more technically, are strongly positively associated. Prove to yourself that you can construct a scatterplot: plot the data for Mother's Education and Family Income in Box 3, putting Mother's Education on the horizontal axis.[9]

We can summarize the relationship in Box 5 numerically with a **correlation coefficient** (symbolized by the letter r), which indicates the strength of the linear relationship between two variables. You can find the arithmetic formula for the correlation coefficient in any elementary statistics text. At this point, it is more important for you to have an intuitive feel for **r**. A correlation coefficient may range from –1 to 0 to +1. A value of 0 signifies no linear relationship between two variables. As **r** tends to –1, the two variables are more strongly negatively associated; as **r** tends to +1, the two variables are more strongly positively associated.

Real-world correlations never attain a value of –1 or +1: First, anything that happens outside of the laboratory does so for many reasons. To account for all of the changes we might observe in a particular Y, we need to have many Xs (independent variables). Second, even if we were totally convinced that a single X could explain a particular Y, we would never obtain a correlation of + or –1 because of measurement error; that is, we can never measure any variable precisely. The line

drawn through the scatterplot points in 5 represents the theoretical relationship between the respondent's Father's Education (X) and Mother's Education (Y). The vertical distance between the line and any particular point represents the missing effects of other causes of Y, as well as errors in measuring the variables. The closer the points tend to cluster near this line, the stronger the absolute value of **r**.

For a relationship to be considered "statistically significant," conventional standards require that the probability of it being due to chance is less than 5 percent. Statistical significance depends upon both the strength of the relationship and the size of the sample. For example, if the sample size is 45 or more, a correlation of + or –.25 is statistically significant (i.e., it would be obtained by chance alone less than 5 times in a 100). Although the scatterplot in Box 5 is based on a relatively small number of cases (N=20), the relationship is strong enough to be statistically significant. (An **r** of .75 is very strong in any sociological study; this particular relationship could be expected to appear by chance alone fewer than 1 in 1,000 times.)

Box 6 shows a variety of relationships between a hypothetical X and Y, along with accompanying correlation coefficients. Ideally, a researcher would show you both a scatterplot and its accompanying correlation coefficient. (At the very least, you could check to make sure that **r** was appropriate—that is, that the data were related in a straight-line manner.) Unfortunately, to conserve space in scholarly books and journals, this is rarely done. Nevertheless, you will have a deeper understanding of correlation coefficients now that you know how scatterplots are constructed and have a mental image of the connection between a particular correlation and what its scatterplot should look like.

Basic Tabular Analysis

A second method for assessing whether a change in X is associated with a change in Y is a special kind of table called a **crosstab** (short for crosstabulation). Although easy to construct, a crosstab can produce powerful insights. Most importantly, like the scatterplot, it allows us to establish whether change in one variable is associated with

Box 6. Scatterplot Examples with Accompanying Correlation Coefficients

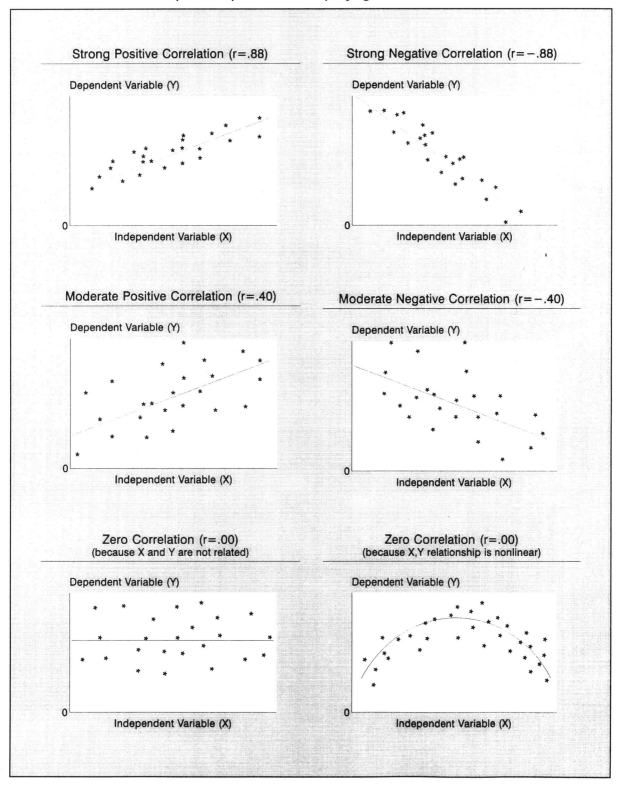

change in another. Let's use the table in Box 7 (constructed from the GSS data in Box 3) to detail the elements and the logic of a properly constructed crosstab.

Box 7. Crosstab of Family Income* by Parents' Education**

		Parents' Education	
		Low (< 26)	High (≥ 26 Yrs)
Family Income	**High (> $56,250)**	12.5% (1)	75.0% (9)
	Low (< $56,250)	87.5% (7)	25.0% (3)
		100% (8)	100% (12)
			N=20

Prediction: Parents' Education and Family Income are positively related.

Finding: Strongly confirmatory, i.e., those respondents whose parents possess "high" amounts of education (≥ 26 years) have a (75.0%–12.5%=) 62.5% greater chance of having a "high" (>$56,250) Family Income

*Family Income has been dichotomized at the median

**Parents' Education = Mother's Education + Father's Education; the values of 6–25 fall below the median for this variable, while the values 26–34 are at or above the median

First, note the **title**. Often the best title is simply the "<dependent variable> by <independent variable>"; thus, here it would be "Family Income by Parents' Education."

Next, note the **footer**, that material at the base of the table. Footers vary greatly in content; however, in this workbook we will stress the kind used in Box 7—that is, a *prediction* and a *finding*. The prediction is simply our hypothesis or best guess about the functional form of the relationship (which variable is independent, which is dependent, and the expected relationship between the two—here we expect the two variables to fall and rise together, so we are predicting a "positive" relationship). Using this kind of footer will train you to (a) look for relationships between

variables (your "prediction") and (b) recognize them when they exist (your "finding").

Next, note the **variable labels** and the associated **value labels**. The row variable label here is *Family Income*, with the values *High (>$56,250)* and *Low (<$56,250)*. The column variable label is *Parents' Education*, with the values *Low (<26 Yrs)* and *High (≥26 Yrs)*. Note that the many values of both of these variables (e.g., 26 years of parents combined education, 28 years, 32 years, and so on; $27,500, $67,500, and so on) have been collapsed into only two key values or categories: for Parents' Education, less than 25 years versus more than 25 years (in other words: less than the median versus greater than or equal to the median); for Family Income, less than 56,250 dollars per year and more than 56,250 thousand dollars per year (in other words: less than the median versus greater than the median). Often the categories of a many-valued variable are collapsed into a smaller number of categories for simplification and to allow us to begin seeing patterns that may exist in the data.

You must be clear whether the values of the independent variable are placed in the rows or in the columns. (Even if the author does not tell us which of the variables is the independent, you should be able to figure it out theoretically. Here, obviously, Parents' Education is a possible determinant of Family Income—not vice versa.) Most commonly, you will find the independent variable placed on the column and the dependent variable on the rows. Moreover, you will find the table constructed as in Box 7—that is, with the values *increasing* from the first column to the last column (here, the first column is < 26, and the last column is ≥ 26), but with the values *decreasing* from the first row to the last row (row #1 is >$56,250, and row #2 is <$56,250). The logic of this construction relates to the format of a scatterplot—the means for finding a relationship between X and Y that you just learned. Notice in Box 5 how the values increase reading from left to right and from down to up, just like the values in the Box 7 crosstab. Box 8 shows the close connection between a properly constructed crosstab and its respective scatterplot, as well as their similar capacity to describe a relationship between X and Y.

Next, note the direction (row or column) in which cell percentages have been calculated. To achieve

Box 8. A Crosstab Overlaying Its Equivalent Scatterplot, and Crosstab by Itself

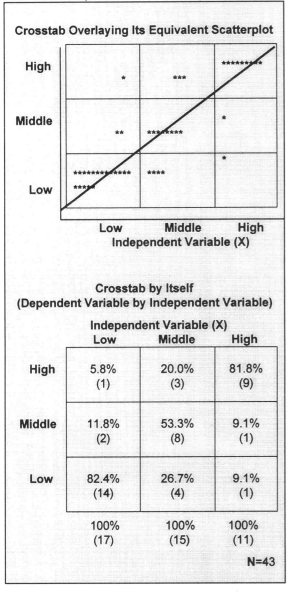

Crosstab Overlaying Its Equivalent Scatterplot

Crosstab by Itself
(Dependent Variable by Independent Variable)

	Independent Variable (X)		
	Low	Middle	High
High	5.8% (1)	20.0% (3)	81.8% (9)
Middle	11.8% (2)	53.3% (8)	9.1% (1)
Low	82.4% (14)	26.7% (4)	9.1% (1)
	100% (17)	100% (15)	100% (11)
			N=43

our ultimate aim — to see whether a change in X is associated with a change in Y — the hard-and-fast rule is to *calculate cell percentages in the direction of the independent variable.* Thus, in our Box 7 table, the **column sum** of 8 was used to calculate the percentages in the cells for the first column (*not either of the **row sums,** nor the total **N** of 20*). Similarly, the sum for the second column, 12, is

used to calculate the cell percentages for that column (*not* either of the row sums, nor the total **N** of 20).

The rule for reading or interpreting cell percentages is to *compare them in the opposite direction from that used to calculate them.* Let us proceed using this rule. Seven of those GSS respondents having parents with "low" education (<25 years) live in homes where family income is "low" (see the Row 2/Column 1 cell); that is, 87.5 percent (7/8) of those with parents having a low amount of education are in families where earnings are less than $56,250 per year. Recall that our ultimate aim (which cannot be repeated too often!) is to discover whether a change in X is associated with a change in Y. If we stay on Column 1 (comparing the 87.5% with the 12.5%), we cannot answer this question because we have not changed values in X! Only by comparing "low" versus "high" parental education (that is, by reading across a row) can we discover whether changes in X lead to a change in Y. Our final conclusion? Indeed, Parent's Education and Family Income are related: Those respondents having parents with "high" levels of education (combined years of schooling greater than 25) have a 62.5 percent (75%–12.5%) greater chance of being part of a family where income exceeds $56,250 per year.

Although there are many ways to determine the strength of an association between two variables in a crosstab, one of the easiest and most powerful is simply to compare percentage differences: given a change in X, what is the percentage change in being at a particular value of Y? Recall that statistical significance depends upon both the strength of the relationship (here, defined as percentage difference) and the size of the sample Thus, even though we only have a very small sample of 20, the relationship is strong enough to meet conventional standards of significance — usually defined as the probability of the relationship being due to chance is less than 5 percent. According to the **chi-square** test for statistical significance, an option under the **Table** command of Student CHIP, the probability here is only 6 in 1,000.[10] Regardless of statistical significance, you should be developing an ability to recognize percentage-difference relationships between variables in crosstabs. Obviously, I used a small sample in this chapter so you could practice data analysis by hand. (Whether a sample is "small" or "large" depends on the needs of the particular research project; in general, however, the further below 100 or so, the less likely a sample will yield statistically significant results.)

Prove to yourself that you can construct and read a crosstab. Let X be Family Income as recoded in Box 7. Let Y be Health Status. Crosstab these two variables. Put the two values of Family Income on the columns (let Column 1 = "low" Family Income, i.e., <$56,250; let Column 2 = "high" Family Income, i.e., >$56,250); put the three values of Health Status on the rows (let Row 1 = Excellent). Is there a relationship using a percentage-difference comparison? Does it seem weak or strong, especially given the sample size? Focus your analysis on those with Excellent health—in other words, does the probability of reporting "excellent health" vary with Family Income?[11]

Criteria for Establishing Causality in Nonexperimental Situations

The **experimental method** is the most persuasive means that human beings have developed for establishing that a change in X truly generates a change in Y. The logic of an experiment is simple, yet powerful: the experimenter controls for—that is, holds constant—all possible determinants of Y save one, the suspected causal factor X. Thus, if a change in X is followed by a change in Y, then the only possible cause must be X. One possible confounding factor is the passage of time; perhaps Y changes not in response to X, but simply because of aging. To make sure that the effects of X are not confused with the simple passage of time, the experimenter sets up two groups at the beginning of the study: one that receives X, called the **experimental** or **treatment group**, and one that does not receive X, called the **control group**. If the two groups differ on Y at the end of the experiment, then the only possible cause must be the presence or absence of X.

Of course, the idea of control or holding everything constant implies that the two groups are alike. For example, if we wanted to learn whether the artificial sweetener saccharin causes cancer in rats, we could not put white lab rats in the control group and your basic East Coast wood rat in the experimental group. (From my personal experience, nothing makes these guys sick. They eat aluminum foil, barbed wire, pesticides, and all forms of garbage—*without* any ill effects!). When dealing with human subjects, experimenters employ one of two key methods to ensure the sameness of experimental and control groups. Occasionally, they use **matched samples**, in which they try to match key characteristics between the two groups. For example, if the experimental group is all female, then so is the control group; if the experimental group contains all young adults, then so does the control group.

Where does one draw the line? That is, how does one know that the experimental and the control group have been truly "matched" on everything essential? It is hard, perhaps impossible, to determine this. To avoid this problem, experimenters more commonly use the second method to ensure equality between groups. In this procedure, called **randomization**, they assign an equal number of subjects randomly to an experimental group and to an accompanying control group. On any particular trial of an experiment, the two groups may not have characteristics that are exactly equal. If the experiment is repeated many times, however, and if randomization is employed, then the differences between the experimental and the control groups will tend to cancel each other out and any significant differences between the groups on Y can safely be attributed to differences on X.

Despite the great power of the experimental method to ascertain causation, it is rarely used in sociology (except in the subfield of social psychology). A key reason is that in the real world people's lives are not influenced by isolated independent variables. We are complex beings who live in a complex world. Our individual and collective attitudes and behavior are subjected to a barrage of influences. To understand more clearly the effects of many factors, simultaneously and relative to one another, sociologists use surveys and censuses, both of which include many items or questions measuring many variables. Given these kinds of data, how does one go about ascertaining that a change in X produces a change in Y? Box 9 contains the answer. Take special notice of Criterion 3, which draws its logic from the experimental method (getting rid of possible confounding influences on Y by holding them constant).

Box 9. The Criteria for Establishing Causality in Nonexperimental Situations

1. X and Y are associated.
2. X precedes Y.
3. The X–Y relationship is nonspurious. That is, it is resistant to controls; it maintains itself when a reasonable competing independent variable is held constant.
4. The X–Y relationship is intuitively pleasing. That is, it fits with our current understanding of how the world functions.

Let's explicate the criteria in Box 9 with an example drawn from Rodney Stark's introductory sociology text.[12] Surveying a large sample of teenagers in Richmond, California, Stark and fellow sociologist Travis Hirschi tested the seemingly reasonable model that religiosity and juvenile delinquency are inversely related. We may sketch their bivariate model as follows:

$$\text{Religiosity} \xrightarrow{\ -\ } \text{Delinquency}$$

Indeed, the following table (adapted from Stark's text) seems to support their model:

Church Attendance

Delinquency Problem		Infrequent	Frequent
	Yes	38%	22%
	No	62%	78%
		100%	100%

Prediction: Church Attendance and Delinquency Problem are negatively related.

Finding: Moderately confirmatory, i.e., those teenagers who attend church "infrequently" have a (38%–22%=) 14% greater chance of having a delinquency problem.

At this point, we have a strong case for causality. We have met Criteria 1 (the table shows an association), 2 (most people are introduced to religion before the adolescent years, when delinquency problems peak), and 4 (it seems plausible that a very religious person would be less delinquent, as all the major religions forbid stealing,

lying, cheating, and similar reprehensible acts). However, perhaps the world looks like the model below; it represents a reasonable competing explanation, allowing for a reasonably strong check for the possible spuriousness of the original X–Y relationship:

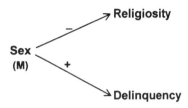

This model also is backed by reason. Girls are more likely than boys to attend church and are raised to be less aggressive (to wit, consider the prison data cited earlier). Furthermore, if this model is true, then we should not find any significant association between religiosity and delinquency after holding sex constant (examining the relationship just for boys, then just for girls). Finally, if this alternative model is true, then we would be forced to look elsewhere for causal factors, perhaps family income or the degree to which an adolescent's closest friends are delinquent.

Indeed, a check for spuriousness reveals the original relationship between religiosity and delinquency to be noncausal (i.e., spurious):

Partial Table #1: Boys

Church Attendance

Delinquency Problem		Infrequent	Frequent
	Yes	50%	50%
	No	50%	50%
		100%	100%

Partial Table #2: Girls

Church Attendance

Delinquency Problem		Infrequent	Frequent
	Yes	10%	10%
	No	90%	90%
		100%	100%

The notion of checking for spuriousness is also applicable to nonquantitative research, studies reported in the popular media, and everyday thinking.[13] In these instances, the idea is expressed as a search for alternatives to the interpretation given to a particular interaction, happening, activity, attitude, sentiment, or pattern in the data.

Prove to yourself that you can analyze data with crosstabs and check findings for spuriousness. For the data in Box 3, operationally define (a) "low" Family Income as below $56,250 and (b) "high" Family Income as greater than $56,250. Transform Mother's Education into a similar dichotomy, defining (a) "low" as equal to or less than 12 years of schooling, and (b) "high" as greater than 12 years. Then, crosstabulate Family Income by Mother's Education (putting the values of Family Income on the rows, and writing in a footer with a *prediction* and *finding*). Is there an association between Family Income and Mother's Education? (Box 9, Criterion 1)?[14] Can we argue readily that "education" precedes "income" (Box 9, Criterion 2)?[15] Can we give a reasonable interpretation for why we should find the data patterned in this way (i.e., that the more educated are more likely to be prosperous — Box 9, Criterion 4)?[16] Check your findings for spuriousness (Box 9, Criterion 3), using Race as the control variable. Did the original relationship maintain itself?[17]

The Art of Reading Partial Tables

To check for spuriousness, you must use at least one control variable — as we have discussed above. In the *Advanced* exercises in this workbook, you will be asked to test many relationships for spuriousness, and you will, therefore, be examining many partial tables. Although it takes many years of experience to be able to recognize the many subtleties that can be obtained in partial tables, you should be able to learn some common patterns very quickly. The patterns discussed here will be labeled *Causality, Spuriousness, Multivariable Model, Intervening Variable,* and *Interaction Effects.*

Causality As noted in Box 9, an X–Y relationship can only be considered causal if one can rule out

the possibility that it has not been generated by a third variable — often called an *antecedent* variable because it precedes in time both X and Y. Examine the X–Y relationship in Footnote #14. Perhaps income is not changing in response to changes in education, but rather both are responding to changes in the antecedent variable Race. That is, perhaps the actual relationships look like this:

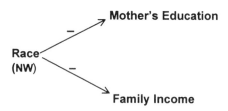

In other words, the relationship between Mother's Education and Family Income exists *not* because education is promoting income but simply because both variables are related to the antecedent variable Race. Observe that there is no arrow between Mother's Education and Family Income, denoting that there is no causal relationship. More generally, whenever we find a relationship between X and Y that we suspect is causal, we must test to see if the following model is true:

This model implies a relationship between Z and X, and between Z and Y; but no relationship between X and Y once Z has been controlled for. Remember, in such a case the only reason the original X–Y relationship is found is that Z is not held constant ("controlled for"). Allowed to vary, Z imparts its effects on X and Y; if we are unaware of Z, we may be fooled into thinking that X and Y are related causally — because changes in X are associated with changes in Y. Thus, in short, to discover whether the X–Y relationship is spurious or causal, one must hold Z constant and reexamine the X–Y relationship. If it maintains itself, we can conclude, at least for the moment, that the X–Y relationship is "nonspurious" or "causal."

In the example at hand, when we control for Z, that is Race, we find that the original relationship maintains. The large percentage difference in the original table (41.7%) is found to be in the same direction ("high" education means a higher probability of being in the "high" income row) and to still be quite large in *both* partial tables — even though it increases for whites and decreases for nonwhites. Note that these crosstabulations are called "*partial* tables" because they only deal with part of the sample; the existence of a partial table always implies that at least one Z variable is being held constant. The direction of the relationship must be the same if we are to conclude nonspuriousness (e.g., if the original relationship is "positive," the relationship in each of the partial tables must also be "positive"). However, the percentage difference may be stronger or weaker, as long as it does not weaken greatly or even totally disappear. Thus, for example, if the original percentage difference of 41.7 had weakened to, say, 30 in one or both of the partial tables, we would still make the conclusion of "nonspurious" or "causal." This would not be the case, however, if the percentage difference weakened dramatically (say went down to 5), disappeared all together (reduced to zero), or even started heading in the opposite direction (say, from positive to negative); then, we may have an example of spuriousness.

Spuriousness We have already seen an example of what happens in the partial tables if the original relationship is spurious — that is, we saw above that when Sex was held constant, the relationship between Church Attendance and Delinquency did not maintain itself. Let us use our imaginations and fill in percentages in the Footnote #17 table shells appearing in the next column that would have shown the original X–Y relationship (between Mother's Education and Family Income) to be spurious. Concoct percentages for each table that would support the spuriousness model sketched above; that is, your percentages must show no relationship between education and income in each of the partial tables; moreover, your percentages must reveal that Race is, indeed, the key independent variable here and is

determinative of income. Note, too, that your percentages must add up to 100 for each column in each table. For this mental exercise, forget about sample size and cell frequencies; just try to come up with the percentages. Pause now, ponder the question marks, and replace them with eight numbers that will demonstrate the desired (non!)relationship between X and Y. There are no right or wrong answers here in terms of finding any exact number or numbers (e.g., one of them does not have to be "40") — what is important are the relationships that they manifest (and do not manifest). Try hard, then check your answer by examining that given in Footnote #18.

Family Income by Mother's Education for Whites[18]

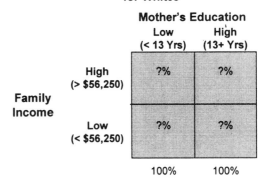

Family Income by Mother's Education for Nonwhites[18]

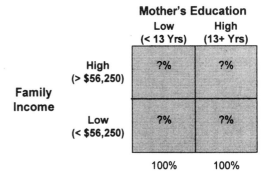

Multivariable Model We do not just pull an antecedent Z variable out of thin air; rather, we choose a particular Z because we think that it will fit the Z-to-X and Z-to-Y model as sketched above. That is, we can make reasonable interpretations as to why we think the world looks this way. For example, we could argue that the historically severe segregation of the races resulted in nonwhite mothers having acquired lower levels of education. As for the Z–to–Y relationship, it could be argued that nonwhites suffer greater discrimination in the workplace and would therefore be more likely to end up in the "low" income column.

Given that we have strong reason to believe that Z may be a cause of Y, it should come as no surprise that many times when checking for spuriousness we find not only X maintaining its effect on Y (thus we reject the spuriousness model) but also Z affecting Y. Indeed, this is the case in the partial tables displayed in Footnote #17. For now, forget about sample size (which is intentionally very small so that you could do your work in this chapter by hand). We have already discussed how, regardless of the value of Z (Race)—that is to say "independent" of Z—the X–Y (mother's education—family income) relationship maintains itself. But take a close look. Regardless of X (level of Mother's Education), Z (Race) has consistent effects on Y (Family Income). For those respondents whose mothers possess low levels of education (< 13 years of schooling), whites have a (37.5%–25.0%=) 12.5% greater chance of being in the "high" Family Income column (> $56,250). Similarly, for those GSS respondents whose mothers possess "high" education (13+ years), whites have a (83.3%–50.0%=) 33.3% greater chance of being in high income-earning families. Thus, regardless of Mother's Education—that is to say "independent" of Mother's Education—whites are more likely to have high Family Income. We may sketch the empirical model evident in these tables as follows:

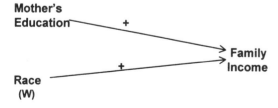

Now, let us do a mental experiment again. Forget about sample sizes and fill in percentages below that would show a multivariable model—that is, both Mother's Education and Race having independent effects on Family Income (of course you

cannot use the "true" percentages that are present in the partial tables in Footnote #17!). Then compare your results to those given in Footnote #19 (again, there are no right or wrong answers with regard to any exact number or numbers).

Family Income by Mother's Education for Whites[19]

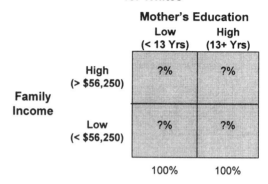

Family Income by Mother's Education for Nonwhites[19]

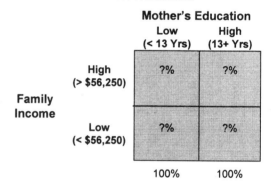

Intervening Variable It is time to throw a little monkey wrench into your thinking. As of this moment, if someone were to ask you "What does it mean if after controlling for Z we find that the original relationship between X and Y weakens greatly or even disappears?", what would you reply? Think a minute, write down your reply, then compare it to the answer given in Footnote #20.[20] But there is another possible interpretation of the partial tables. More specifically, perhaps the world looks like this:

$$X \longrightarrow Z \longrightarrow Y$$

That is, a change in X produces a change in Z, which, in turn, produces a change in Y. Now think: If this model is true, what will happen to the relationship between X and Y if Z is held constant? Pause here to figure this out (stop reading!). If you said "The X–Y relationship will weaken greatly or disappear," you are correct! If a change in X produces a change in Y via changes in Z, and if Z is not allowed to vary, then X cannot have any effect on Y. At the very least, those effects of X on Y that occur via Z will be absent, and the X–Y relationship will at minimum weaken (i.e., reveal smaller percentage differences in the partial tables).

Empirically, that is to say, with what is revealed in the partial tables, one cannot distinguish between the situation where Z is the antecedent variable (spuriousness) and where Z is the intervening variable. Then how do we know whether the partial tables above for Church Attendance and Delinquency by Sex demonstrate that the X–Y relationship is spurious, as opposed to demonstrating that Z simply intervenes between X and Y, and that the X,Y relationship is causal—with the effects of X on Y being transmitted via Z? Again, the partial tables cannot answer this question. What does answer it is simply thinking logically about the world. Which makes more sense: that Church Attendance causes Sex, that in turn causes a Delinquency Problem $(X-Z-Y)$? or that Sex determines both the odds of one's going to church as well as the odds of one's having a delinquency problem (Z-to-X and Z-to-Y, with no relationship between X and Y, i.e., Spuriousness.)? Of course, the first alternative makes no sense (one's "Sex" cannot be caused by one's "Church Attendance"), so we would say that our partial tables have revealed that the X,Y relationship is spurious. Similarly, the partial tables you created for Footnote #17 would be indicative of spuriousness, not that Z was an intervening variable between X and Y.

Interaction Effects Sometimes when checking for spuriousness, the partial tables will reveal that the relationship has maintained itself in at least one partial table and has weakened greatly or disappeared in at least one other partial table. What should we make of this? On the one hand, we have argued that if the relationship maintains itself then we have evidence for causality. On the other hand, we have contended that if the rela-

tionship weakens greatly or disappears then we have evidence for spuriousness (or that Z intervenes between X and Y). In brief, here is the answer: We would have evidence of causality but only under certain conditions, that is, only given certain values of Z. Scientists label such a situation "interaction"—in other words, X and Z "interact" in producing their effects on Y. Because our primary focus is on the X–Y relationship, in our examination of the partial tables we are especially interested in seeing how the effects of X on Y vary by the value of Z. Let us do one last mental experiment. In the following tables, fill in percentages that would show that the effect of X on Y depends upon the value of Z; more specifically, conjure up percentages that would show Family Income to be sensitive to changes in Mother's Education for nonwhites but not for whites. (Again, there are no right or wrong answers in terms of designating any exact percentages—rather the problem is to invent percentages that show interaction in the manner specified.)

Family Income by Mother's Education for Whites[21]

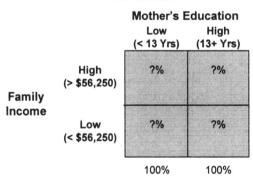

Family Income by Mother's Education for Nonwhites[22]

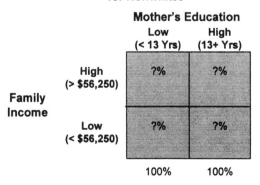

The discovery of interaction effects poses special problems of interpretation. You must be able to think up an interpretation that would account for X affecting Y for some values of Z but not for others. Developing such an interpretation is much more than simple mental gymnastics—for this is the process of science, including social science. When anomalous or unexpected findings arise, findings that challenge our views of the world, we must try to interpret them. We then must go out and test our new interpretations, refining them as necessary. Try your hand at the process of science now: come up with a brief interpretation that would account for our finding that Mother's Education was predictive of Family Income, but only for nonwhites.[22]

Endnotes for *Elementary Data Analysis Tools Needed to Study Social Issues*

1. James A. Davis and Tom W. Smith, *General Social Survey, 1998* (Chicago: NORC). Distributed by Roper Public Opinion Research Center (Storrs, CT). Box 3 contains all 18- and 19-year olds for whom information was available on the educational levels of their mothers and fathers. Mother's Education for CaseId 5 has been altered for demonstration purposes of the exercises that appear later in this chapter.

2. Answer: 16+2+12+16+13+14+12+12+9+12+12+12+16+13+14+12+12+12+12+18=251; this sum divided by 20 equals 12.55.

3. Answer: the new sum of 362 divided by 20 equals 18.1.

4. Answer: The values for Family Income need to be reordered to put them in a low-to-high ranking:

500	32,500	45,000	67,500	100,000
500	37,500	<u>45,000</u>	67,500	111,000
9,000	37,500	67,500	67,500	111,000
27,500	45,000	67,500	82,000	111,000

Thus, the average of the middle two values is 56,250 (45,000 + 67,5000 = 112,500; divided by 2 = 56,250), which is the median for Family Income.

5. The values for Family Income for CaseIDs 1–4, 6, 12, 15, 16, and 20 need to be rank-ordered:

37,500	67,500
45,000	100,000
45,000	111,000
<u>67,500</u>	111,000
<u>67,500</u>	

For an odd-numbered distribution, the median is middle value after rank ordering; thus, it is 67,500 here.

6. Answer: Aries, Aquarius, Cancer, Pisces, and Scorpio appear only once. Leo, Gemini, Taurus, and Virgo appear twice. Capricorn appears three times. Libra appears the most often, four times; therefore, it is the mode.

7. Answer: 18–4 = 14.

8.

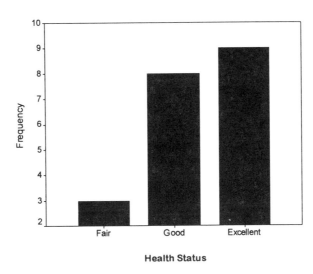

9. The scatterplot confirms what you may have already presumed: Mother's Education and Family Income are positively associated: those from better-educated backgrounds tend to be in families with higher levels of income. (This relationship is found consistently in national survey data).

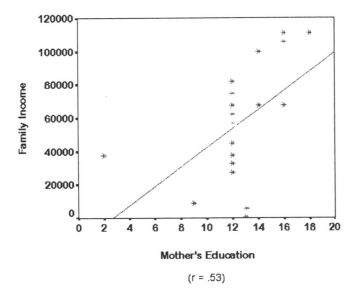

10. As a test of statistical significance for crosstabs, chi-square compares the *actual* cell frequencies with the *expected* cell frequencies if there were no relationship between X and Y. The larger the sample size, the larger the table size, and the larger the difference between the percentage of one value of X possessing a particular value of Y and the percentage of another value of X possessing that value of Y, the more likely the value of chi-square will be statistically significant. See any elementary statistics textbook for a more detailed discussion of chi-square (e.g., Jack Levin and James Fox, *Elementary Statistics in Social Research* , 8th Edition. Boston: Allyn & Bacon, Chapter 9).

11. Answers: Yes, there is a relationship (a change in X yields a 30% difference in being in the "Excellent" Health Status category). Because the sample size is relatively small (N=20), it does not approach conventional standards of statistical significance, even though the relationship might seem substantively significant. Note, I made the prediction that those from a higher-income background would more likely report being in excellent health because of their greater access to medical care, as well as the likelihood that their jobs involve less physical risk (exposure to machinery, environmental pollutants, inclement weather, and so on.).

Health Status by Family Income

Family Income

		Low (<56,250)	High (>56,250)
	Excellent	30% (3)	60% (6)
Health Status	**Good**	50% (5)	30% (3)
	Fair	20% (2)	10% (1)
		100% (10)	100% (10)

N=20

Prediction: Family Income and the Health Status are positively related.

Finding: Moderately confirmatory, e.g., those respondents with "high" Family Income (>$56,250) have a (60%–30%=) 30% greater chance of reporting being in "Excellent" health.

12. Rodney Stark, *Sociology* 3rd ed. (Belmont, CA: Wadsworth, 1990, pp. 93–95.

13. Despite the objections of some nonquantitative sociologists, "the moral for qualitative researchers is the same. When two variables look correlated, especially when you think they are causally associated, wait a beat, and consider whether some third variable might be underlying/influencing/causing them both" (Matthew B. Miles and A. Michael Huberman, *Qualitative Data Analysis*. Beverly Hills, CA: Sage, 1984, p. 239).

14. Answer: Yes, there is a moderately strong association between the dichotomized Father's Education variable and Family Income. Individuals whose fathers have 13 or more years of schooling have a 40% greater chance of being in the "high" Family Income (>$56,250) category. Not surprisingly, even when larger samples are analyzed (e.g., all GSS respondents), the relationship remains highly significant.

Original Table (has no controls; other variables therefore may be confounding the relationship, perhaps even to the point of making it spurious):

Family Income by Mother's Education

Mother's Education

		Low (< 13 Yrs)	High (13+ Yrs)
Family Income	High (> $56,250)	33.3% (4)	75.0% (6)
	Low (< $56,250)	66.7% (8)	25.0% (2)
		100% (12)	100% (8) N=20

Prediction: Mother's Education and Family Income are positively related.

Finding: Moderately confirmatory, i.e., those respondents whose mothers possess a "high" amount of education (13+ Yrs) have a (75.0%–33.3%=) 41.7% greater chance of having a "high" (> $56,250) Family Income

15. Answer: Yes, it is highly plausible to argue that "education" precedes "income." Most individuals complete their schooling before embarking on full-time employment.

16. Answer: Yes, the relationship is plausible. One of the more powerful interpretations: Better educated individuals can compete better in the job market. Being a high school graduate and having gone on to college demonstrate to potential employers the individual's willingness to learn and to persevere—qualities highly predictive of productivity and therefore highly valued by employers. Contrast this relationhip with one that might appear between Zodiac Sign and Family Income. Even if we were to find a significant relationship (say, individuals born under summer signs having a 75% greater chance of being in the "high" income category compared to individuals born under winter signs), would we be able to meet Criterion 4 in Box 9? We could not do so without a revolution in our current thinking about the rationales underlying pay scales and the value of labor.

17. **Partial Tables #1** and **#2** (controlling for, or holding constant, Race; if the relationship in the original table maintains itself, we will have strong evidence for nonspuriousness—i.e., for a causal relationship between Mother's Education and Family Income):

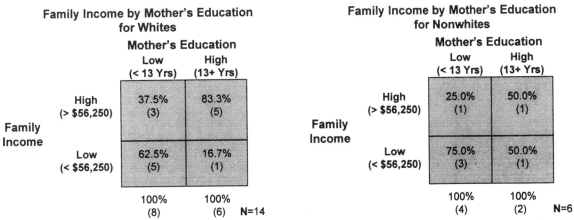

Family Income by Mother's Education for Whites

Mother's Education

		Low (< 13 Yrs)	High (13+ Yrs)
Family Income	High (> $56,250)	37.5% (3)	83.3% (5)
	Low (< $56,250)	62.5% (5)	16.7% (1)
		100% (8)	100% (6) N=14

Family Income by Mother's Education for Nonwhites

Mother's Education

		Low (< 13 Yrs)	High (13+ Yrs)
Family Income	High (> $56,250)	25.0% (1)	50.0% (1)
	Low (< $56,250)	75.0% (3)	50.0% (1)
		100% (4)	100% (2) N=6

Finding: The partial tables reveal that the direction of the original relationship between Mother's Education and Family Income has maintained itself. Even though the relationship has strengthened slightly for whites and reduced moderately for nonwhites, we can still conclude that the Mother's Education→Family Income relationship is nonspurious or causal.

18. There are no "right" and "wrong" answers here; the key is that you have reduced the original percentage difference from 41.7 to zero. Note very carefully the wording of the *Finding* below

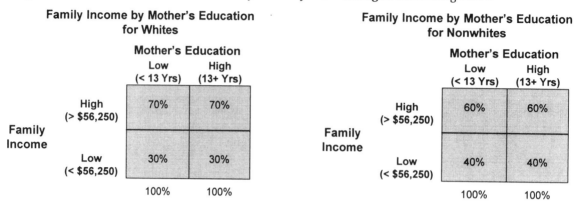

Finding: The partial tables reveal that the original positive relationship between Mother's Education and Family Income has **not** maintained itself; we may therefore conclude that this relationship was spurious or non-causal.

19. Again, there are no "right" and "wrong" answers here; the key is that you have maintained both the direction (positive!) and approximate strength of the original percentage difference (which was 41.7). Note very carefully the wording of the *Finding* below.

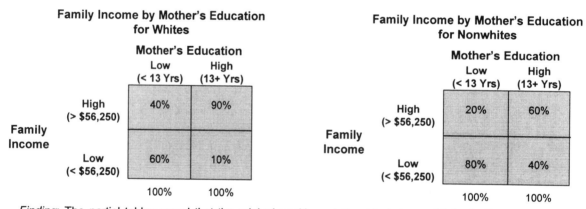

Finding: The partial tables reveal that the original positive relationship between Mother's Education and Family Income has maintained itself in both tables; we may therefore conclude that this relationship was nonspurious or causal. Moreover, the tables reveal the independent-variable effects of Race on Family Income: for those whose mothers possess less than 13 years of education, whites have (40%–20%=) 20% greater chance of being in the "high" (>$56,200) income row; similarly, for those having mothers with 13+ years of education, whites have a (90%–60%=) 30% greater chance of being in the "high" income row. We may sketch the empirical model evident in these tables as follows:

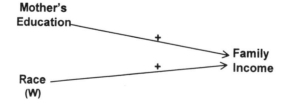

(Obviously, the sketch for the actual results in the footnote #17 would be the same as this one.)

20. As of this moment, you would answer: "If after controlling for Z we find that the original relationship between X and Y weakens greatly or even disappears, then we must conclude the this relationship was spurious or noncausal.

21. Again, there are no "right" and "wrong" answers here; the key is that you have reduced the original percentage difference from 41.7 to zero or some small number in one of the partial tables, while maintaining both the direction (positive!) and approximate strength of the original percentage difference (41.7). Note very carefully the wording of the *Finding* below.

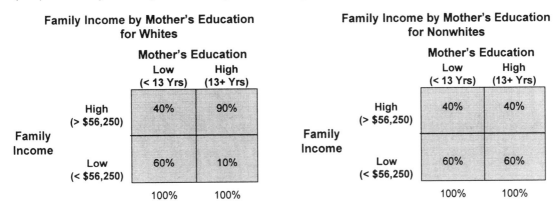

Finding: The partial tables reveal that the original positive relationship between Mother's Education and Family Income has maintained itself, but only for whites; we may therefore conclude that there is an interaction effect between Mother's Education and Race in determining Family Income. We may sketch the empirical model evident in these tables as follows:

$$\text{Mother's Education} \xrightarrow{+} \text{Family Income}$$
(but only for whites)

22. Perhaps whites are evaluated more on the basis of their educations, while nonwhites suffer discrimination and are assumed to have lower levels of productivity, regardless of educational attainment. Of course, this is only conjecture that must be rigorously assessed empirically before it is accepted. You need not have made the same conjecture; however, your speculation must be reasonable and must give an accounting of why education would be predictive of family income for whites, but not for nonwhites.

Chapter 1. The Sociological Study of Contemporary Social Issues and Problems

The authors of sociology textbooks warn students that there is seldom unanimity in a society on what actually constitutes its contemporary "social problems." Sullivan observes that "the mere existence of a social condition does not make it problematic, no matter how harmful it may be. For example, smoking tobacco has been a contributing factor in lung cancer for as long as humans have used the substance, but it was not defined as a social problem until biomedical research made people aware of the link between smoking and lung cancer."[1] Eitzen and Zinn make the same point when they note that environmental pollution comes and goes in being considered a social problem.[2] So, too, does Blumer in his classic essay on the nature of social problems when he observes: "Racial injustice and exploitation in our society were far greater in the 1920s and 1930s than they are today; yet the sociological concern they evoke was little until the chain of happenings following the Supreme Court decision on school desegregation and the rioting" that has occurred off and on in African-American neighborhoods since the mid-1960s.[3]

In a pluralistic society—like that of the United States—the definition of social problems is even more problematic: People from different social classes and other social positions (such as region, occupation, race, gender, and age) "differ in their perceptions of what a social problem is, and once defined, how it should be solved."[4] Is school prayer a social problem? Is abortion? Is pervasive income inequality a social problem? There is much disagreement in U.S. society on these and other social issues.

However, even when there is agreement, we need to be wary: Virtually every sociology textbook author agrees that what does constitute a social problem varies by social class—that is, the prosperous and the needy view the social landscape differently; and because the more prosperous hold more sway in public discourse—for example, they have greater access to the media and to government officials—public opinion is not always the best guide to determining what is and is not a truly important social problem. Social problems that have solutions which can disrupt the current social order are not popular with the prosperous (if the prosperous are on top, why would they want to change the way things are now?). For example, should the federal government take from those who have and give to those who have not? Should economic inequality even be considered a problem? One can imagine that the answers a person might give to such questions would depend upon the level of his or her current prosperity.

The CHIP exercises in this chapter allow you to see how a variety of social issues are conceived differently by those from different social locations—including income (social class), race, gender, age, family status, and religious persuasion. Other data files appearing elsewhere in this workbook can be assigned at the instructor's discretion to make the same point (e.g., see "Busing" in Chapter 10).

Is It the Government's Responsibility to Reduce Income Differences Between the Rich and the Poor?

File: **Equal98** (Should gov't reduce income differences between rich & poor? '96 & '98 GSS)

Info: Region→ Race→ Sex→Age→Ed→FamInc→PolView→Party→Equalize
(4)　　(2)　　(2)　(3)　(4)　(3)　　(3)　　(3)　　(3)

---

[1] Thomas J. Sullivan, *Introduction to Social Problems*, 5th ed. (Boston: Allyn & Bacon, 2000), p. 5.

[2] D. Stanley Eitzen and Maxine Baca Zinn, *Social Problems*, 8th ed. (Boston: Allyn & Bacon, 2000), p. 4.

[3] Hubert Blumer, "Social Problems as Collective Definition and Collective Behavior," pp. 15–20 in Gregg Lee Carter (ed.), *Perspectives on Current Social Problems* (Boston: Allyn & Bacon, 1997).

[4] Eitzen and Baca Zinn., *op.cit.*, p. 5.

Region	Northeast (CT, ME, MA, NH, NJ, NY, PA, RI, and VT)
	Midwest (IL, IN, IA, KS, MI, MN, MO, NE, ND, OH, SD, and WI)
	South (AL, AR, DE, FL, GA, KY, LS, MD, MS, NC, OK, SC, TN, TX, VA, and WV)
	West (AK, AZ, CA, CO, HI, ID, MT, NV, NM, OR, UT, WA, and WY)
Race	White, Black
Sex	Male, Female
Age	18–39, 40–64, 65+
Ed	(Years of education) <12yrs, 12yrs, 13–15yrs, 16+yrs
FamInc	(Annual family income) <$25K, $25K–$60K, $60K+
PolView	(Political view — conservatism scale; On a 7-point scale on which the political views that people might hold are arranged from extremely liberal to extremely conservative, "where would you place yourself?") Liberal (1–3), Moderate (4), Conservative (5–7)
Party	Democrat, Independent, Republican
Equalize	(Government should do something to reduce income differences between rich and poor: 1=should . . . 7=should not) No (5–7), Neutral (4), Yes (1–3)

Basic

1. Crosstabulate Equalize (Y) by each of the following:

(a) Race   (b) Sex   (c) Age   (d) Ed

(e) FamInc   (f) Party

(a) Equalize (Y) by Race (X)

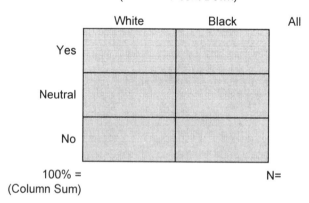

CrossTab: Equalize / Race

(**Table**: Percent Down)

(Percentage difference between Black and White for the "Yes" row =   )

Prediction:

Finding:

(b) Equalize (Y) by Sex (X)

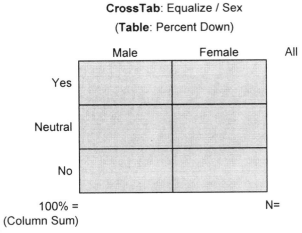

CrossTab: Equalize / Sex
(**Table**: Percent Down)

	Male	Female	All
Yes			
Neutral			
No			

100% =   N=
(Column Sum)

(Percentage difference between Female and Male for the "Yes" row =   )

Prediction:

Finding:

(c) Equalize (Y) by Age (X)

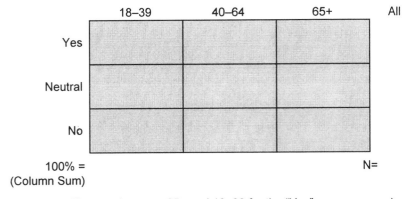

CrossTab: Equalize / Age
(**Table**: Percent Down)

	18–39	40–64	65+	All
Yes				
Neutral				
No				

100% =   N=
(Column Sum)

(Percentage difference between 65+ and 18–39 for the "Yes" row =   )

Prediction:

Finding:

(d) Equalize (Y) by Ed (X)

CrossTab: Equalize / Ed
(**Table**: Percent Down)

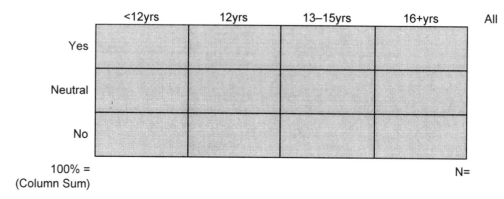

	<12yrs	12yrs	13–15yrs	16+yrs	All
Yes					
Neutral					
No					

100% =
(Column Sum)   N=

(Percentage difference between 16+yrs and <12yrs for the "Yes" row =   )

Prediction:

Finding:

(e) Equalize (Y) by FamInc (X)

CrossTab: Equalize / FamInc
(**Table**: Percent Down)

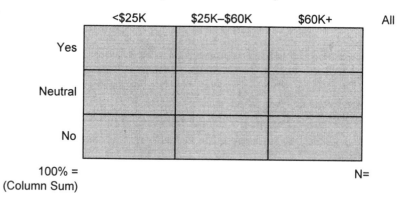

	<$25K	$25K–$60K	$60K+	All
Yes				
Neutral				
No				

100% =
(Column Sum)   N=

(Percentage difference between $60K+ and <$25K for the "Yes" row =   )

Prediction:

Finding:

(f) Equalize (Y) by Party (X)

CrossTab: Equalize / Party

(**Table**: Percent Down)

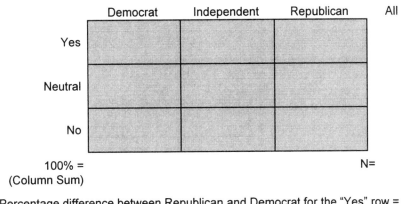

100% =
(Column Sum)

N=

(Percentage difference between Republican and Democrat for the "Yes" row =　　　　)

Prediction:

Finding:

(Note: for the following questions, concentrate your answers on the "Yes" column of Equalize.)

2.　Are all of the Xs associated with Equalize?

3.　Are all of the associations in the directions you would have predicted? (If one or more are not, discuss why you would have thought the association to be different, e.g., why you would have thought whites would have been more likely than blacks to be in the "yes" category of Equalize.)

4. Examining the crosstab for Equalize and FamInc, why do you think the data are patterned in this way (i.e., that the more prosperous are less likely to agree that the government should try to be an "equalizer")?

Prayer in Public Schools

File: **NoPray98** (Do you approve of the Supreme Court's ruling of no prayer in public schools? '96 & '98 GSS)

Info: Region→Urban→Race→Sex→Age→Ed→Religion→PolView→Party→NoPrayer
(4)   (3)   (3)   (2)   (3)   (4)   (4)   (3)   (3)   (2)

Region   Northeast (CT, ME, MA, NH, NJ, NY, PA, RI, and VT)
Midwest (IL, IN, IA, KS, MI, MN, MO, NE, ND, OH, SD, and WI)
South (AL, AR, DE, FL, GA, KY, LS, MD, MS, NC, OK, SC, TN, TX, VA, and WV)
West (AK, AZ, CA, CO, HI, ID, MT, NV, NM, OR, UT, WA, and WY)

Urban   Rural/Small-Town, Suburb, City

Race   White, Black, Other

Sex   Male, Female

Age   18–39, 40–64, 65+

Ed   (Years of education) <12yrs, 12yrs, 13–15yrs, 16+yrs

Religion   Other (e.g., Jewish, Hindu, Buddhist, no religion), Catholic, Mod-LibProt (Moderate or Liberal Protestant, FundProt (Fundamentalist Protestant)[5]

PolView   (Political view — conservatism scale; On a 7-point scale on which the political views that people might hold are arranged from extremely liberal to extremely conservative, where would you place yourself?) Liberal (1–3), Moderate (4), Conservative (5–7)

Party   Democrat, Independent, Republican

NoPrayer   (The United States Supreme Court has ruled that no state or local government may require the reading of the Lord's Prayer or Bible verses in public schools; what are your views on this — do you approve or disapprove of the court ruling?) Disapprove, Approve

Basic

1. Crosstabulate NoPrayer (Y) by each of the following:

---

[5]Whether a Protestant denomination falls into a "fundamentalist," "moderate," or "liberal" category is based on the conservatism of its theology. With only a few key exceptions, *conservative* is tantamount to *fundamentalist* according to the GSS's coding scheme. Fundamentalists are generally opposed to the growth of secular influence in society. They believe in the inerrancy of the Bible, personal salvation by accepting Christ as their savior (and being "born again"), the imminent return of Christ, evangelism/revivalism to reach out to save and convert others, the Holy Trinity, and the Virgin birth. Liberal denominations tend to emphasize concerns about this world more than salvation in the next, which leads them to support social action and progressive reform. They also tend to accept secular change and science, and do not accept the literal message of the Bible (seeing, for example, Biblical miracles as metaphorical in nature and not as historical facts). Denominations that fall between these extremes have been deemed moderate." Most denominations can readily be placed in one of these three categories; for example, the Assembly of God and the Church of Christ are clearly fundamentalist, while Congregationalists and Unitarians are clearly liberal. Other fundamentalist denominations include all Baptists (except the Northern Baptists), Missouri Synod Lutherans, and Jehovah's Witnesses, while other liberal denominations include the United Methodist Church and the United Presbyterian Church in the USA. Two denominations, that pose difficulty are the Mormons (Church of Jesus Christ of Latter-day Saints) and the Christian Scientists. Based on a variety of historical and sociological facts, the GSS eventually placed both in the *fundamentalist* category. For the details of this decision and for an in-depth analysis of the GSS coding scheme, see Tom W. Smith, "Classifying Protestant Denominations," GSS Methodological Report No. 43, July, 1987 (available from the National Opinion Research Center, University of Chicago; also downloadable from the Internet: http://www.icpsr.umich.edu/gss/report/m-report/meth43.html); a revised edition of this report appears in the *Review of Religious Research* 31 (March 1990), pp. 225–245.

(a) Region   (b) Race   (c) Urban   (d) Age
(e) Ed   (f) Religion   (g) PolView   (h) Party

(a) NoPrayer (Y) by Region (X)

CrossTab: NoPrayer / Region
(**Table**: Percent Down)

	Northeast	Midwest	South	West	All
Approve					
Disapprove					

100% =   N=
(Column Sum)

(Percentage difference between the South and the West for the "Approve" row =   )
(Percentage difference between the South and the Midwest for the "Approve" row =   )
(Percentage difference between the South and the Northeast for the "Approve" row =   )
Prediction:

Findings:

(b) NoPrayer (Y) by Race (X)

CrossTab:NoPrayer / Race
(**Table**: Percent Down)

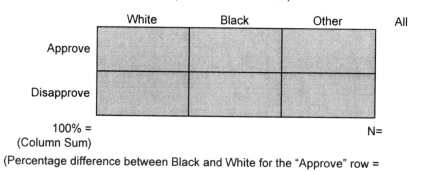

	White	Black	Other	All
Approve				
Disapprove				

100% =   N=
(Column Sum)

(Percentage difference between Black and White for the "Approve" row =   )

Prediction:

Finding:

(c) NoPrayer (Y) by Urban (X)

CrossTab:NoPrayer / Urban

(**Table**: Percent Down)

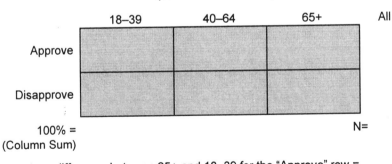

(Percentage difference between City and Rural/Small-Town for the "Approve" row =   )

Prediction:

Finding:

(d) NoPrayer (Y) by Age (X)

CrossTab:NoPrayer / Age

(**Table**: Percent Down)

	18–39	40–64	65+	All
Approve				
Disapprove				
100% = (Column Sum)				N=

(Percentage difference between 65+ and 18–39 for the "Approve" row =   )

Prediction:

Finding:

(e) NoPrayer (Y) by Ed (X)

CrossTab: NoPrayer / Ed
(**Table**: Percent Down)

	<12yrs	12yrs	13–15	16+yrs	All
Approve					
Disapprove					
100% = (Column Sum)					N=

(Percentage difference between 16+yrs and <12yrs for the "Approve" row =   )

Prediction:

Finding:

(f) NoPrayer (Y) by Religion (X)

CrossTab: NoPrayer / Relgion
(**Table**: Percent Down)

	Other	Catholic	Mod-LibProt	FundProt	All
Approve					
Disapprove					
100% = (Column Sum)					N=

(Percentage difference between FundProt and Mod-LibProt for the "Approve" row =   )

(Percentage difference between FundProt and Catholic for the "Approve" row =   )

Prediction:

Findings:

(g) NoPrayer (Y) by PolView (X)

CrossTab:NoPrayer / PolView

(**Table**: Percent Down)

	Liberal	Moderate	Conservative	All
Approve				
Disapprove				

100% =
(Column Sum)

N=

(Percentage difference between Conservative and Liberal for the "Approve" row =   )

Prediction:

Finding:

(h) NoPrayer (Y) by Party (X)

CrossTab:NoPrayer / Party

(**Table**: Percent Down)

	Democrat	Independent	Republican	All
Approve				
Disapprove				

100% =
(Column Sum)

N=

(Percentage difference between Republican and Democrat for the "Approve" row =   )

Prediction:

Finding:

(Note: for the following questions, concentrate your answers on the "Approve" column of NoPrayer.)

2. Are all of the Xs associated with NoPrayer?

3. Are all of the associations in the directions you would have predicted? (If one or more are not, discuss why you would have thought the association to be different, e.g., why you would have thought blacks would have been more likely than whites to be in the "Approve" category of NoPrayer.)

Should Abortion Be Legal for Any Reason?

File: **Abort98** (Should abortion be legal if a woman wants it for any reason? '96 & '98 GSS)

Info: Region→Urban→Race→Sex→Age→Ed→Religion→PolView→Party→Abortion
  (4)　　　(3)　　　(3)　　(2)　　(3)　　(4)　　(4)　　　　(3)　　　(3)　　　(2)

Region	Northeast (CT, ME, MA, NH, NJ, NY, PA, RI, and VT) Midwest (IL, IN, IA, KS, MI, MN, MO, NE, ND, OH, SD, and WI) South (AL, AR, DE, FL, GA, KY, LS, MD, MS, NC, OK, SC, TN, TX, VA, and WV) West (AK, AZ, CA, CO, HI, ID, MT, NV, NM, OR, UT, WA, and WY)
Urban	Rural/Small-Town, Suburb, City
Race	White, Black, Other
Sex	Male, Female
Age	18–39, 40–64, 65+
Ed	(Years of education) <12yrs, 12yrs, 13–15yrs, 16+yrs
Religion	Other (e.g., Jewish, Hindu, Buddhist, no religion), Catholic, Mod-LibProt (Moderate or Liberal Protestant, FundProt (Fundamentalist Protestant; see footnote on the "Religion" variable for the preceding data file (*NoPray98*), p. 43)
PolView	(Political view — conservatism scale; On a 7-point scale on which the political views that people might hold are arranged from extremely liberal to extremely conservative, where would you place yourself?) Liberal (1–3), Moderate (4), Conservative (5–7)
Party	Democrat, Independent, Republican
Abortion	(Should abortion be legal if a woman wants it for any reason?) No, Yes

Basic

1. Crosstabulate Abortion (Y) by each of the following:

    (a) Sex　　(b) Region　　(c) Race　　(d) Urban　　(e) Age
    (f) Ed　　(g) Religion　　(h) PolView　　(i) Party

(a) Abortion (Y) by Sex (X)

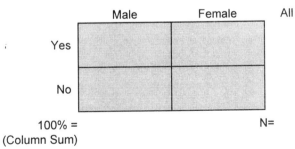

CrossTab: Abortion / Sex
(**Table**: Percent Down)

(Percentage difference between Male and Female for the "Yes" row =　　　　　)

Prediction:

Finding:

(b) Abortion (Y) by Region (X)

CrossTab: Abortion / Region
(**Table**: Percent Down)

	Northeast	Midwest	South	West	All
Yes					
No					

100% =
(Column Sum)   N=

(Percentage difference between the South and the West for the "Yes" row =   )

(Percentage difference between the South and the Midwest for the "Yes" row =   )

(Percentage difference between the South and the Northeast for the "Yes" row =   )

Prediction:

Findings:

(c) Abortion (Y) by Race (X)

CrossTab:Abortion / Race
(**Table**: Percent Down)

	White	Black	Other	All
Yes				
No				

100% =
(Column Sum)   N=

(Percentage difference between Black and White for the "Yes" row =   )

Prediction:

Finding:

(d) Abortion (Y) by Urban (X)

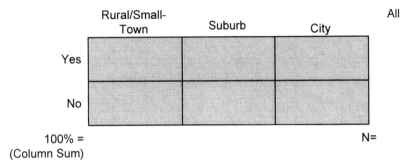

CrossTab:Abortion / Urban
(**Table**: Percent Down)

(Percentage difference between City and Rural/Small-Town for the "Yes" row =   )
Prediction:

Finding:

(e) Abortion (Y) by Age (X)

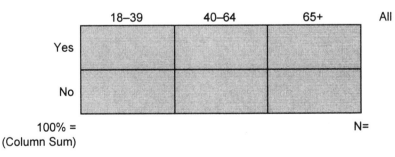

CrossTab:Abortion / Age
(**Table**: Percent Down)

(Percentage difference between 65+ and 18–39 for the "Yes" row =   )

Prediction:

Finding:

(f) Abortion (Y) by Ed (X)

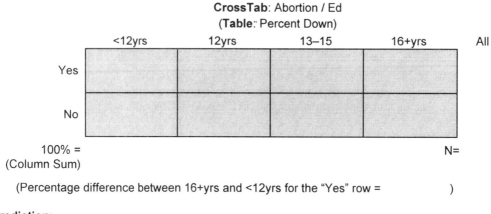

CrossTab: Abortion / Ed
(**Table**: Percent Down)

	<12yrs	12yrs	13–15	16+yrs	All
Yes					
No					
100% = (Column Sum)					N=

(Percentage difference between 16+yrs and <12yrs for the "Yes" row =   )

Prediction:

Finding:

(g) Abortion (Y) by Religion (X)

CrossTab: Abortion / Religion
(**Table**: Percent Down)

	Other	Catholic	Mod-LibProt	FundProt	All
Yes					
No					
100% = (Column Sum)					N=

(Percentage difference between FundProt and Mod-LibProt for the "Yes" row =   )

(Percentage difference between FundProt and Catholic for the "Yes" row =   )

Prediction:

Findings:

(h) Abortion (Y) by PolView (X)

CrossTab:Abortion / PolView
(**Table**: Percent Down)

	Liberal	Moderate	Conservative	All
Yes				
No				

100% =
(Column Sum)   N=

(Percentage difference between Conservative and Liberal for the "Yes" row =   )

Prediction:

Finding:

(i) Abortion (Y) by Party (X)

CrossTab:Abortion / Party
(**Table**: Percent Down)

	Democrat	Independent	Republican	All
Yes				
No				

100% =
(Column Sum)   N=

(Percentage difference between Republican and Democrat for the "Yes" row =   )
Prediction:

Finding:

(Note: for the next three questions, concentrate your answers on the "Yes" column of Abortion.)

2. Are all of the Xs associated with Abortion? Which two variables appear to be most weakly associated with Abortion?

3. Are all of the associations in the directions you would have predicted? (If one or more are not, discuss why you would have thought the association to be different, e.g., why you would have thought poorer people would have been more likely than better-off people to be in the "yes" category of Abortion.)

4. Perhaps women of varied backgrounds hold varied positions on abortion. Using your **Modify** command, **Omit** the "Male" category of Sex; then crosstabulate Abortion (Y) by Age (X) and control for Urban (Z).

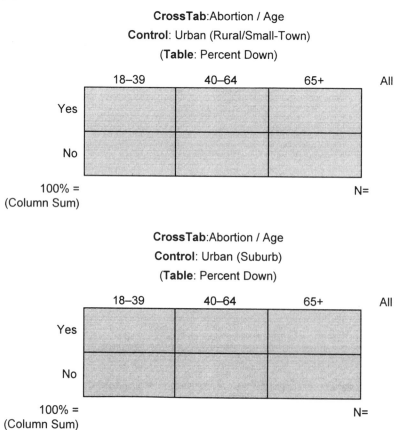

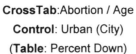

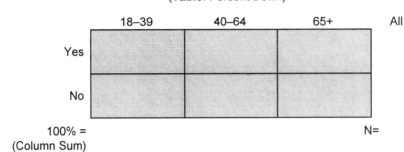

(a) Does a woman's attitude toward abortion depend upon her location and age?

(b) Which kind of woman is most likely to agree with unrestricted abortion (e.g., an older, city woman . . . , or a . . ., or a . . .)? And which kind of woman is most likely to agree?

(c) Did your answers in (b) turn out as you had expected? Briefly discuss.

5. Does the pattern of your CHIP findings for your analyses of attitudes toward government actions regarding income-equalization, school prayer, and abortion support the argument that in a pluralistic society — like that of the United States — the definition of "social problems" is problematic? Discuss.

Advanced

1. Perhaps the relationship between Party and Equalize that you found on page 40 is spurious. More specifically, it is very plausible that the relationship only exists because of the common association that Party and Equalize have with FamInc. It could be that those who are more prosperous are more likely to be Republican (the "conservative" party in the United States that favors the status quo) and, at the same time, less likely to favor income equalization (quite naturally because families with "high" incomes would be the "losers" in such a situation). Thus, it could be that the process motivating the inverse association between Republican Party membership and "Equalize" has nothing to do with being "Republican" *per se*, but rather simply reflects the relationship that family income has with these two variables. Sketch this alternative model—that is, that Party and Equalize are only related because of their common association with FamInc (note: you may want to review the section "The Art of Reading Partial Tables" in the preceding chapter).

2. Test the alternative model that you have just sketched by crosstabulating Equalize (Y) by Party (X) and controlling for FamInc (Z). To simplify your analysis, first use your **Modify** command to **Omit** the "Independents" from Party, then to **Omit** the "Neutral" value for Equalize (you can verify that you have correctly done these modifications by doing an **Info** command: You should now see just "2" values under the Party and Equalize variables, and have the smaller sample size of 1,981).

(a)

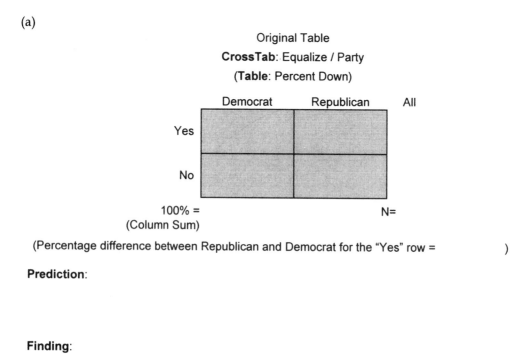

Original Table

CrossTab: Equalize / Party

(**Table**: Percent Down)

(Percentage difference between Republican and Democrat for the "Yes" row =   )

Prediction:

Finding:

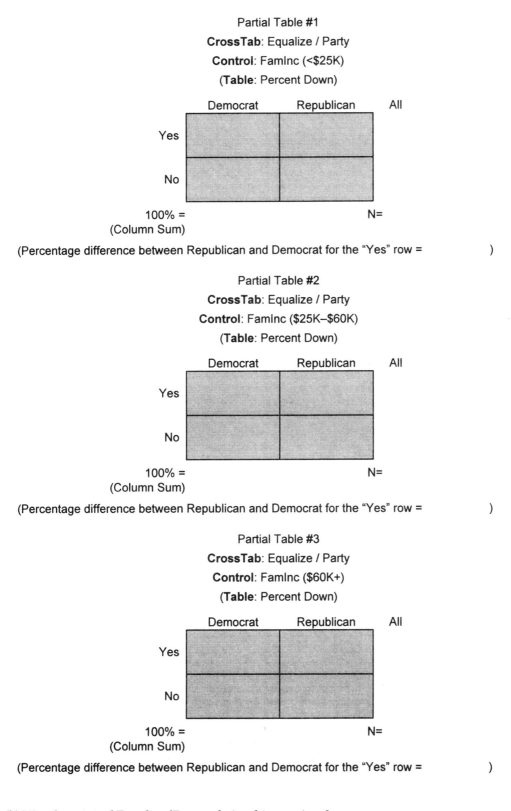

Partial Table #1
CrossTab: Equalize / Party
Control: FamInc (<$25K)
(**Table**: Percent Down)

	Democrat	Republican	All
Yes			
No			

100% =   N=
(Column Sum)

(Percentage difference between Republican and Democrat for the "Yes" row =   )

Partial Table #2
CrossTab: Equalize / Party
Control: FamInc ($25K–$60K)
(**Table**: Percent Down)

	Democrat	Republican	All
Yes			
No			

100% =   N=
(Column Sum)

(Percentage difference between Republican and Democrat for the "Yes" row =   )

Partial Table #3
CrossTab: Equalize / Party
Control: FamInc ($60K+)
(**Table**: Percent Down)

	Democrat	Republican	All
Yes			
No			

100% =   N=
(Column Sum)

(Percentage difference between Republican and Democrat for the "Yes" row =   )

(b) Was the original Equalize/Party relationship spurious?

(c) Is a multivariable model apparent—that is, do both Party and FamInc have independent effects on Equalize? Refer to the correct percentage-differences to support your answer.

3. Let's elaborate on our analysis of the relationship between Race and NoPrayer that we found earlier (see p. 45). Why is it, do you suppose, that blacks are more likely than whites to disapprove of the Supreme Court's ruling that no state or local government may require reading the Lord's Prayer or Bible verses in public schools? Perhaps it is because blacks are more likely to be fundamentalists (who are strongly religious and believe that the Bible *is* the word of God), who, in turn, are more likely to disapprove of the ruling.

(a) Sketch the model that would show Race and NoPrayer being connected by the intervening variable Religion.

(b) If the model that you have just sketched is true, what should happen to the Race→NoPrayer relationship if we were to control for Religion? (Hint: you may want to review the section "The Art of Reading Partial Tables" in the preceding chapter).

(c) Test your expectation in (b) by crosstabulating NoPrayer (Y) by Race (X) and controlling for Religion (Z). To simplify your analysis, first use your **Modify** command to **Omit** the "Others" from Race. Then use **Modify** again, but this time to **Combine** the "Other," "Catholic," and "Mod-LibProt" categories of Religion; label this new category "NonFund." (You can verify that you have correctly done these modifications by doing an **Info** command: you should now see just "2" values under the Race and Religion variables, and have a reduced sample size of 3,177). What did you find? Was this what you expected?

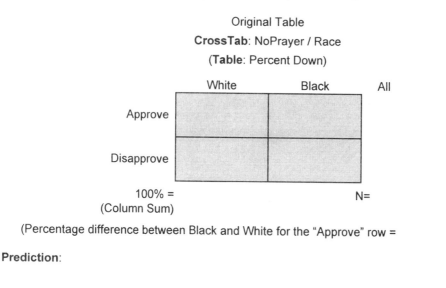

Original Table
CrossTab: NoPrayer / Race
(**Table**: Percent Down)

(Percentage difference between Black and White for the "Approve" row =)

Prediction:

Finding:

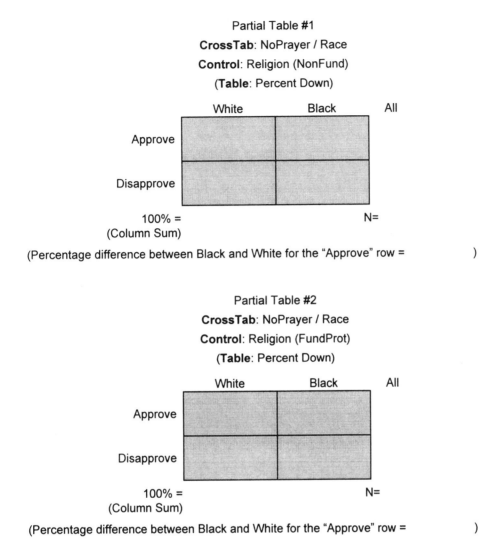

Partial Table #1
CrossTab: NoPrayer / Race
Control: Religion (NonFund)
(**Table**: Percent Down)

	White	Black	All
Approve			
Disapprove			
100% = (Column Sum)			N=

(Percentage difference between Black and White for the "Approve" row =   )

Partial Table #2
CrossTab: NoPrayer / Race
Control: Religion (FundProt)
(**Table**: Percent Down)

	White	Black	All
Approve			
Disapprove			
100% = (Column Sum)			N=

(Percentage difference between Black and White for the "Approve" row =   )

Answer/Discussion

Suggestions for Further Study

Herbert Blumer emphasizes that social problems lie less in objective reality and more in the minds of the general public. Moreover, he observes that sociologists are notoriously bad at predicting which forms of deviance and which objective conditions will be deemed insidious enough to be called "social problems." Blumer contends that the task of the social scientist is to study objective conditions less and to study the processes by which they became labeled as social problems more. These processes involve the public's initial recognition that some objective situation is a problem, the public's subsequent framing and interpretation of it, and, finally, the reasons why the public sees a problem as being resolvable along some lines of action rather than others. See his classic essay "Social Problems as Collective Definition & Collective Behavior," pp. 15–20 in Gregg Lee Carter (ed.), *Perspectives on Current Social Problems* (Boston: Allyn & Bacon, 1997).

In another essay in *Perspectives on Current Social Problems* ("The Intersection Between Social Conflict and Collective Definitions of Reality: Why African-American Rioting Ended," pp. 23–32), I argue that the nonAfrican-American riots that flourished toward the end of the Civil Rights movement belie the image propagated during the early 1960s that American society consisted of only two key groups, African-Americans (the have-nots) and whites (the haves). Analysis of trends in African-American and non-African-American rioting and a review of public opinion polls and commentary in African-American newspapers support the contention that non-African-American disorders robbed the African-American movement of part of its ideological justification and thus contributed to its decline. As emphasized in the Blumer article above, this essay reveals the importance of collective definitions in the emergence and decline of a social problem.

Relevant World Wide Web Sites

The General Social Survey — the source of all three data files used in this chapter — is available on the Web (as of the spring of 2000, through the 1994; the 1996 and 1998 surveys will be added during the year 2001). Simple analyses may be done on-line, but data may also be downloaded for investigation with SPSS or similar statistical analysis software: www.icpsr.umich.edu/gss.

Other public opinion data sources — such as the Harris Poll, the International Social Survey, and a variety of university-sponsored surveys — on a wide range of issues (including those examined in this chapter) can be found at the Survey Research Center at Princeton University. As with the GSS site listed above, simple analyses can be done on-line, or the data downloaded for further investigation with SPSS or similar software. The Princeton site also has links to the most important on-line sources for public opinion data: www.princeton.edu/~abelson/index.html

The Gallup Organization offers useful on-line summaries of its public opinion polls, including findings on abortion, crime, school prayer, gun control, education, and government anti-poverty programs: www.gallup.com/poll

A host of religious, political, and privately funded organizations have websites dedicated to particular social issues. Although the writing on these sites is highly opinionated, they can be useful for updates of political activities, court decisions, and other news on the issue at hand. For the issues examined in this chapter — governmental equalization, school prayer, and abortion — see:

Income Equalization	www.tcf.org www.clasp.org	www.welfareinfo.org www.childrensdefense.org
School Prayer	www.religiousfreedom.house.gov www.freedomforum.org/religion	www.adl.org/ www.atheists.org/courthouse
Abortion	www.aclu.org/issues/women/hmwo.html www.abortionfacts.com	www.prolifeinfo.org www.voters4choice.org

Exploratory

I.   Using one of the CHIP data files for this chapter (*Equal98, NoPray98,* or *Abort98*), state a hypothesis relating an X and a Y variable that have not already been analyzed together.

II. Sketch the bivariate model.

III. Give a brief interpretation of your hypothesis—that is, describe what is going on in the world such that we would expect to find data patterned in the way in which you have predicted.

IV. (a) Test your hypothesis with a **CrossTab**, putting your Y variable on the rows. Was your hypothesis confirmed? (Note: you may need to delete one or two rows and/or one or two columns; the following 4x4 table shell is simply a starting point.)

Original Table

CrossTab: _____(Y) /_____ (X)

(**Table**: Percent Down)

All

100% =
(Column Sum)   N=

(Percentage difference between the highest and lowest values of X on the highest value of Y =   )

Prediction:

Finding:

(b) Use **Plot** under the **Table** option to display the above relationship graphically. Feel free to be creative—trying out each of the plot types (line, bar, pie, stacked). Print out and attach the plot that you think best captures the relationship between your X and Y.

Do *either* parts V–VIII *or* parts IX–XII below.

V. Perhaps the relationship you uncovered in #IV is spurious; that is, perhaps a third variable is predictive of both X and Y; if this is so, then the relationship between X and Y would exist **not** because X is causing Y, but simply because of their covariation with this third variable. If this third variable is held constant, then the relationship between X and Y will weaken greatly or disappear. Choose a third variable that might possibly be generating a spurious relationship between X and Y. Sketch the model showing the relationship between this third variable and X, and between this third variable and Y, as well as the lack of causal relationship between X and Y. Hint: refer back to the discussion on page 25 in the introductory chapter entitled "Elementary Data Analysis Tools Needed to Study Social Issues."

VI. A good social scientist does not choose just any variable to test for spuriosity. Just as you were able to defend the hypothesized relationship between X and Y in #III, develop a brief interpretation to defend the hypothesized relationship between Z and X, then between Z and Y.

   (a) Interpretation of the Z–X relationship:

   (b) Interpretation of the Z–Y relationship:

VII. Test the alternative model sketched in #V by crosstabulating Y by X and controlling for Z—using the appended table shells.

VIII. What are your conclusions? For example, is the original X–Y relationship spurious? Is it nonspurious (i.e., causal)? Is a multivariable model evident?

IX. Examining all the variables in your data set, which one do you think might be serving as a causal mechanism connecting your X with your Y? In other words, which variable would you choose as "Z" in the following sketch: X→Z→Y? Hint: refer back to the discussion on page 26 in the introductory chapter entitled "Elementary Data Analysis Tools Needed to Study Social Issues."

X. A good social scientist does not choose just any variable to test as a causal mechanism (intervening variable). Just as you were able to defend the hypothesized relationship between X and Y in #III, develop a brief interpretation to defend the hypothesized relationship between X and Z, then between Z and Y.

(a) Interpretation of the X–Z relationship:

(b) Interpretation of the Z–Y relationship:

XI. Test the alternative model sketched in #IX by crosstabbing X and Y and controlling for Z—using the appended table shells. (Note: you may need more than the four partial tables provided; of course, you will need one partial table for each value of Z.)

XII. What are your conclusions? Most importantly, do your findings support the notion that your Z is acting as an intervening variable (causal mechanism) connecting your X and your Y?

Use the following 4x4 table shells to record your findings from *either* VII *or* XI above. Note: you may need fewer partial tables; you will need one partial table for each value of Z. Also, you may need to delete 1 or 2 rows and/or 1 or 2 columns. The appended shells simply provide you with a starting point.

Partial Table #1

Cross Tab: _____ (Y) / _____ (X)

Control: _____ (Z value)

(Table: Percent Down)

				All
				N=

100% = _____
(Column Sum)
(Percentage difference between the highest and lowest values of X
on the highest value of Y = _____)

Partial Table #2

Cross Tab: _____ (Y) / _____ (X)

Control: _____ (Z value)

(Table: Percent Down)

				All
				N=

100% = _____
(Column Sum)
(Percentage difference between the highest and lowest values of X
on the highest value of Y = _____)

Partial Table #3

Cross Tab: _____ (Y) / _____ (X)

Control: _____ (Z value)

(Table: Percent Down)

				All
				N=

100% = _____
(Column Sum)
(Percentage difference between the highest and lowest values of X
on the highest value of Y = _____)

Partial Table #4

Cross Tab: _____ (Y) / _____ (X)

Control: _____ (Z value)

(Table: Percent Down)

				All
				N=

100% = _____
(Column Sum)
(Percentage difference between the highest and lowest values of X
on the highest value of Y = _____)

SELECTED ANSWERS FOR CHAPTER 1 EXERCISES

It is expected that you will learn fairly quickly how to use Student CHIP and have the ready capacity to do crosstabulations and plots (transcribing your findings from your computer screen to your workbook). This is not the true test, however, of what you are learning about sociology and its applications to the study of contemporary social issues and problems. The true test comes in your ability to concisely and incisively fill-in the "white space" provided for your written answers. To give you an idea of what is expected of you, selected questions from above are answered in this section. These answers will provide "exemplars" that you can refer to from time to time as your "white-space" abilities blossom. Please note that this section is *not* repeated in the remaining chapters of this workbook.

Is It the Government's Responsibility to Reduce Income Differences Between the Rich and the Poor?

Basic

1. Crosstabulate Equalize (Y) by each of the following:

      (a) Race   (b) Sex   (c) Age   (d) Ed
          (e) FamInc   (f) Party

(a) Equalize (Y) by Race (X)

CrossTab: Equalize / Race
(**Table**: Percent Down)

	White	Black	All
Yes	41.0	55.7	43.1
Neutral	21.0	26.0	21.7
No	38.0	18.3	35.0
100% = (Column Sum)	2,515	415	N= 2,930

(Percentage difference between Black and White for the "Yes" row = 14.7)

Prediction: Blacks are more likely to be in the "Yes" row.

Finding: Moderately confirmatory, i.e., compared to Whites, Blacks have a (55.7%–41.0%=) 14.7%* greater chance of being in the "Yes" row.

*(Note: if you use the "Percent Diff" option under the **Table** command, you will generally come up with a slightly different percentage-difference answer, as this command carries out calculations to two decimal places; either answer—that given by "Percent Diff" or that obtained by doing the calculation from the single-decimal place percentages in the crosstab—is acceptable.)

(e) Equalize (Y) by FamInc (X)

CrossTab: Equalize / FamInc

(Table: Percent Down)

	<$25K	$25K–$60K	$60K+	All
Yes	51.0	41.7	33.4	43.1
Neutral	24.1	21.1	19.2	21.7
No	24.9	32.7	47.4	35.2
100% = (Column Sum)	1,035	1,228	667	N= 2,930

(Percentage difference between $60K+ and <$25K for the "Yes" row = −17.6)

Prediction: FamInc and Equalize are negatively related.

Finding: Moderately confirmatory, e.g., those individuals with a FamInc of $60K+ have a 17.6% smaller chance of being in the "Yes" row compared to those with a FamInc of <$25K.

Comments on the Footers for the Above Crosstabulations: In general, you will make a prediction that X is either positively related to Y, or that X is negatively related to Y (as we have done in the second crosstabulation involving FamInc). Remember, "positive" implies that the two variables increase and decrease together (as X increases, so does Y; as X decreases, so does Y), and "negative" implies that the two variables change in opposite directions (increases in one are associated with decreases in the other). If X is a nominal variable (as is the case in the first crosstabulation involving Race), then one must specify a category of X when making the prediction (see p. 12 in the earlier chapter entitled "Reading and Thinking Critically About Contemporary Social Issues"). Recall that a "nominal" variable is one whose values cannot be rank-ordered "more than" or "less than." Thus, in the General Social Survey, "Race" would be a nominal variable ("black" is not more than "white," or vice versa), while "family income" is not ("$20,000" is less than "$30,000" is less than "$40,000"). Variables having values that can be rank ordered, that is, that have gradients or weight, are called "quantitative" variables. Thus, when our prediction involves the X variable "Race" and the Y variable "Equalize" we would *not* say "Race is negatively related to Equalize" (this does not make any sense); rather, we must specify a value of Race and say something like we did: "Blacks are more likely to be in the 'Yes' row of Equalize" (or some such phrasing, e.g., "Blacks are more likely to agree with the idea that 'government should do something to reduce income differences between rich and poor'.").

Your finding should be stated in the form:
  ➢ MODIFIER (Weakly, Moderately, or Strongly), followed by the word
  ➢ CONFIRMATORY (or NONCONFIRMATORY), followed by either
  ➢ E.G., or I.E., followed by a
  ➢ PERCENTAGE DIFFERENCE (a change in X produces how much of a change in Y; you can calculate this by hand or use the *Percent diff* option of Student CHIP—one of your choices under **Table**)

Thus, say that the percentage difference in our first crosstabulation had been "4.7" instead of 14.7, then our finding would read:

Weakly confirmatory, i.e., Blacks have a 4.7% greater chance of being in the "Yes" row.

Although your instructor may have you assess the degree of confirmation by having you calculate the Chi Square statistic, you should be developing your own internal standards of assessing whether a percentage difference is confirmatory or nonconfirmatory and the degree to which it is one of these (e.g., weakly, moderately, or strongly). As sample size increases and as the percentage-difference becomes greater, the degree of confirmation becomes stronger. Thus, for example, given a relatively small sample of, say, 50, and given a relatively small percentage difference of, say 7, we would give the assessment "weakly" confirmatory (or nonconfirmatory). If the relationship is in the expected direction, then it is confirmatory. Thus, for example, if we hypothesize that it is positive and it turns out to be positive, then the finding is confirmatory. Again, the degree to which it is confirmatory will depend upon sample size and the strength of the relationship (percentage difference). When we use the General Social Survey, sample size is often in the thousands, thus a relatively small percentage difference will be both statistically and substantively significant (at least "moderately" confirmatory) — that is, any percentage difference above 9 or 10 should be considered important. When we use U.S. states (where N=50) or crossnational data (where N is typically between 150 and 200, then we need larger percentage differences to give an assessment of "moderately" or "strongly" confirmatory — well into double digits (15, 20, 25 percentage points).

Whether you use the connecting abbreviation "i.e." versus "e.g." depends upon the dimensions of your crosstab. Two-by-two (2 row / 2 column) crosstabs have only one correct percentage difference (comparing columns on either row yields the same percentage difference), and thus you use "i.e." ("that is"). For crosstabs of larger dimensions (anything greater than 2x2, e.g., 3x2 or, say, 3x3), you would use "e.g." ("for example") because there is more than one possibility for comparing percentages. In these situations, you are instructed which percentage difference to compute; in general, it will be the difference between the "highest" and "lowest" values of X on the "highest" value Y.

Sometimes there will be a second part to this kind of question — that is, you will be asked to do a line plot to depict the relationship graphically. Had this been asked, you would have hand-drawn a straight line between the percentage value for Equalize = "Yes" for the FamInc value of <$25K and the percentage value for Equalize = "Yes" for the FamInc value of $25K–$60K; and in the same manner, drawn the line between $25K–$60K and $60K+. (Redo the **CrossTab**, then select the **Line** alternative for the **Plot** option under the **Table** command and highlight the "Yes" category):

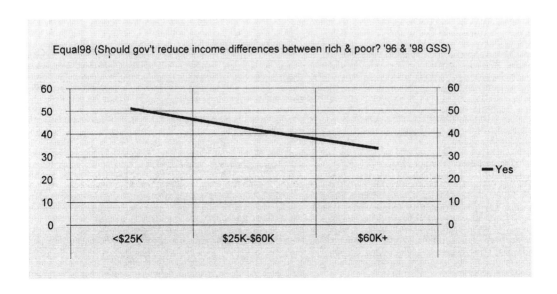

(Note: for the following questions, concentrate your answers on the "Yes" column of Equalize.)

2. Are all of the Xs associated with Equalize?

    Yes, every X has a modest association with Equalize.

3. Are all of the associations in the directions you would have predicted? (If one or more are not, discuss why you would have thought the association to be different, e.g., why you would have thought whites would have been more likely than blacks to be in the "yes" category of Equalize.)

    Yes, the direction of the relationship between each X and Equalize is as we would predict:

    Equalize/Race: We would expect those suffering from discrimination and from current social arrangements to be more likely to favor government redistribution of income; indeed, blacks are significantly more likely than whites to favor redistribution.

    Equalize/FamInc: We would expect those benefiting from current social arrangements to be less likely to favor government redistribution of income; indeed, those in the most prosperous group (with incomes over $60,000 per year) are much less likely than those in the least prosperous group (with incomes under $25,000 per year) to favor redistribution. Inspection of the line plot reveals that the relationship is negative and linear.

4. Examining the plot and crosstab for Equalize and FamInc, why do you think the data are patterned in this way (i.e., that the more prosperous are less likely to agree that the government should try to be an "equalizer")?

    We would expect those benefiting from current social arrangements to be less likely to favor government redistribution of income—as they would be the ones to have to "give up" something under such a policy.

Note that in our answer to this question we are required to give an "interpretation" to our finding. This will be required of you quite often—in this workbook, in the workplace, and in life in general! Although not present here, many times you will see a white-space section entitled "**Answer/Discussion**" following your crosstabs and plots. Whenever you see such a heading, you should demonstrate your understanding of the finding at hand by doing the following:

> ➤ stating the hypothesis that motivated the particular analysis (e.g., crosstab or line plot)—this amounts to the "prediction" in the crosstab;
>
> ➤ stating the finding—and in doing so, assess the degree to which it is in line with the hypothesis;
>
> ➤ generating a brief interpretation that makes sense out of the hypothesis and finding.

Let us say that your Equalize/FamInc crosstabulation and plot had been followed by an **Answer/Discussion** section. Applying the above steps, we would fill-in the "white space" with something like:

    It was hypothesized that Equalize and FamInc would be negatively associated; indeed, the crosstab and plot both reveal a moderately strong negative relationship. This was expected because those benefiting from current social arrangements—here, the most prosperous—would be the ones to have to "give up" something under a policy of governmental redistribution of income.

Note that all three steps are incorporated into this brief paragraph. The amount of "white space" to do your writing is small, so you must learn to be concise and "cut to the chase" quickly.

Advanced

1. Perhaps the relationship between Party and Equalize that you found on page 40 is spurious. More specifically, it is very plausible that the relationship only exists because of the common association that Party and Equalize have with FamInc. It could be that those who are more prosperous are more likely to be Republican (the "conservative" party in the United States that favors the status quo) and, at the same time, less likely to favor income equalization (quite naturally because families with "high" incomes would be the "losers" in such a situation). Thus, it could be that the process motivating the inverse association between Republican Party membership and "Equalize" has nothing to do with being "Republican" *per se*, but rather simply reflects the relationship that family income has with these two variables. Sketch this alternative model—that is, that Party and Equalize are only related because of their common association with FamInc (note: you may want to review the section "The Art of Reading Partial Tables" in the preceding chapter).

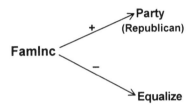

This type of question is asked many times in *Analyzing Contemporary Social Issues*. Note that the model sketch will always look the same: Z–to–X, Z–to–Y; and no connection between X and Y.

2. Test the alternative model that you have just sketched by crosstabulating Equalize (Y) by Party (X) and controlling for FamInc (Z). To simplify your analysis, first use your **Modify** command to **Omit** the "Independents" from Party, then to **Omit** the "Neutral" value for Equalize (you can verify that you have correctly done these modifications by doing an **Info** command: You should now see just "2" values under the Party and Equalize variables, and have the smaller sample size of 1,981).

(a)

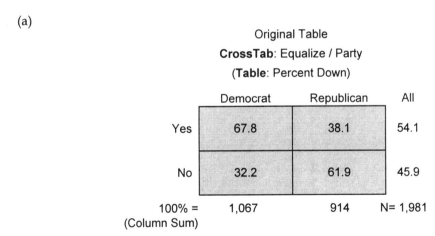

Original Table

CrossTab: Equalize / Party

(**Table**: Percent Down)

	Democrat	Republican	All
Yes	67.8	38.1	54.1
No	32.2	61.9	45.9
100% = (Column Sum)	1,067	914	N= 1,981

(Percentage difference between Republican and Democrat for the "Yes" row = –29.7)

Prediction: Republicans are less likely to be in the "Yes" row.

Finding: Strongly confirmatory, i.e., compared to Democrats, Republicans have a 29.7% smaller chance of being in the "Yes" row.

Partial Table #1
CrossTab: Equalize / Party
Control: FamInc (<$25K)
(**Table**: Percent Down)

	Democrat	Republican	All
Yes	73.4	54.5	66.7
No	26.6	45.5	33.3
100% = (Column Sum)	425	233	N= 658

(Percentage difference between Republican and Democrat for the "Yes" row = −18.9)

Partial Table #2
CrossTab: Equalize / Party
Control: FamInc ($25K–$60K)
(**Table**: Percent Down)

	Democrat	Republican	All
Yes	67.6	36.3	52.2
No	32.4	63.7	47.8
100% = (Column Sum)	423	411	N= 830

(Percentage difference between Republican and Democrat for the "Yes" row = −31.3)

Partial Table #3
CrossTab: Equalize / Party
Control: FamInc ($60K+)
(**Table**: Percent Down)

	Democrat	Republican	All
Yes	57.1	26.7	40.3
No	42.9	73.3	59.7
100% = (Column Sum)	219	270	N= 489

(Percentage difference between Republican and Democrat for the "Yes" row = −30.4)

(b) Was the original Equalize/Party relationship spurious?

No. Although the relationship has weakened somewhat in the first partial table (the absolute value of the key percentage-difference dropping from 29.7 in the original table to 18.9), and has strengthened slightly in the second and third partial tables (the absolute values increasing to 30.4 and 31.3 respectively), it is still strong and in the same direction; we may therefore conclude that it is nonspurious or causal.

(c) Is a multivariable model apparent—that is, do both Party and FamInc have independent effects on Equalize? Refer to the correct percentage-differences to support your answer.

Yes—as we have just shown, the partial tables reveal that regardless of ("independent of") FamInc that Party influences Equalize in a consistent and strong manner (with Republicans less likely to favor income equalization). Moreover, the tables reveal the independent-variable effects of FamInc on Equalize: for Democrats, "high" FamInc individuals ($60K+) have (57.1%–67.6%) 10.5% smaller chance of being in the "Yes" row compared to "middle" FamInc individuals ($25K–$60K); similarly the "middle" FamInc individuals have a (67.6%–73.4%) 5.8% smaller chance of being in the "Yes" row compared to those with "low" FamInc (<$25K). Likewise, for Republicans, "high" FamInc individuals have (26.7%–36.3%) 9.6% smaller chance of being in the "Yes" row compared to "middle" FamInc individuals; similarly the "middle" FamInc individuals have a (36.3%–54.5%) 18.2% smaller chance of being in the "Yes" row compared to those with "low" FamInc. Thus, regardless of political Party affiliation—that is to say, "independent" of Party—FamInc has a negative effect on Equalize. We may sketch the causal mode evident in these partial tables as follows:

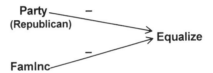

3. Let's elaborate on our analysis of the relationship between Race and NoPrayer that we found earlier (see p. 45). Why is it, do you suppose, that blacks are more likely than whites to disapprove of the Supreme Court's ruling that no state or local government may require reading the Lord's Prayer or Bible verses in public schools? Perhaps it is because blacks are more likely to be fundamentalists (who are strongly religious and believe that the Bible *is* the word of God), who, in turn, are more likely to disapprove of the ruling.

(a) Sketch the model that would show Race and NoPrayer being connected by the intervening variable Religion.

(b) If the model that you have just sketched is true, what should happen to the Race→NoPrayer relationship if we were to control for Religion? (Hint: you may want to review the section "The Art of Reading Partial Tables" in the preceding chapter).

If the model sketched in (a) were completely accurate, then controlling for Religion would wipe out the relationship between Race and NoPrayer (that is, percentage difference would be zero) because the effects of Race on NoPrayer are being transmitted via Religion—and this can occur only if FamInc is allowed to vary. Realistically, however, there are many intervening variables (e.g., a greater "distrust" in the legal system on the part of blacks) and thus we would only expect a reduction in the relationship—not its complete disappearance. Why should it reduce? It should do so because we have removed one of the causal pathways by which Race transmits its effects on NoPrayer!

(c) Test your expectation in (b) by crosstabulating NoPrayer (Y) by Race (X) and controlling for Religion (Z). To simplify your analysis, first use your **Modify** command to **Omit** the "Others" from Race. Then use **Modify** again, but his time to **Combine** the "Other," "Catholic," and "Mod-LibProt" categories of Religion; label this new category "NonFund." (You can verify that you have correctly done these modifications by doing an **Info** command: you should now see just "2" values under the Race and Religion variables, and have a reduced sample size of 3,177). What did you find? Was this what you expected?

Original Table

CrossTab: NoPrayer / Race

(**Table**: Percent Down)

	White	Black	All
Approve	45.4	30.1	43.2
Disapprove	54.6	69.9	56.8
100% = (Column Sum)	2,712	465	N= 3,177

(Percentage difference between Black and White for the "Approve" row = −15.3)

Prediction: Blacks are less likely to be in the "Approve" row.

Finding: Moderately confirmatory, i.e., compared to Whites, Blacks have a 15.3% smaller chance of being in the "Approve" row.

Partial Table #1

CrossTab: NoPrayer / Race

Control: Religion (NonFund)

(**Table**: Percent Down)

	White	Black	All
Approve	51.5	37.3	50.3
Disapprove	40.5	62.7	49.7
100% = (Column Sum)	2,013	185	N= 2,198

(Percentage difference between Black and White for the "Approve" row = −14.2)

Partial Table #2

CrossTab: NoPrayer / Race

Control: Religion (FundProt)

(**Table**: Percent Down)

	White	Black	All
Approve	27.9	25.4	27.2
Disapprove	72.1	74.6	72.8
100% = (Column Sum)	699	280	N= 979

(Percentage difference between Black and White for the "Approve" row = −2.5)

Answer/Discussion

As predicted in (b), the relationship between Race and NoPrayer has reduced—to a small degree in Partial Table #1, and greatly so in the Partial Table #2. Thus, we have confirmation that our X→Z→Y (Race→ Religion→NoPrayer) model is reasonable. (Whenever you are presented with an "intervening variable" model, this is the key assessment that you must make—that is, did the relationship diminish, per our expectation.)

The findings in the partial tables can also be interpreted as supporting an "interaction" model—that is, that the effects of X on Y depend upon the value of Z (see p. 27 in the earlier chapter "Elementary Data Analysis Tools Needed to Study Social Issues"). Here, Race does influence NoPrayer, but only for those who are not fundamentalists. We can sketch this "interaction" model as follows:

Race (Black) —————————————————→ **NoPrayer**
 (but only for NonFundamentalists)

In general, the Advanced exercises demonstrate the importance of introducing "control" variables in the course of analyzing our X–Y hypotheses. As you have seen, "anything" can happen once a control variable is introduced. What you need to acquire is the set of intellectual tools necessary to interpret whatever happens. Learning to apply the vocabulary of causal analysis—for example, "spuriosity," "intervening variable," "interaction effect," "multivariable model" —will go a long way in giving you these tools. Learning sociology will too.

Exploratory

I. Using either of the CHIP data files for this chapter (*Equal98, NoPray98,* or *Abort98*), state a hypothesis relating an X and a Y variable that have not already been analyzed together.

> Examining the Equalize data file, we might reasonably hypothesize that education would be predictive of family income, that is, Ed and FamInc are positively related.

II. Sketch the bivariate model.

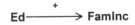

Ed ——————→ FamInc

III. Give a brief interpretation of your hypothesis — that is, describe what is going on in the world such that we would expect to find data patterned in the way in which you have predicted.

> Employers place greater value on more educated individuals because these individuals: (a) tend to have more training in a particular field; (b) have proven that they have perseverance and can "pay the price" it takes to realize significant accomplishment; and (c) will have more in common with the staff in high-paying fields where most workers are highly educated (a basic principle of sociology is that people feel more comfortable around those who are like themselves).

IV. (a) Test your hypothesis with a **CrossTab**, putting your Y variable on the rows. Was your hypothesis confirmed? (Note: you may need to delete one or two rows and/or one or two columns; the following 4x4 table shell is simply a starting point.)

CrossTab: FamInc / Ed
(**Table**: Percent Down)

	<12yrs	12yrs	13–15yrs	16+yrs	All
$60K+	6.1	14.8	21.4	42.2	22.2
$25K–$60K	26.9	45.7	46.6	40.8	41.9
<$25K	67.0	39.5	32.0	17.0	35.3
100% = (Column Sum)	424	891	831	784	N= 2,930

(Percentage difference between 16+yrs and <12yrs for the "$60K+" row = 36.1)

Prediction: Ed and FamInc are positively related.

Finding: Moderately confirmatory, e.g., those individuals with 16+ years of schooling have a (42.2%–6.1%=) 36.1% greater chance of being in the $60K+ row.

(Note that in the tables for this set of exploratory exercises, only 3 rows are needed — and you would, of course, not use the 4th row in the table shells that are provided).

(b) Use **Plot** under the **Table** option to display the above relationship graphically. Feel free to be creative — trying out each of the plot types (line, bar, pie, stacked). Print out and attach the plot that you think best captures the relationship between your X and Y.

Equal98 (Should gov't reduce income differences between rich & poor? '96 & '98 GSS)

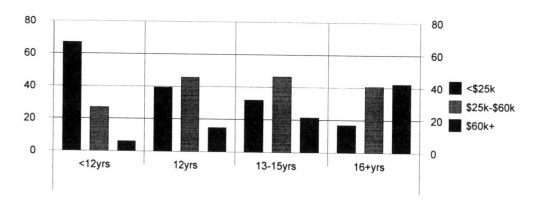

XIII. Perhaps the relationship you uncovered in #IV is spurious; that is, perhaps a third variable is predictive of both X and Y; if this is so, then the relationship between X and Y would exist **not** because X is causing Y, but simply because of their covariation with this third variable. If this third variable is held constant, then the relationship between X and Y will weaken greatly or disappear. Choose a third variable that might possibly be generating a spurious relationship between X and Y. Sketch the model showing the relationship between this third variable and X, and between this third variable and Y, as well as the lack of causal relationship between X and Y. Hint: refer back to the discussion on page 25 in the introductory chapter entitled "Elementary Data Analysis Tools Needed to Study Social Issues."

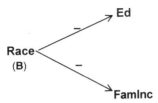

V. A good social scientist does not choose just any variable to test for spuriosity. Just as you were able to defend the hypothesized relationship between X and Y in #III, develop a brief interpretation to defend the hypothesized relationship between Z and X, then between Z and Y.

(a) Interpretation of the Z–X relationship:

> For a variety of reasons we might expect whites to have an educational advantage over blacks, especially when we are examining the entire adult population. For example, due to segregation and lack of choice, blacks have been forced to go to inner-city schools in which much of the student body is poor. Role models for a student considering going on to college are relatively few, while models for a student dropping out of high school are disproportionately high. In addition, education begets itself— with the sons and daughters of educated parents being more likely to become educated themselves (more opportunity; more encouragement). Because of historical discrimination, blacks are less likely to have educated parents and thus lack this advantage.

(b) Interpretation of the Z–Y relationship:

> We might expect whites to have higher incomes because they have faced less current and historical discrimination in the labor force. In addition, many good jobs are acquired through "connections," and because whites have historically been more likely to hold higher prestige jobs, they have an 'inside advantage" denied to blacks.

NOTE that in neither (a) nor (b) was a direct or causal connection ever made between education and family income. Indeed, we are playing the "devil's advocate" here and are trying to see whether it is possible to make a persuasive argument for a *spurious* association between X and Y, not a *causal* one. Thus, we are conjecturing that the reason we might have found an association between Ed and FamInc in the crosstab in #IV above is that both of these variables happen to vary with Race, *not* because X (Ed) is causing Y (FamInc).

VI. Test the alternative model sketched in #V by crosstabbing Y by X and controlling for Z—using the appended table shells.

Partial Table #1

CrossTab: FamInc / Ed

Control: Race (White)

(**Table**: Percent Down)

	<12yrs	12yrs	13–15yrs	16+yrs	All
$60K+	7.2	16.1	22.7	41.9	24.3
$25K–$60K	29.1	48.1	47.9	41.2	43.5
<$25K	63.7	35.7	29.4	16.9	32.2
100% = (Column Sum)	333	750	704	728	N= 2,515

(Percentage difference between 16+yrs and <12yrs for the "$60K+" row = 34.7)

Partial Table #2

CrossTab: FamInc / Ed

Control: Race (Black)

(**Table**: Percent Down)

	<12yrs	12yrs	13–15yrs	16+yrs	All
$60K+	2.2	7.8	14.2	46.4	13.7
$25K–$60K	18.7	32.6	39.4	35.7	32.0
<$25K	79.1	59.6	46.5	17.9	54.2.
100% = (Column Sum)	91	141	127	56	N= 415

(Percentage difference between 16+yrs and <12yrs for the "$60K+" row = 44.2)

(Note that we needed to use only two for the four partial-table shells provided.)

VII. What are your conclusions? For example, is the original X–Y relationship spurious? Is it nonspurious (i.e., causal)? Is a multivariable model evident?

> Inspection of the partial tables reveals that the original positive relationship between Ed and FamInc has maintained itself; we may therefore conclude that this relationship is nonspurious or causal.

A special note on subsample size and searching for multivariable effects: The percentage-differences for the partial tables above do *not* support a multivariable model when we focus on the $60K+ row; to do so, whites would need to have a higher probability of being in this row for every value of education (thus, "independent" of education), but this is not the case for those with 16+yrs of education, where we find blacks more likely to be $60K+ earners. However, there are so few blacks in this row that it becomes both statistically and substantively risky to focus on it (remember from your earlier chapter on "Elementary Data Analysis" that statistical significance is dependent upon sample size—with larger samples much more likely to produce "significant" results). Thus, in this situation, it is advisable to focus on the other end of the income scale—that is, on who is "poorest"—rather than who is "most prosperous." If we focus our attention on those in the poorest row (FamInc = "<$25K"), where the numbers for both black and white are relatively large, the percentage differences *do* support the notion of a multivariable model. More specifically, regardless of level of education, blacks are more likely to be in the "low" FamInc row (<$25K): for those with 16+ years of education, blacks have a (17.9%–16.9%=) 1.0% greater chance of having "low" family income; the same can be said for those with 13–15 years of education (blacks have 17.1% greater chance), 12 years (a 23.9% greater chance), and less than 12 years of education (a 15.4% greater chance). We may sketch the multivariable model evident in these tables as follows:

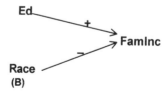

One more key observation to help you along the road of becoming a keen data analyst with a sharp sociological imagination: the effects of Z (in this case "Race") appear small compared to those of X (here, Ed). For example, the average (absolute value) percentage-difference effect of Ed on "low" FamInc equals 54.0% (61.2%+46.8% equals 108.0%, divided by 2 equals 54.0%), while that of Race equals 14.35% (1.0%+17.9%+ 23.9%+15.4% equals 57.4%, divided by 4 equals 14.35%). However, because the direction of this effect is sociologically interpretable (blacks suffer more discrimination and thus should be more likely to be in the lowest income category), it should not be discounted. Moreover, we can see that even if we had chosen to focus on the "most prosperous" row—those with family incomes of greater than $60,000 per year ("$60K+")—the effect of Race is still apparent, with whites being favored in three of the four educational categories (<12yrs, 12yrs, and 13–15yrs).

Take a close look at the last column of the two partial tables. Sociologically speaking, these findings reveal much hope for reducing racial inequality in U.S. society. When blacks become highly educated—that is, graduate from college—they have about the same high probability as whites of becoming prosperous and, likewise, about the same low probability of being poor.

Chapter 2. Social Problems and Social Conflict—The Political Dimension

Many sociology textbook authors emphasize a "conflict" perspective in trying to understand many contemporary problems. The conflict perspective assumes that different individuals and different groups have different interests. Moreover, as they pursue their interests, they increase the likelihood that they will end up in states of competition and conflict. Pick up any daily newspaper and the truth of the assumptions is obvious. Accounts of labor strikes, coups d'etat, wars, business competition, and sporting events abound.

What will determine the outcome of any particular conflict? The answer seems obvious, and it is: Those individuals and those groups with the greatest number of resources will tend to win out, whether the competition is between two men for a woman, or two companies for a contract, or two nations at war. Resources comprise anything that can be of assistance in a fray: money, knowledge, technology, size, experience, and allies are just a few examples.

Eventually, conflicts are resolved; but then the parties will have new conflicting interests: losers will want to try to get back what they've lost, winners will want to solidify their gains. In a closed system, the cycle—repeated over many generations—will result in a social class structure, that is, in stratification: the rich will tend to get richer and the poor poorer. This cycle is diagrammed below.[1]

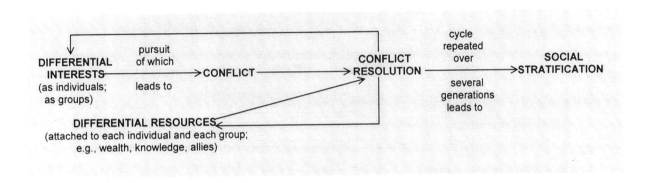

In Chapter 27 of *Capital*, Karl Marx, the father of modern conflict theory, offers the following example of this cyclical process: The landowners of England and Scotland were the heart of the upper class from the 15th through the 18th centuries. As the textile industry developed and they saw more profit in using their land for sheep-grazing rather than for tilling, they used their power and influence to expropriate the peasants from their historic holdings and convert these holdings into sheep pastures. The weaker class, the peasants, were forced into states of privation and compelled to migrate to cities, where they toiled for low wages in the textile mills converting wool and cotton into cloth. In short, the rich stayed rich or got richer, and the poor got more miserably poor.[2]

Most sociology textbook authors concur with Marx's view that coercion and force are pivotal to the maintenance of the contemporary social order, with the lower classes being compelled to accept the dictates of the upper classes. These authors emphasize that the rich and powerful use their wealth, the power of government (over which they have great influence if not outright control), and sometimes force to shape society to meet their economic interests at the expense of the less affluent. For example, Doug McAdam's

---

[1]Adapted from Part 12 in Gregg Lee Carter, *Empirical Approaches to Sociology: Classic and Contemporary Readings* 3rd Edition (Boston: Allyn & Bacon), 2001.

[2]See Karl Marx *Capital, Vol. I* (New York: Vintage Books, 1977[1867]), Chapter 27.

research on the 1960s African-American riots confirms Marx's work on how those in power use force to quash weaker groups that try to rebel against the existing social and economic hierarchy.[3] That the African-American movement of the 1960s was crushed before achieving full victory is manifested by the enduring poverty of many African-Americans and the ever-present threat of black rioting (for example, the 1992 cataclysm in south central Los Angeles, as well as the many other outbreaks in African-American neighborhoods that have happened sporadically over the past 3 decades).

In the first of the following computer exercises, we discover how social conflict is reflected in political ideology and in the political system. More specifically, we will explore how those with social advantages (the "right" skin color; the "right" sex; high incomes) are more likely to be political conservatives (which is related to our CHIP work above, that is, that these same individuals are least likely to favor income redistribution). We will then find that the more advantaged are more likely than the less advantaged to have their interests represented by government because they vote more and have greater control over the political process more generally.

The Social Correlates of Political Party Identification

File: **Equal98** (Should gov't reduce income differences between rich & poor? '96 & '98 GSS)

Info: Region→ Race→ Sex→Age→Ed→FamInc→PolView→Party→Equalize
       (4)   (2)   (2)   (3) (4)   (3)   (3)   (3)   (3)

Region	Northeast (CT, ME, MA, NH, NJ, NY, PA, RI, and VT) Midwest (IL, IN, IA, KS, MI, MN, MO, NE, ND, OH, SD, and WI) South (AL, AR, DE, FL, GA, KY, LS, MD, MS, NC, OK, SC, TN, TX, VA, and WV) West (AK, AZ, CA, CO, HI, ID, MT, NV, NM, OR, UT, WA, and WY)
Race	White, Black
Sex	Male, Female
Age	18–39, 40–64, 65+
Ed	(Years of education) <12yrs, 12yrs, 13–15yrs, 16+yrs
FamInc	(Annual family income) <$25K, $25K–$60K, $60K+
PolView	(Political view—conservatism scale; On a 7-point scale on which the political views that people might hold are arranged from extremely liberal to extremely conservative, where would you place yourself?) Liberal (1–3), Moderate (4), Conservative (5–7)
Party	Democrat, Independent, Republican
Equalize	(Government should do something to reduce income differences between rich and poor: 1=should . . . 7=should not) No (5–7), Neutral (4), Yes (1–3)

Basic

1. The Republican Party (GOP) has traditionally been the political party in the United States for those in favor of the status quo. It would therefore seem plausible that Republicans would consider themselves more conservative. Test this hypothesis by crosstabulating PolView (Y) by Party (X). Is it supported? (*Concentrate your answer on the "Conservative" row of PolView.*)

---

[3]Doug McAdam, *Political Process and the Development of Black Insurgency 1930-1970* (Chicago: University of Chicago Press, 1982), especially Chapter 8.

CrossTab: PolView / Party
(**Table**: Percent Down)

	Democrat	Independent	Republican	All
Conservative				
Moderate				
Liberal				
100% = (Column Sum)				N=

(Percentage difference between Republican and Democrat for the "Conservative" row =   )

(Percentage difference between Republican and Independent for the "Conservative" row =   )

Prediction:

Findings:

Answer/Discussion

2. Since the Republican party has traditionally been the party for those in favor of the status quo, it would seem plausible that those who benefit most from the way things currently are would be most likely to favor the GOP. Test this hypothesis by crosstabulating Party (Y) by FamInc (X). Is it supported? (*Concentrate your answer on the "Republican" row of Party.*)

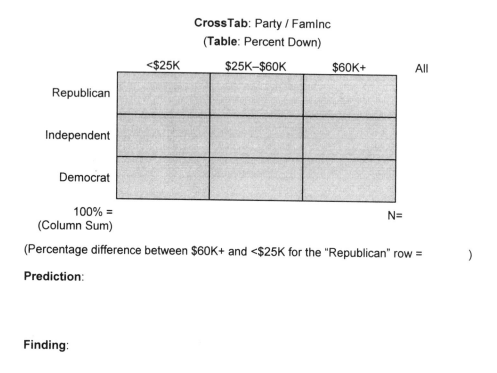

CrossTab: Party / FamInc
(**Table**: Percent Down)

(Percentage difference between $60K+ and <$25K for the "Republican" row =   )

Prediction:

Finding:

Answer/Discussion

3. It would seem plausible that those who benefit most from the way things currently are would be most likely to be conservative (why change the *status quo* if it's currently profiting you?). Test this hypothesis by crosstabulating PolView (Y) by FamInc (X) and; also examine the relationship graphically (after doing the **CrossTab**, select the **Line** alternative for the **Plot** option under the **Table** command and highlight the "Conservative" category). What did you find? (*Concentrate your answer on the "Conservative" row of PolView.*)

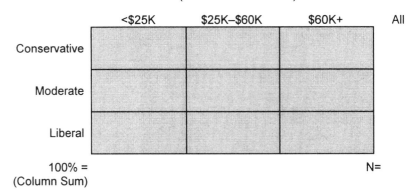

CrossTab: PolView / FamInc
(**Table**: Percent Down)

	<$25K	$25K–$60K	$60K+	All
Conservative				
Moderate				
Liberal				

100% =
(Column Sum)   N=

(Percentage difference between $60K+ and <$25K for the "Conservative" row =   )

Prediction:

Finding:

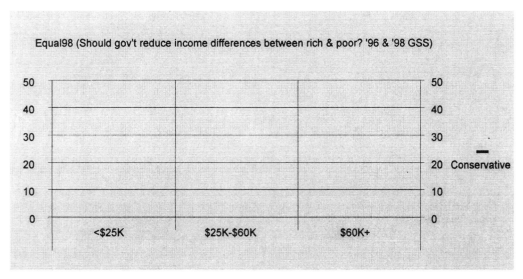

Answer/Discussion

4. Crosstabulate Party (Y) by each of the following: Race (X), Sex (X), and Age (X). Considering these three crosstabulations, along with the one you did in #(2) above, answer the following:

   (a) Who is most likely to be a Republican? (e.g., a black, male, aged . . .)

   (b) Who is most likely to be a Democrat? (e.g., a black, male, aged . . .)

5. Crosstabulate PolView (Y) by each of the following: Race (X), Sex (X), and Age (X). Considering these three crosstabulations, along with the one you did in #(3) above, answer the following:

   (a) Who is most likely to be politically conservative? (e.g., a black, male, aged . . .)

   (b) Who is most likely to be politically liberal? (e.g., a black, male, aged . . .)

6. Do all of your findings above (#s1–5) support the notion that those with social advantages are generally more likely to be politically conservative? Discuss.

Advanced

7. Perhaps the relationship between FamInc and Party is spurious—more specifically, perhaps they are only related because of their common association with Race. Defend this alternative model.

    (a) Sketch the model that would show the relationship between these two variables as spurious, using Race as your antecedent variable (let Party = *Republican*).

    (b) Interpretation of the Race–FamInc relationship:

    (c) Interpretation of the Race–Party relationship:

8. Crosstab Party (Y) by FamInc (X), then control for Race. Does the relationship between FamInc and Party maintain itself? Is an interaction model evident—between FamInc and Race when predicting Party? (Review "The Art of Reading Partial Tables" in your earlier chapter on "Elementary Data Analysis Tools," if necessary.) Refer to the correct percentage differences to support your answer. (*Concentrate your discussion on the "Republican" row of Party.*)

Partial Table #1
CrossTab: Party / FamInc
Control: Race (White)
(**Table**: Percent Down)

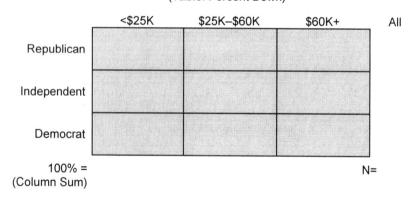

	<$25K	$25K–$60K	$60K+	All
Republican				
Independent				
Democrat				
100% = (Column Sum)				N=

(Percentage difference between $60K+ and <$25K for the "Republican" row =   )

Partial Table #2
CrossTab: Party / FamInc
Control: Race (Black)
(**Table**: Percent Down)

	<$25K	$25K–$60K	$60K+	All
Republican				
Independent				
Democrat				
100% = (Column Sum)				N=

(Percentage difference between $60K+ and <$25K for the "Republican" row =   )

Answer/Discussion

Social Class and Political Participation

Leonard Beeghley writes in the "conflict" tradition of sociological theorizing on socioeconomic inequality and stratification. His research demonstrates how election laws and practices in the United States benefit the more affluent classes.[4] The poor display the lowest rate of all forms of participation for three key reasons: they have fewer political resources, fewer psychological resources, and the organization of the electoral process inhibits their participation:

> **Level of Political Resources**—The most important political resource in the U.S. is clearly money. The budgets of poorer people do not allow much for transportation to meetings, so organizational, electoral, partisan, and governmental participation are difficult. More importantly, the budget for a poor family does not include money for campaign contributions. As a result, they are least likely to appear on candidate or party mailing lists, and least likely to be contacted and mobilized to participate.
>
> **Level of Psychological Resources**—Political participation is also affected by a variety of psychological resources that few poor persons possess: feelings of competence, beliefs that political decisions can be made in one's own interests, and a generalized sense that political issues are important. These resources are distributed differently by class. Measures of political efficacy commonly show that the poor think they have less say in political decisions and less influence over decision-makers than do members of any other class. And they are right, of course, for impoverished persons typically do not control their own destinies. For example, they do not have job protection if they are fired unjustly or legal aid if they are denied unemployment compensation.
>
> **The Structure of the Electoral Process**—Electoral procedures are so designed that the poor are least able to participate: *Election Day*—In the U.S., election day is Tuesday and, partly as a result, participation rates are much lower and class differences are great. Voting during the week is a structural barrier to participation. Those who overcome this obstacle in the greatest numbers have longer lunch hours, leave-time built into their jobs, more physical energy at the end of the day, child care available, and belief in their own competence. These traits, however, are class related, which is why participation is also class related. *Registration Requirements*—In Western European nations, the state automatically registers all citizens to vote, a fact that partly accounts for high electoral participation rates. In the U.S., citizens are responsible for their own registration. Requiring the first act as a condition for the second is a barrier to electoral participation.

There are other barriers to electoral participation, and they affect the poor the most: *Separation of Local, State, and Federal Elections*—Americans go to the polls for different purposes in different elections. Partly as a result, participation rates are very low and class differences are great. State and federal elections are generally separated: only fourteen states ever schedule gubernatorial contests in presidential election years. Similarly, local elections are usually separated from other contests: only 17 percent of all cities larger than twenty-five thousand people hold elections concurrently with either state or federal campaigns. Finally, many areas hold bond and special district elections at different times. With so much diverse election activity, many people find it difficult to obtain information about candidates and issues and to maintain an interest in voting.

In sum, while individuals can choose to vote or not, the process is so organized that low rates of participation by the poor seem almost inevitable. Given their location in society, members of this stratum

---

[4]"Social Class and Political Participation," *Sociological Forum* 1(Summer 1986):496–513; reprinted in Part 9 of Gregg Lee Carter, *Empirical Approaches to Sociology*, 3rd edition (Boston: Allyn & Bacon, 2001). The paragraphs that follow—with some modifications—are taken from this article and are reprinted by permission of the author and Plenum Publishing.

are least capable of voting on Tuesdays, coping with voting procedures, getting registered, overcoming the problem posed by separate elections, and getting to the polls frequently. As noted in one popular sociology textbook: "non-voters are mostly young, poor, black, and uneducated. High-income individuals are [much more] likely to vote [than] low-income individuals. By defaulting on their voting privileges, the lower- and working-class nonvoters have created a *voter elite* that elects our government leaders."[5] James M. Henslin eloquently expresses the most important interpretation that can account for these racial and social-class patterns in voting behavior: "The more that people feel they have a stake in the political system, the more likely they are to vote. They have more to protect, and feel that voting can make a difference. In effect, people who have been rewarded by the political system feel more socially integrated. They vote because they perceive that elections directly affect their own lives and the type of society in which they and their children live."[6]

The following computer exercises allow you to test Beeghley's fundamental hypothesis that social class and voting are positively related. The variables in the CHIP file *Voter98* also allow you to examine a variety of social circumstances — beyond social class — that can predict voting behavior.

File: **Voter98** (Social characteristics of voters and nonvoters. *Source:* 1993–98 cumulative GSS)

Info: Immigrant→Latino→RaceHH→Sex→Age→Ed→TypeHH→FamInc→Voter
   (2)   (2)   (4)   (2) (3) (3)   (5)   (3)   (2)

Immigrant	No, Yes
Latino	(Latino heritage) No, Yes (GSS coding for "Ethnicity" = 17, 22, 25, or 38)
RaceHH	(Race of household) White, Black, Asian, Other
Sex	Male, Female
Age	18–39, 40–64, 65+
Ed	<12yrs, 12yrs, 13–15yrs, 16+yrs
TypeHH	(Type of Household) Other (e.g., cohabitators, extended families, roommates), SingParent (Single Parent), SingAdult (Single Adult), MarrParent (Married-Couple with children), MarrNoKids (Married-Couple with no children)
FamInc	(Family Income) <$20K, $20K–$60K, $60K+
Voter	(Did you vote in the last presidential election?) No, Yes

Basic

1. Test the basic hypothesis that income and likelihood of voting are positively related by crosstabulating Voter (Y) by FamInc (X); also examine the relationship graphically (after doing the **CrossTab**, select the **Line** alternative for the **Plot** option under the **Table** command and highlight the "Yes" category). Did you find the expected relationship? (*Concentrate your discussion on the "Yes" row of Voter for all questions in this section.*)

---

[5]Vincent N. Parrillo, John Stimson, and Ardyth Stimson, *Contemporary Social Problems*, 2nd ed. (NY: Macmillan, 1989), p. 417.

[6]*Sociology: A Down-to-Earth Approach*, 4th ed. (Boston: Allyn & Bacon, 1999), p. 415.

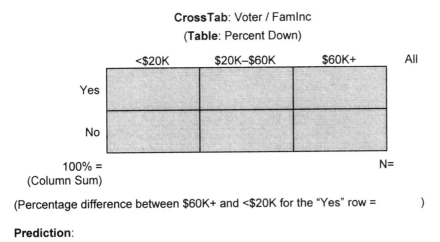

CrossTab: Voter / FamInc
(**Table**: Percent Down)

(Percentage difference between $60K+ and <$20K for the "Yes" row =   )

Prediction:

Finding:

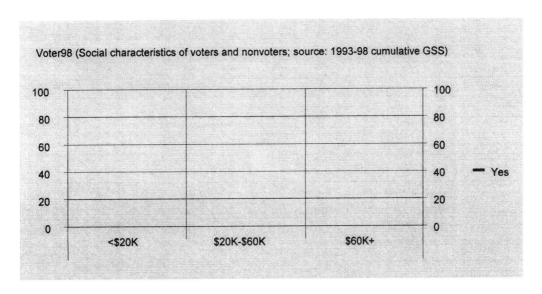

Answer/Discussion

2. Letting Y=Voter, do individual crosstabulations for each of the following:

        (a) Immigrant   (b) Latino   (c) RaceHH   (d) Sex   (e) Age

(a)   Voter (Y) by Immigrant (X)

CrossTab: Voter / Immigrant
(**Table**: Percent Down)

	No	Yes	All
Yes			
No			
100% = (Column Sum)		N=	

(Percentage difference between the Yes and No columns for the "Yes" row =   )

Prediction:

Finding:

(b)   Voter (Y) by Latino (X)

CrossTab: Voter / Latino
(**Table**: Percent Down)

	No	Yes	All
Yes			
No			
100% = (Column Sum)		N=	

(Percentage difference between the Yes and No columns for the "Yes" row =   )

Prediction:

Finding:

(c) Voter (Y) by RaceHH (X)

CrossTab: Voter / RaceHH
(**Table**: Percent Down)

	White	Black	Asian	Other	All
Yes					
No					
100% = (Column Sum)					N=

(Percentage difference between White and Black for the "Yes" row =   )
(Percentage difference between White and Asian for the "Yes" row =   )
(Percentage difference between White and Other for the "Yes" row =   )

Prediction:

Findings:

(d) Voter (Y) by Sex (X)

CrossTab: Voter / Sex
(**Table**: Percent Down)

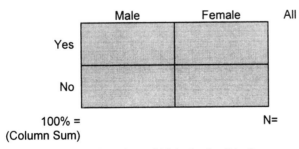

	Male	Female	All
Yes			
No			
100% = (Column Sum)			N=

(Percentage difference between the Female and Male for the "Yes" row =   )

Prediction:

Finding:

(e)   Voter (Y) by Age (X)

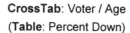

CrossTab: Voter / Age
(**Table**: Percent Down)

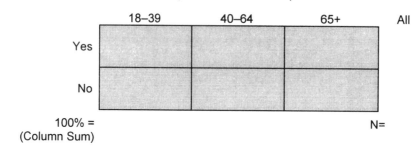

	18–39	40–64	65+	All
Yes				
No				

100% =   N=
(Column Sum)

(Percentage difference between 65+ and 18–39 for the "Yes" row =   )

Prediction:

Finding:

Given your findings here in #(2), as well as in #(1), what is the profile of the person most likely to vote (e.g., an older, white, female . . .)? Are those with social advantages more likely than their less advantaged counterparts to maintain their advantages because of their involvement in the political system?

Advanced

3. Perhaps the relationship between social class—as measured by family income—and voting uncovered above is spurious. Sketch the model that would show this relationship is spurious when controlling for the antecedent variable Latino. Defend this alternative model, then test it by crosstabulating Voter (Y) by FamInc (X) and control for Latino (Z).

   (a) Model sketch:

   (b) Interpretation of the Latino–FamInc relationship:

   (c) Interpretation of the Latino–Voter relationship:

4. If the model sketched above in #3(a) is true, then what will happen to the relationship between FamInc and Voter when Latino is held constant? Why?

5. Check out the alternative model sketched in #3(a):

   (a) Crosstabulate Voter (Y) by FamInc (X), then control for Latino (Z).

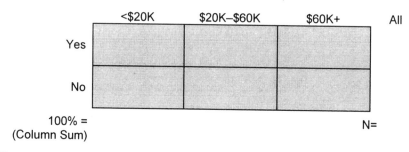

Original Table
CrossTab: Voter / FamInc
(**Table**: Percent Down)

	<$20K	$20K–$60K	$60K+	All
Yes				
No				
100% = (Column Sum)				N=

(Percentage difference between $60K+ and <$20K for the "Yes" row =   )

Prediction:

Finding:

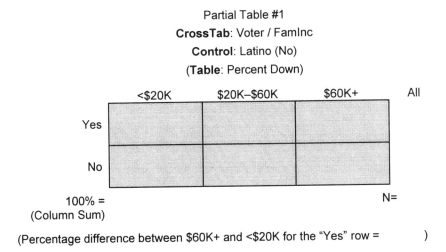

Partial Table #1
CrossTab: Voter / FamInc
Control: Latino (No)
(**Table**: Percent Down)

(Percentage difference between $60K+ and <$20K for the "Yes" row =   )

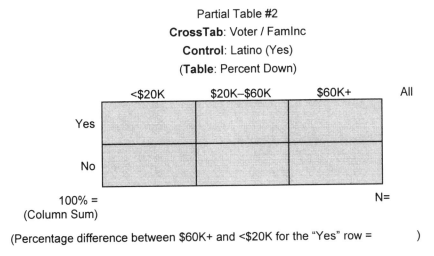

Partial Table #2
CrossTab: Voter / FamInc
Control: Latino (Yes)
(**Table**: Percent Down)

(Percentage difference between $60K+ and <$20K for the "Yes" row =   )

(b) Was the original relationship between FamInc and Voter causal or spurious?

(c) Is a multivariable model evident? That is, do both FamInc and Latino have independent effects on Voter? Refer to the correct percentage-differences to support your answer.

Suggestions for Further Study

Jeffrey Reiman argues that the inverse relationship between social class and political participation hurts the poor when it comes to the criminal justice system. That the poor vote less and have few officials from their ranks results in the "police mainly arresting those with the least political clout, those who are least able to focus public attention on police practices or bring political influence to bear, and these happen to be the members of the lowest social and economic classes." This bias continues throughout the system, with poorer people—compared to their more prosperous counterparts—more likely to be convicted of crimes, and if convicted, more likely to serve jail time. See his classic essay "And the Poor Get Prison," pp. 269–301 in Gregg Lee Carter (ed.), *Perspectives on Current Social Problems* (Boston: Allyn & Bacon, 1997).

Relevant World Wide Web Sites

Several organizations that recognize the differences in political attitudes and participation of the poor and working class compared to their more prosperous counterparts maintain web sites. Although the writings on these sites are highly opinionated, they are still useful sources for the history, court decisions, political activities, and related information concerning voting/social class issues. Most importantly, see:

Project Vote Smart	www.vote-smart.org
National Voting Rights Institute	www.nvri.org
National Urban League	www.nul.org
National Coalition for the Homeless	www.nch.ari.net
AFL-CIO	www.aflcio.org

For more attitudinal data on the relationship between social class and political conservatism, see the GSS and other public-opinion sources listed in the "Suggestions for Further Study" section in Chapter 1 (p. 64).

Exploratory exercises for the *Equal98* and *Voter98* data files have been included with those for Chapter 3; see p. 125.

Chapter 3. Inequality and Poverty

The authors of sociology textbooks are in near unanimity that the root of many of the most pressing social problems in virtually every nation is inequality—and that, indeed, inequality itself is the greatest social problem. Poverty is associated with prejudice, discrimination, segregation, inferior housing, inadequate diet, ill health, exposure to crime, bad schools, and maltreatment of children, women, and the elderly—to list just a few contemporary problems.

Among the more important issues in the study of inequality are the following: First, why are all societies—capitalist and socialist, democratic and totalitarian, small and large, historical and contemporary—*stratified*, that is, contain gross inequalities in income, wealth, power, and prestige? Second, given any particular system of social stratification, who is most likely to succeed? who is most likely to fail? Finally, what are the consequences of being located in one or another position in the social class system, i.e., what does it mean to be poor? working class? middle class? upper middle class? rich?

In the last half of the nineteenth century, Karl Marx addressed the first issue when he developed the basic ideas behind what today is known as the **conflict perspective** on social stratification. Its explanation as to why all societies are stratified was developed in Chapter 2. (Right now, you should pause for a few minutes and review the introduction to Chapter 2). An alternative explanation, the **functionalist perspective**, starts with the fundamental and true assumption that society's most important positions—those critical to the survival and well-being of its members—cannot be filled by just anyone. Thus, for example, many people can mow grass but few can perform heart surgery. Moreover, society's most important positions are very demanding; they require major investments of time, study, hard work, talent, and skill. The question then becomes: How do we get individuals to "pay the price" it takes to pursue careers in society's most important jobs? The answer seems obvious: We motivate them by rewarding them unequally, that is, we accord each of these important positions great amounts of income, power, and prestige. In time, a society finds certain positions more or less permanently established near the top of its reward system and others near the bottom. Those individuals who fill the former become members of the more affluent classes, while those that fill the latter are relegated to the less affluent classes. We may sketch the causal logic of the functionalist perspective as follows:

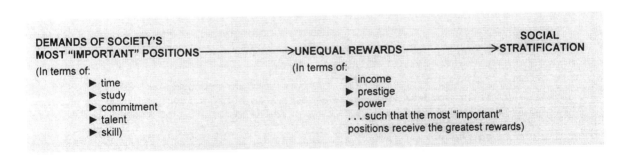

There is truth in the functionalist perspective. Consider yourself. Why are you in college? Most likely because you believe the time and energy spent studying will pay off, and you intend to place yourself in a position that will garner significant income, prestige, and power.

However, to fully understand the social stratification within a country one needs to combine both the conflict and functionalist perspectives. Physicians and corporate executives don't get high salaries just because their positions are so important and demanding and capable of being filled by so few. Once a position becomes invested with a degree of income, prestige, and power, individuals filling it will use its resources to help maintain its resources (i.e., the income, prestige, and power). Thus, for example, at the beginning of the twentieth century medical doctors used their resources to influence state legislatures to outlaw and/or highly restrict other healing practitioners such as chiropractors and homeopathic doctors. And, true to the conflict perspective, it was only when the latter increased their resources and made effective use of them that laws and social conventions were changed allowing for the freer practicing of the healing arts. Thus, for example, in the 1970s chiropractors courted public opinion, lobbied legislatures and used the courts to promote and eventually win their right to receive medical insurance benefits such as Blue Cross.

Moving from the intra-national level (e.g., the United States) to international level of analysis, the conflict perspective becomes absolutely essential if one is to make any sense out of the gross inequalities among countries (e.g., compare the 1997 per capita GNP of the U.S. [$29,080], Burundi [$140], Cambodia [$300], and Gambia [$340]).[1] Much of the poverty in "Third World" nations is a result of colonialism and of economic domination by developed nations in the post-colonial era. As Eitzen and Zinn explain: "As recently as 1914, approximately 70 percent of the world's population lived in colonies (in those areas now designated as the Third World). As colonies of super-powers, their resources and labors were exploited. Leadership was imposed from outside. . . . Raw materials were extracted for exports." Wealth that was created became concentrated in the hands of local elites and the colonizers. "Population growth was encouraged because the colonizer needed a continuous supply of low-cost labor. Colonialism destroyed the cultural patterns of production and exchange by which these societies once met the needs of their peoples. Thriving industries that once served indigenous markets were destroyed. The capital generated by the natural wealth in these countries was not used to develop local factories, schools, sanitation systems, agricultural processing plants, or irrigation systems. Colonialism also promoted a two-class society by increasing landholdings among the few and landlessness among the many."[2]

The legacy of colonialism continues to promote poverty today. The two-class system has been slow to dissolve (which would be predicted by the conflict perspective as diagrammed in Chapter 2). Multinational corporations, headquartered in First World countries, strip Third World nations of their resources and retard the growth of domestic industries. Finally, developing countries are heavily dependent on aid from economic superpowers. This aid—in the form of direct, government-to-government assistance, as well as bank loans—has generated one of the most serious economic problems in the Third World, their debt crisis, which in turn serves to lock the Third World into persistent under-development and poverty (as of the late 1990s, poor nations owed $1.4 trillion). Indeed, "this debt, which is more than half the collective GNP of [Third World countries], is so large for some nations that they cannot spend for needed public works, education, and other social services. Available monies must be spent, rather, on servicing the debt."[3]

The computer exercises in Chapter 3 begin with an examination of inequality in the United States—addressing the issue of who is most likely to succeed economically. The exercises then move on to the analysis of cross-national data, focusing on the relationships among economic development, wealth, political structure, disease, famine, and death.

---

[1] *World Population Data Sheet.* (Washington, D.C.: Population Reference Bureau, 1999).

[2] D. Stanley Eitzen and Maxine Baca Zinn, *Social Problems*, 8th ed. (Boston: Allyn & Bacon, 2000), p. 68.

[3] Eitzen and Baca Zinn, *ibid*, p. 69; also see the *Report on the World Situation*, (New York: United Nations, 1997), as well as Daniel J. Curran and Claire M. Renzetti, *Social Problems: Society in Crisis*, 5th ed. (Boston: Allyn & Bacon, 2001), chap. 4.

An Examination of the "Status Attainment" Model and the Predictors of Individual Economic Success

The following computer exercises address the issue of who is most likely to succeed economically in U.S. society. The CHIP file *Status98* contains many of the key variables associated with *status attainment* research begun by Blau and Duncan[4] and continued by Jencks[5] and others at Harvard University and by the Duncans and Featherman[6] and their colleagues at the University of Michigan and the University of Wisconsin. The models for status attainment developed by these investigators are among the most rigorously tested in all of sociology; you can test the most significant aspects of them with the GSS data in *Status98*.

File: **Status98** (Status attainment model; *source:* '96 and '98 GSS; **Note:** *full-time workers only*)

Info: Region→Race→Sex→Age→Married→Papres→Sibs→Ed→Income
(4)   (2)   (2)   (3)   (3)   (3)   (3)   (4)   (3)

Region   Northeast (CT, ME, MA, NH, NJ, NY, PA, RI, and VT)
Midwest (IL, IN, IA, KS, MI, MN, MO, NE, ND, OH, SD, and WI)
South (AL, AR, DE, FL, GA, KY, LS, MD, MS, NC, OK, SC, TN, TX, VA, and WV)
West (AK, AZ, CA, CO, HI, ID, MT, NV, NM, OR, UT, WA, and WY)

Race   White, Black

Sex   Male, Female

Age   18–39, 40–64, 65+

Married   Never Married, DivSepWid (Divorced/Separated/Widowed), Married

Papres   (Hodge-Segal-Rossi occupational prestige score for father's occupation): Low (17–38), Medium (39–47), High (48–86); for example, on this scale, Janitors=22, Cashiers=29, Apparel Sales Workers=30, Accountants=65, Architects=73, Teachers=74, Lawyers=75, Physicians=86

Sibs   ("How many brothers and sisters did you have? Please count those born alive, but no longer living, as well as those alive now. Also include step-brothers and step-sisters, and children adopted by your parents."): 0–1, 2–3, 4+

Ed   (Years of schooling): <12yrs, 12yrs, 13–15yrs, 16+yrs

Income   (Respondent's individual income): <$17.5K, $17.5–$35K, $35K+

Basic

1.   Who is most likely to succeed economically in American society? Develop a profile of this individual by crosstabbing Income (Y) by each of the following, focusing your attention on the $35K+ row.

(a) Region	(b) Race	(c) Sex	(d) Age
(e) Sibs	(f) Papres	(g) Ed	(h) Married

---

[4]Peter M. Blau and Otis Dudley Duncan, *The American Occupational Structure* (NY: Free Press), 1967.

[5]Christopher Jencks, et al., *Inequality: A Reassessment of the Effect of Family and Schooling in America* (NY: Basic Books), 1972.

[6]Otis Dudley Duncan, David L. Featherman, and Beverly Duncan, *Socioeconomic Background and Achievement* (NY: Seminar Press), 1972.

CrossTab: Income / Region
(**Table**: Percent Down)

	Northeast	Midwest	South	West	All
$35K+					
$17.5K–$35K					
<$17.5K					
100% = (Column Sum)					N=

(Percentage difference between West and South for the "$35K+" row =   )

(Percent difference between Midwest and South for the "$35K+" row =   )

(Percent difference between Northeast and South for the "$35K+" row =   )

Prediction:

Findings:

CrossTab: Income / Race
(**Table**: Percent Down)

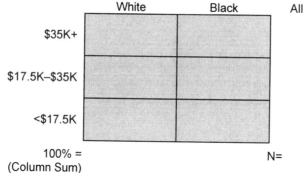

	White	Black	All
$35K+			
$17.5K–$35K			
<$17.5K			
100% = (Column Sum)			N=

(Percentage difference between White and Black for the "$35K+" row =   )

Prediction:

Finding:

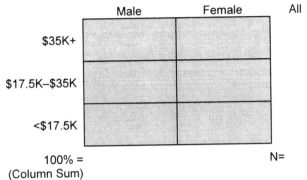

CrossTab: Income / Sex
(**Table**: Percent Down)

(Percentage difference between Male and Female for the "$35K+" row =   )

Prediction:

Finding:

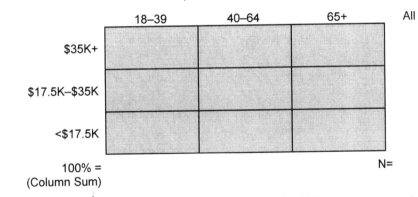

CrossTab: Income / Age
(**Table**: Percent Down)

(Percentage difference between 40–64 and 65+ for the "$35K+" row =   )

(Percentage difference between 40–64 and 18–39 for the "$35K+" row =   )

Prediction:

Findings:

CrossTab: Income / Sibs
(**Table**: Percent Down)

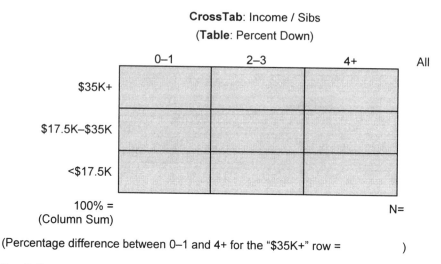

(Percentage difference between 0–1 and 4+ for the "$35K+" row =   )

Prediction:

Finding:

CrossTab: Income / Papres
(**Table**: Percent Down)

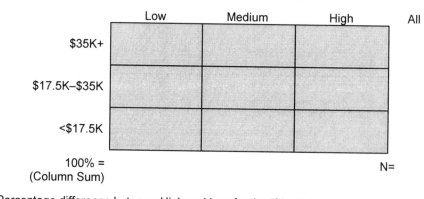

(Percentage difference between High and Low for the "$35K+" row =   )

Prediction:

Finding:

CrossTab: Income / Ed
(**Table**: Percent Down)

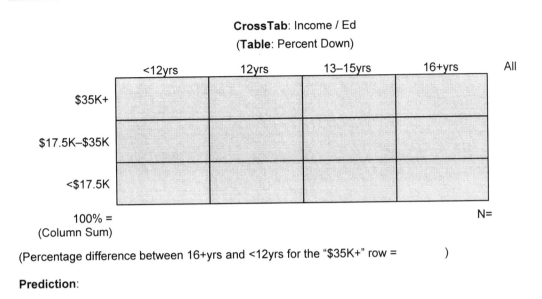

	<12yrs	12yrs	13–15yrs	16+yrs	All
$35K+					
$17.5K–$35K					
<$17.5K					
100% = (Column Sum)					N=

(Percentage difference between 16+yrs and <12yrs for the "$35K+" row =   )

Prediction:

Finding:

CrossTab: Income / Married
(**Table**: Percent Down)

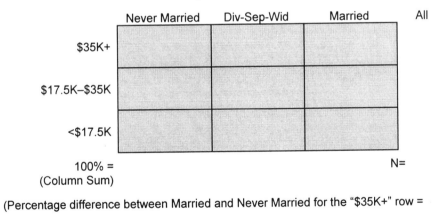

	Never Married	Div-Sep-Wid	Married	All
$35K+				
$17.5K–$35K				
<$17.5K				
100% = (Column Sum)				N=

(Percentage difference between Married and Never Married for the "$35K+" row =   )

(Percentage difference between Married and Div-Sep-Wid for the "$35K+" row =   )

Prediction:

Findings:

Who is most likely to succeed? (e.g., a western, white, female . . . 8 characteristics must be noted):

2. Using "percentage difference" as your criterion,

    (a) which independent variable above best predicts Income? That is, given a change in the value of X, in which crosstab did you observe the greatest percentage change in the $35K+ row?

    (b) which independent variable is the second best predictor?

3. Based on your reading, class discussion, and/or your own intuition:

    (a) why do you think *Region* is related to *Income* in the way in which it is?

    (b) why do you think *Race* is related to *Income* in the way in which it is?

(c) why do you think *Sex* is related to *Income* in the way in which it is?

(d) why do you think *Age* is related to Income in the way in which it is?

(e) why do you think *Sibs* is related to *Income* in the way in which it is?

(f)   why do you think *Papres* is related to *Income* in the way in which it is?

(g)   why do you think *Ed* is related to *Income* in the way in which it is?

(h)   why do you think *Married* is related to *Income* in the way in which it is?

(a)   Does the Ed→Income relationship make you glad that you're in college? ☺

Advanced

4. Perhaps the relationship between education and status attainment uncovered above is spurious. Sketch the model that would show this relationship as spurious when controlling for the antecedent variable Race. Defend this alternative model.

(a) Model sketch:

(b) Interpretation of the Race–Ed relationship:

(c) Interpretation of the Race–Income relationship:

5. Check out your alternative model in #(4):

(a) Crosstabulate Income (Y) by Ed (X), then control for Race (Z).

Original Table
CrossTab: Income / Ed
(**Table**: Percent Down)

	<12yrs	12yrs	13–15yrs	16+yrs	All
$35K+					
$17.5K–$35K					
<$17.5K					
100% = (Column Sum)					N=

(Percentage difference between 16+yrs and <12yrs for the "$35K+" row =   )

Prediction:

Finding:

Partial Table #1
CrossTab: Income / Ed
Control: Race (White)
(**Table**: Percent Down)

	<12yrs	12yrs	13–15yrs	16+yrs	All
$35K+					
$17.5K–$35K					
<$17.5K					
100% = (Column Sum)					N=

(Percentage difference between 16+yrs and <12yrs for the "$35K+" row =   )

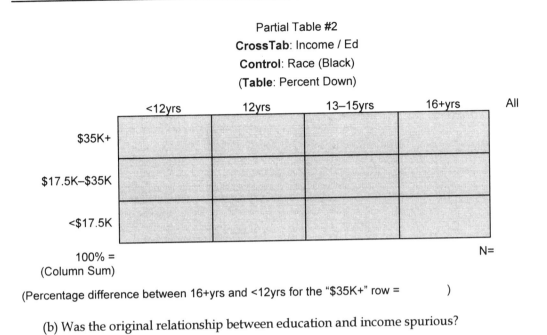

Partial Table #2
CrossTab: Income / Ed
Control: Race (Black)
(**Table**: Percent Down)

(Percentage difference between 16+yrs and <12yrs for the "$35K+" row =   )

(b) Was the original relationship between education and income spurious?

(c) Who is most likely to be in the $35K+ category? Does this surprise you? Why or why not?

(d) Who is most likely to be in the <$17.5K category? Does this surprise you? Why or why not?

6. In research on status attainment (that is, on who becomes most prosperous and who gets the best jobs), the relationship between the prestige of a respondent's father's occupation and the respondent's income—as uncovered in #(1f) above—is accounted for, in part, by the relationship between father's occupational prestige and respondent's education. That is, fathers with high job prestige tend to raise children who get a lot of schooling; in turn, those with a lot of schooling tend to make higher incomes. This causal pathway describes the "indirect" effect of a father's occupational prestige on a respondent's income attainment. The argument here is that children from higher social classes tend to end up making more money *not* because of who they are or whom they know, but because of the education that their parents were able to afford for them. Thus, the upper middle-class child who does *not* take advantage of the educational opportunities afforded him or her—say by dropping out of school—will likely wind up

in a low prestige, low-paying job. On the other hand, the child from humble roots who manages to get an education is not hindered by his or her humble beginnings (e.g., the medical school doesn't ask who the parents of an applicant are—rather, the applicant is asked to provide his or her GPA and standardized test scores).

In addition to the indirect effects of father's occupation on respondent's income, there is also a direct effect. That is, beyond educational opportunities (or lack of opportunities for poorer children), parents also can bequeath their children income directly—through, for example, the inheritance of income-producing wealth (e.g., stocks, bonds, trust funds) or actual jobs (e.g., taking over a family business or being able to enter a field through the intervention of a parent). Sketch the model that would represent both the direct and indirect effects of Papres on Income.

7. If the model sketched above is true, then what will happen to the relationship between Papres and Income when Ed is held constant? Why?

8. Test your prediction in #(7) by crosstabulating Income (Y) by Papres (X), then control for Ed (Z). What did you find?

Original Table

CrossTab: Income / Papres

(**Table**: Percent Down)

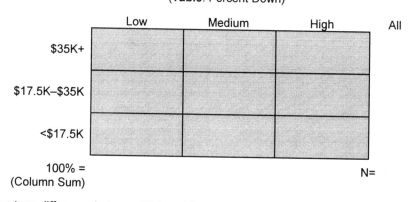

(Percentage difference between High and Low for the "$35K+" row =   )

Prediction:

Finding:

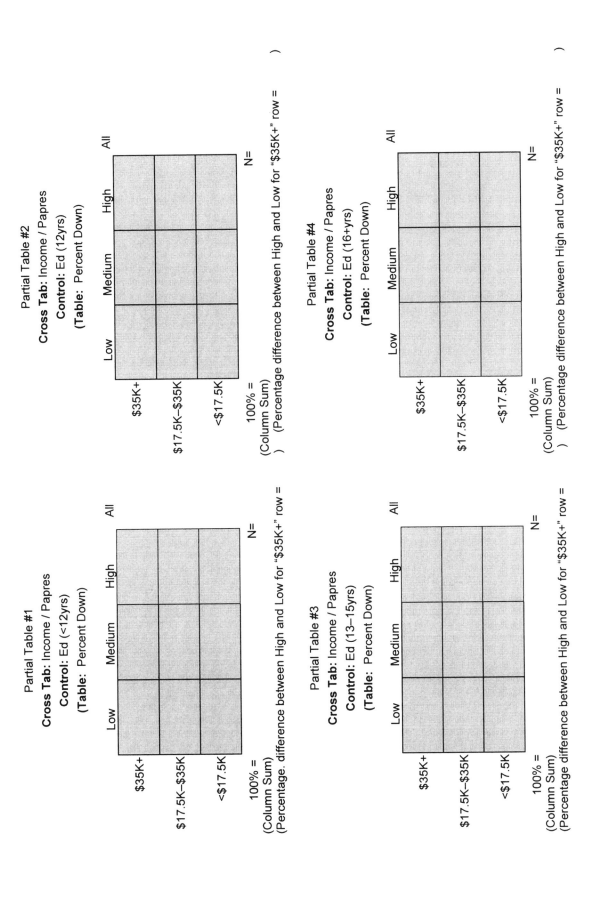

Partial Table #1

Cross Tab: Income / Papres

Control: Ed (<12yrs)

(Table: Percent Down)

	Low	Medium	High	All
$35K+				
$17.5K–$35K				
<$17.5K				
100% =
(Column Sum)				N=

(Percentage. difference between High and Low for "$35K+" row =)

Partial Table #2

Cross Tab: Income / Papres

Control: Ed (12yrs)

(Table: Percent Down)

	Low	Medium	High	All
$35K+				
$17.5K–$35K				
<$17.5K				
100% =
(Column Sum)				N=

(Percentage difference between High and Low for "$35K+" row =)

Partial Table #3

Cross Tab: Income / Papres

Control: Ed (13–15yrs)

(Table: Percent Down)

	Low	Medium	High	All
$35K+				
$17.5K–$35K				
<$17.5K				
100% =
(Column Sum)				N=

(Percentage difference between High and Low for "$35K+" row =)

Partial Table #4

Cross Tab: Income / Papres

Control: Ed (16+yrs)

(Table: Percent Down)

	Low	Medium	High	All
$35K+				
$17.5K–$35K				
<$17.5K				
100% =
(Column Sum)				N=

(Percentage difference between High and Low for "$35K+" row =)

Answer/Discussion

9. If the relationship between X and Y disappears or greatly weakens when we control for Z, the situation is most likely one of the following: (a) the X,Y relationship was spurious—that is, the antecedent variable Z was related to both X and Y, and X and Y had no other association except that due to their common association with Z; or, (b) a change in X produces a change in Z, which, in turn, produces a change in Y—and if Z is not allowed to vary, then the effects of X on Y will not be apparent. Does #(9a) or #(9b) most closely describe what you found in (8)? Defend your answer.

The Wealth of Nations: Associations Among Economic Development, Political Structure, Literacy, Fertility, Hunger, and Infant Mortality

During the 1990s, approximately one-quarter of the world lived in dire poverty, with 840 million people in developing countries being undernourished. Some fifty million people died annually—most of them in developing nations—from easily preventable infectious diseases. One-third of the world's population lacked access to safe drinking water, and the number of children not attending primary school varied up and down between 80 and 109 million.[1]

Cross-national comparisons are risky, especially when lesser-developed nations are included. The problem is that a seemingly identical variable (e.g., "urbanization") may receive different definitions in different countries. In addition, censuses and other data collection efforts are of varying quality and are done during different years. Despite such measurement errors, differences among and between countries can often be calculated (the real differences exceeding all conceivable measurement error), especially when we are confident—as we are here—that the data are the best available. *World98* is intended to let you discover what kinds of structural factors are related to cross-national differences in prosperity, fertility, and mortality.

File: **World98** (Cross-national data, late 1990s)[2]

Info: Region→Freedom→GNP→Farmers→Electric→Literate→Unemploy→
    (6)   (3)   (3)   (3)   (3)   (3)   (3)

Calories→InfDeath→Fertility→LifeExp→FemLife→FemAdv
   (3)   (3)   (3)   (3)   (3)   (3)

(Note: all variables, except Region and Freedom, are divided into three categories: bottom, middle, and top third.)

Region	(United Nations regional designation) Industrial, East-Europe, Africa-SubSaharan, Arab, Asia, Latin-America
Freedom	(Type of political regime) Not Free, Partly Free, Free
GNP	(Per capita GNP in 1997 U.S. dollars) <$1,100; $1,100–$3,400; >$3,400
Farmers	(Percentage of the workforce in agriculture) <14%, 14–40%, >40%
Electric	(Kilowatt hours per capita) <860kw; 860–3,300kw; >3,300kw
Literate	(% of pop. literate) <83%, 83–97%, >97%
Unemploy	(Unemployment Rate) <7.7%, 7.7–15%, >15%
Calories	(Average calories consumed per day) <2,500; 2,500–3,000; >3,000
InfDeath	(Infant deaths per 1,000 births) <15, 15–45, >45
Fertility	(Total Fertility Rate, which is the number of children an adult woman, aged 15–44, can expect to have during her lifetime) <2.0, 2.0–3.7, >3.7
LifeExp	(Life Expectancy) <67.3yrs, 67.3–72.5yrs, >72.5yrs
FemLife	(Female Life Expectancy) <70yrs, 70–75yrs, >75yrs
FemAdv	(Female Life Expectancy − Male Life Expectancy, i.e., "female advantage" over males in life expectancy) <4.1yrs, 4.1–5.9yrs, 6+yrs

[1] See *Report on the World Social Situation*, op. cit.; also see *Report of the United Nations Summit for Social Development*, Copenhagen, Denmark, March, 1995—as cited in *The Providence Sunday Journal*, March 12, 1995, p. A–4.

[2] *Sources*: Central Intelligence Agency, *The World Factbook 1999* (Dulles, VA.: Brassey's Inc., 1999); Robert L. Bartley (ed.), *Freedom in the World: The Annual Survey of Political Rights and Civil Liberties, 1998-1999* (Piscataway, NJ: Transaction Publishers, 1999); and *World Population Data Sheet*, op. cit.

Country	Freedom	GNP	Farmers	Electric	Literate	Unemploy	Calories	InfDeath	Fertility	LifeExp	Femlife	FemAdv
Albania	Partly	360	49.5	1,801	93.0	21.0	2,523	33.2	2.80	72.5	75.5	5.9
Algeria	Not Free	1,690	22.0	708	61.6	30.0	3,020	55.0	4.26	67.3	67.8	0.9
Angola	Not Free	260	85.0	169	42.0	50.0	1,983	137.0	6.48	46.0	48.0	4.0
Ant.& Barbuda	Partly	6,970	11.0	1,485	89.0	9.0	2,365	17.6	1.70	73.0	74.9	4.1
Argentina	Free	8,060	12.0	2,076	96.2	12.0	3,136	22.9	2.70	72.1	75.7	7.1
Armenia	Partly	670	38.0	1,708	99.0	20.0	2,147	15.1	1.70	71.2	74.4	6.5
Australia	Free	17,980	5.0	9,820	99.0	8.1	3,001	5.8	1.82	78.0	80.9	5.9
Austria	Free	24,950	8.1	6,882	99.0	7.0	3,343	5.5	1.42	76.6	79.7	6.4
Azerbaijan	Partly	500	32.0	2,308	97.0	20.0	2,139	25.2	2.21	70.5	74.5	8.2
Bahamas	Free	11,790	5.0	4,718	98.2	9.0	2,443	23.8	1.91	71.8	75.3	7.0
Bahrain	Not Free	7,500	1.0	8,800	85.2	15.0	3,054	19.4	3.70	73.2	76.1	5.0
Barbados	Free	6,530	10.0	2,490	97.4	12.0	3,207	9.1	1.63	75.5	77.9	5.0
Belarus	Not Free	2,160	19.0	3,119	98.0	2.3	3,101	12.9	1.39	69.3	74.3	10.8
Belgium	Free	22,920	2.6	7,904	99.0	12.0	3,543	7.6	1.55	76.5	79.8	6.8
Belize	Free	2,550	30.0	808	70.3	13.0	2,862	34.0	4.50	72.1	74.1	4.1
Brazil	Partly	3,370	31.0	2,026	83.3	8.5	2,938	58.0	2.79	66.4	68.7	4.7
Brunei	Not Free	14,240	4.0	5,250	88.2	4.8	2,886	7.4	3.07	74.2	76.3	3.8
Bulgaria	Free	1,160	18.0	4,991	98.0	12.2	2,756	15.5	1.37	71.4	75.0	7.3
Cambodia	Not Free	300	80.0	20	35.0	31.5	1,974	111.0	5.81	49.3	50.8	3.0
Cameroon	Not Free	680	74.4	203	63.4	30.0	2,175	65.0	5.91	56.0	57.5	3.0
Canada	Free	19,570	3.0	20,904	97.0	7.8	3,056	6.2	1.60	77.8	81.0	6.6
Cape Verde	Free	910	57.0	104	71.6	3.5	3,135	65.0	4.06	64.7	65.5	2.0
Cen. Afr. Rep	Partly	370	85.0	31	60.0	6.0	1,938	97.0	5.10	49.4	51.9	5.0
Chile	Free	3,560	19.2	2,169	95.2	6.4	2,810	13.1	2.54	72.1	75.6	7.1
China	Not Free	530	50.0	891	81.5	7.0	2,844	44.0	1.80	70.1	72.0	3.6
Colombia	Partly	1,620	30.0	1,228	91.3	15.7	2,800	28.0	3.00	69.4	72.3	5.9
Comoros	Partly	510	80.0	27	57.3	20.0	1,824	80.0	6.79	57.8	60.1	4.5
Costa Rica	Free	2,380	21.6	1,428	94.8	5.6	2,822	13.0	3.10	76.3	78.6	4.6
Cuba	Not Free	2,000	20.0	1,201	95.7	6.8	2,357	9.4	1.50	74.8	76.8	3.9
Denmark	Free	28,110	5.0	7,510	99.0	6.5	3,808	5.4	1.81	75.2	77.8	5.3
Dominica	Free	2,830	40.0	521	94.0	15.0	3,093	18.4	2.07	77.5	80.3	5.9
Dominic. Rep.	Free	1,320	50.0	860	82.1	16.0	2,316	51.5	3.31	68.4	70.6	4.4
Ecuador	Free	1,310	29.0	792	90.1	12.0	2,592	40.0	3.60	68.9	71.4	5.0
Egypt	Not Free	710	40.0	801	51.4	10.0	3,289	62.0	3.59	63.6	64.8	2.4
El Salvador	Free	1,480	40.0	599	71.5	7.7	2,515	41.0	3.80	67.8	70.4	5.3
Estonia	Free	2,820	11.0	5,604	99.9	9.6	3,004	14.5	1.38	69.9	75.0	10.9
Ethiopia	Partly	130	80.0	22	35.5	30.5	1,845	120.0	6.80	50.2	51.9	3.5
Fiji	Partly	2,320	67.0	684	91.6	6.0	3,038	19.0	3.00	63.2	65.2	3.9
Finland	Free	18,850	8.6	15,515	99.9	12.0	2,916	4.7	1.85	76.6	80.2	7.4
France	Free	23,470	5.0	7,508	99.0	11.5	3,551	6.1	1.65	77.8	81.8	8.2
Georgia	Partly	580	25.0	1,344	99.0	16.0	2,184	18.3	1.29	72.6	76.1	7.4
Germany	Free	25,580	2.7	6,605	99.0	10.6	3,330	5.5	1.26	75.8	79.0	6.6
Ghana	Partly	430	61.0	326	64.5	20.0	2,560	66.0	5.50	56.0	57.8	3.6
Greece	Free	7,710	19.8	4,632	95.0	10.0	3,575	8.3	1.34	77.4	79.9	5.0
Grenada	Free	2,620	24.0	1,033	98.0	20.0	2,731	12.0	3.82	70.9	73.3	5.0
Guatemala	Partly	1,190	58.0	320	55.6	5.2	2,191	51.0	5.10	64.8	67.3	4.9
Guyana	Free	530	30.2	408	98.1	12.0	2,392	48.0	2.55	65.2	68.0	5.6
Haiti	Partly	220	66.0	87	45.0	60.0	1,855	74.0	4.80	56.6	58.3	3.4
Honduras	Free	580	37.0	485	72.7	6.3	2,368	50.0	5.20	68.2	70.7	4.9
Hungary	Free	3,840	8.3	3,624	99.0	10.8	3,402	11.5	1.64	69.7	74.2	9.4
Iceland	Free	24,590	5.1	18,934	99.0	3.0	3,104	3.4	2.14	78.8	80.7	3.8
India	Free	310	67.0	459	52.0	20.0	2,415	78.5	3.40	58.8	59.3	1.0

Country	Freedom	GNP	Farmers	Electric	Literate	Unemploy	Calories	InfDeath	Fertility	LifeExp	Femlife	FemAdv
Indonesia	Partly	880	41.0	368	83.8	17.0	2,930	66.0	2.85	63.1	64.9	3.7
Iran	Not Free	1,780	33.0	1,180	72.1	30.0	2,824	57.0	5.10	66.5	67.7	2.3
Iraq	Not Free	1,940	30.0	1,439	58.0	5.0	2,252	67.0	6.70	65.8	66.7	1.8
Ireland	Free	13,630	10.0	5,358	98.0	7.7	3,636	5.9	1.86	76.3	79.0	5.4
Israel	Free	14,410	2.6	5,678	95.0	8.7	3,272	6.9	2.88	76.8	78.5	3.4
Italy	Free	19,270	7.0	4,870	97.0	12.5	3,504	8.3	1.19	77.2	80.4	6.6
Jamaica	Free	1,420	22.5	2,424	85.0	16.5	2,575	24.0	3.00	73.6	75.8	4.4
Japan	Free	34,630	6.0	8,074	99.0	4.4	2,905	4.2	1.50	79.8	83.0	6.4
Jordan	Partly	1,390	7.4	1,085	86.6	25.0	2,681	34.0	4.60	67.9	70.0	4.0
Kazakhstan	Not Free	1,110	23.0	3,894	98.0	13.7	3,007	27.4	2.25	68.6	73.1	9.3
Kenya	Not Free	260	80.0	141	78.1	50.0	1,971	62.0	5.40	50.5	52.2	3.4
Kyrgyzstan	Partly	610	40.0	2,551	97.0	6.0	2,489	29.1	3.12	68.3	72.2	8.0
Laos	Not Free	320	80.0	103	60.0	5.7	2,143	102.0	6.07	51.7	53.3	3.1
Latvia	Free	2,290	16.0	2,536	99.0	9.2	2,861	18.8	1.25	67.2	72.9	12.2
Lebanon	Not Free	3,350	7.0	1,879	86.4	18.0	3,279	28.0	2.90	75.2	77.9	5.4
Liberia	Not Free	2,260	70.0	480	38.3	70.0	2,294	113.0	6.36	57.7	60.3	5.0
Lithuania	Free	1,350	20.0	3,120	98.0	6.7	2,805	14.1	1.54	69.2	74.9	12.1
Luxembourg	Free	39,850	2.5	15,075	99.9	3.0	3,485	5.3	1.72	75.9	79.1	6.5
Malta	Free	7,970	2.0	4,103	88.0	5.0	3,417	9.1	1.89	76.7	78.6	3.9
Mauritania	Not Free	480	47.0	66	37.7	23.0	2,653	101.0	5.01	51.5	53.1	3.2
Mauritius	Free	3,180	14.0	1,112	82.9	2.0	2,952	18.1	2.35	69.3	73.0	8.0
Mexico	Partly	4,010	21.8	1,754	89.6	2.6	3,137	33.9	3.10	72.5	75.5	6.0
Moldova	Partly	870	40.2	1,739	96.0	2.0	2,562	22.6	1.97	67.9	71.1	6.8
Morocco	Partly	1,150	50.0	490	43.7	19.0	3,244	57.0	4.04	68.2	70.2	3.8
Mozambique	Partly	80	80.0	66	40.1	50.0	1,799	148.0	6.50	46.4	48.0	3.1
Namibia	Free	2,030	49.0	850	38.0	35.0	2,168	57.0	5.40	58.8	60.0	2.5
Nepal	Partly	200	81.0	56	27.5	5.0	2,339	98.0	5.20	54.7	53.4	−2.5
Netherlands	Free	21,970	4.0	6,143	99.0	4.1	3,259	5.5	1.56	77.0	80.0	6.1
New Zealand	Free	13,190	9.8	9,976	99.0	7.6	3,405	7.0	2.03	75.8	78.7	5.8
Nicaragua	Free	330	31.9	454	65.7	14.0	2,328	49.0	4.60	65.0	67.8	5.9
Nigeria	Partly	280	50.0	129	57.1	28.0	2,609	87.0	6.00	56.3	57.6	2.6
Norway	Free	26,480	6.0	23,830	99.0	2.6	3,350	5.2	1.87	77.8	80.6	5.7
Pakistan	Partly	440	47.0	407	37.8	4.0	2,408	91.0	5.60	60.7	60.6	−0.2
Panama	Free	2,670	26.8	1,486	90.8	13.1	2,556	17.7	2.96	72.9	75.0	4.1
Peru	Partly	1,890	17.0	837	88.7	8.2	2,310	60.0	3.54	66.0	67.9	3.8
Philippines	Free	960	39.8	502	94.6	9.6	2,356	34.0	4.09	64.6	66.4	3.6
Poland	Free	2,470	26.0	3,541	99.0	10.0	3,344	13.5	1.66	71.9	76.1	8.6
Portugal	Free	9,370	12.0	3,532	85.0	5.0	3,658	7.9	1.39	74.8	78.2	7.0
Romania	Free	1,230	36.4	2,744	97.0	9.0	2,943	23.9	1.35	69.7	73.3	7.4
Russia	Partly	2,650	20.0	5,588	98.0	11.5	2,720	17.5	1.36	64.8	71.1	13.6
Saudi Arabia	Not Free	7,240	5.0	5,528	62.8	6.5	2,735	24.0	5.50	69.9	72.3	3.4
Seychelles	Partly	6,210	10.0	1,730	58.0	15.0	2,424	12.9	2.71	70.4	73.2	5.7
Singapore	Partly	23,360	11.4	6,932	91.1	5.0	3,228	4.0	1.75	76.0	79.0	5.0
South Africa	Free	3,010	30.0	3,888	81.8	30.0	2,933	46.0	4.11	66.0	68.0	5.0
South Korea	Free	8,220	21.0	5,022	98.0	7.9	2,905	11.0	1.73	71.6	75.7	8.0
Spain	Free	13,280	8.0	4,368	96.0	20.0	3,295	7.2	1.22	77.2	80.9	7.6
Sri Lanka	Partly	640	37.0	241	90.2	11.0	2,263	18.4	2.28	72.5	74.8	4.7
Sudan	Not Free	290	80.0	49	46.1	30.0	2,391	80.0	6.09	54.3	55.2	1.8
Sweden	Free	23,630	3.2	16,423	99.0	6.3	3,160	4.4	1.88	78.2	80.8	5.3
Switzerland	Free	37,180	4.0	7,734	99.0	3.6	3,280	5.1	1.49	78.4	81.6	6.5
Syria	Not Free	1,120	40.0	1,186	70.8	13.5	3,339	44.0	6.90	66.1	67.4	2.5
Tajikistan	Not Free	350	52.0	2,581	98.0	5.7	2,129	47.0	3.66	68.3	71.1	5.7

Country	Freedom	GNP	Farmers	Electric	Literate	Unemploy	Calories	InfDeath	Fertility	LifeExp	Femlife	FemAdv
Thailand	Free	2,210	54.0	1,570	93.8	4.5	2,334	34.5	2.20	70.0	72.0	4.0
Trinid. & Tob.	Free	3,740	9.5	3,501	97.9	14.0	2,751	12.2	2.19	70.6	73.2	5.2
Tunisia	Not Free	1,800	22.0	857	66.7	15.6	3,250	43.0	3.36	67.8	68.7	1.8
Turkey	Partly	2,450	42.5	1,468	82.3	10.0	3,568	47.0	2.69	67.6	70.0	4.6
Turkmen'tan	Not Free	640	44.0	1,757	98.0	15.8	2,563	46.4	3.87	65.9	69.3	7.0
Ukraine	Partly	1,570	24.0	3,482	98.0	3.7	2,753	14.3	1.50	68.4	73.2	10.4
Un. Kingdom	Free	18,410	1.1	6,249	99.0	7.5	2,753	6.2	1.71	76.5	79.1	5.3
United States	Free	25,860	2.7	12,977	97.0	4.5	3,642	7.5	2.00	75.7	79.0	6.7
Uruguay	Free	4,650	11.0	2,041	97.3	10.5	2,830	20.1	2.34	72.6	75.7	6.4
Uzbekistan	Not Free	950	44.0	2,004	99.0	5.0	2,550	28.2	3.55	69.3	72.4	6.3
Venezuela	Free	2,760	13.0	3,251	91.1	11.5	2,398	23.5	3.10	71.8	74.7	5.8
Vietnam	Not Free	190	65.0	217	93.7	25.0	2,502	42.0	3.73	65.2	67.3	4.4
Yemen	Partly	280	92.0	70	38.0	30.0	2,034	83.0	7.70	51.7	52.9	2.3
Yugoslavia*	Not Free	1,100	35.0	2,985	90.5	30.0	2,336	18.6	1.86	71.5	74.4	5.8
Zaire**	Not Free	110	65.0	94	77.3	32.5	1,815	108.0	6.64	47.6	49.6	3.8
Zimbabwe	Partly	490	74.0	961	85.0	45.0	2,083	52.8	4.40	61.5	62.0	1.0

*Macedonia; **Republic of Congo

Basic

1. The authors of sociology textbooks argue that one reason poor nations are poor is that they have nondemocratic political structures which, in turn, allow a small number of elites to control most of the land and other resources of production; this results in the rest of the population being squeezed onto small plots or marginal land, or to actually leave them landless.[3] Test the proposition that political responsiveness and prosperity are positively related by crosstabbing GNP (Y) by Freedom (X); also examine the relationship graphically (after doing the **CrossTab**, select the **Line** alternative for the **Plot** option under the **Table** command and highlight the ">$3,400" category). Does your finding confirm this proposition? *Concentrate your discussion on the ">$3,400" row for all questions in this section.*

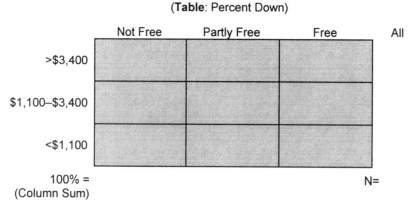

CrossTab: GNP / Freedom
(**Table**: Percent Down)

(Percentage difference between Free and Not Free for the ">$3,400" row =   )
Prediction:

Finding:

---

[3] D. Stanley Eitzen and Maxine Baca Zinn, *Social Problems*, 8th ed. (Boston: Allyn & Bacon, 2000), p. 64.

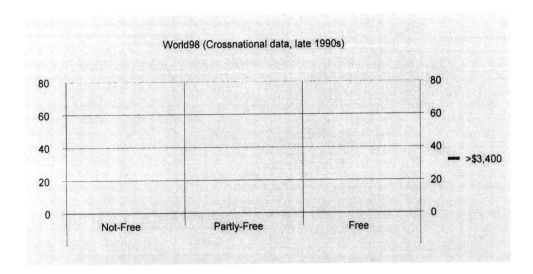

World98 (Crossnational data, late 1990s)

2. The authors of sociology textbooks argue that another reason poor nations are poor is that they have poor economic infrastructures — they lack, for example, schools to educate their children; they lack the banks to supply credit and money for investments in land and machinery; they lack a well-developed transportation system; they lack the energy supplies to run industries.

(a) Test the proposition that education and prosperity are positively related by crosstabbing GNP (Y) by Literate (X); also examine the relationship graphically (after doing the **CrossTab**, select the **Line** alternative for the **Plot** option under the **Table** command and highlight the ">$3,400" category). Does your finding confirm this proposition?

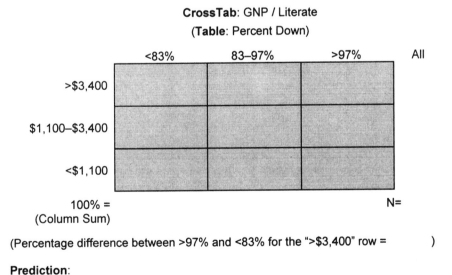

CrossTab: GNP / Literate
(**Table**: Percent Down)

(Percentage difference between >97% and <83% for the ">$3,400" row =   )

Prediction:

Finding:

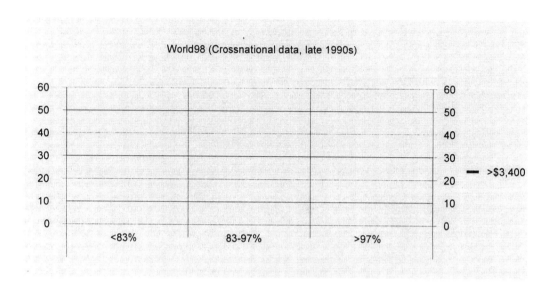

World98 (Crossnational data, late 1990s)

(b) Test the proposition that industrial/technological development and prosperity are positively related by crosstabbing (i) GNP (Y) by Electric (X), and (ii) GNP (Y) by "Farmers" (X); *note*: a large proportion of a nation's workforce devoted to agricultural pursuits would be indicative of a low level of technological development; also examine each of the relationships graphically (after doing each **CrossTab**, select the **Line** alternative for the **Plot** option under the **Table** command and highlight the ">$3,400" category). Do your findings confirm this proposition?

CrossTab: GNP / Electric

(**Table**: Percent Down)

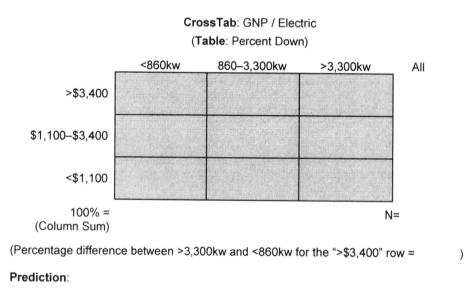

(Percentage difference between >3,300kw and <860kw for the ">$3,400" row =   )

Prediction:

Finding:

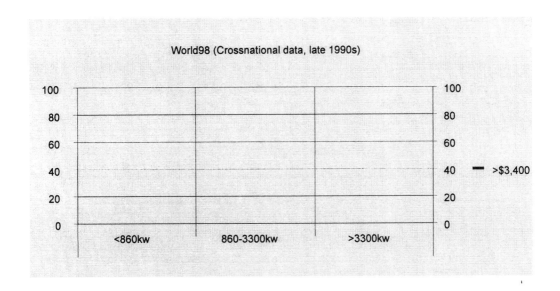

CrossTab: GNP / Farmers
(**Table**: Percent Down)

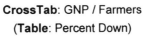

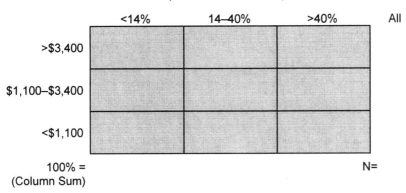

	<14%	14–40%	>40%	All
>$3,400				
$1,100–$3,400				
<$1,100				
100% = (Column Sum)				N=

(Percentage difference between >40% and <14% for the ">$3,400" row =   )

Prediction:

Finding:

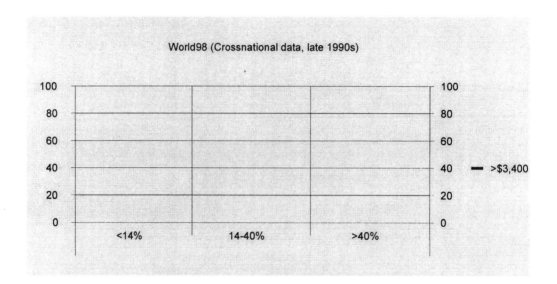

3. High population growth rates make it difficult for a country to provide adequate employment, housing, energy, food, and health care. If this population growth is fueled by women having many children, it magnifies these problems, as children are usually not economically productive until their ages reach double digits (10, 11, 12 . . .) and not until well after adolescence if they go to school. In short, too many children leads to poverty. Test this proposition by crosstabbing GNP (Y) by Fertility (X); also examine the relationship graphically (after doing the **CrossTab**, select the **Line** alternative for the **Plot** option under the **Table** command and highlight the ">$3,400" category). Does your finding confirm this proposition?

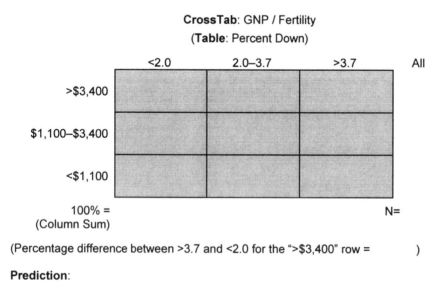

(Percentage difference between >3.7 and <2.0 for the ">$3,400" row =   )

Prediction:

Finding:

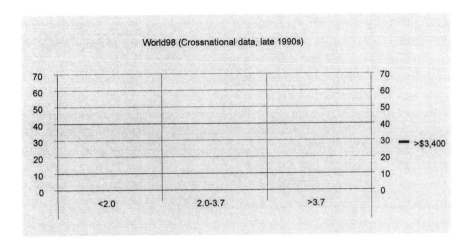

World98 (Crossnational data, late 1990s)

4. Some authors argue that the causal order for the variables in #3 is *not* Fertility→Poverty, but, rather that it is Poverty→Fertility. That the people least able to afford children have the greatest number of children "is not as irrational as it first appears. Poor parents want many children so that the children will help them economically and take care of them in their old age. Because so many children die, the parents must have a large number to ensure several surviving children. Large families make good economic sense to the poor, because children are a major source of labor and income. . . . That poor people are breeding themselves into poverty out of ignorance, religious superstition, poor economic judgment, or lack of handy contraception is a persistent, but a false notion. Poor parents have large families because they are poor—they are not poor because they have large families."[4]

    (a) Test the proposition that nations with many economically distressed individuals will also be nations with high fertility rates by crosstabbing (a) Fertility (Y) by Unemploy (X), and (b) Fertility (Y) by GNP (X); also examine each of the relationships graphically (after doing each **CrossTab**, select the **Line** alternative for the **Plot** option under the **Table** command and highlight the ">3.7" category). Do your findings confirm this proposition?

CrossTab: Fertility / Unemploy
(**Table**: Percent Down)

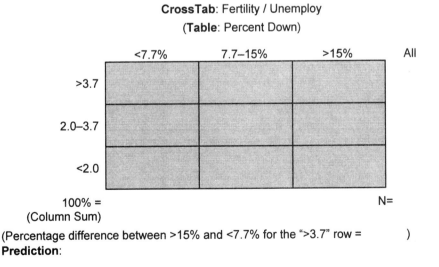

(Percentage difference between >15% and <7.7% for the ">3.7" row =   )
Prediction:

Finding:

4 Eitzen and Zinn, p. 55.

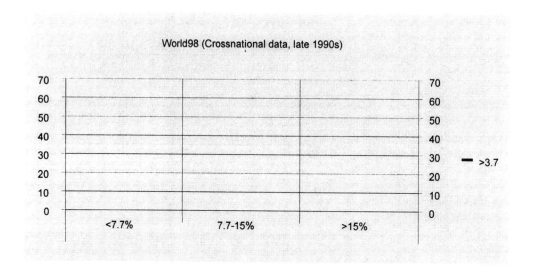

World98 (Crossnational data, late 1990s)

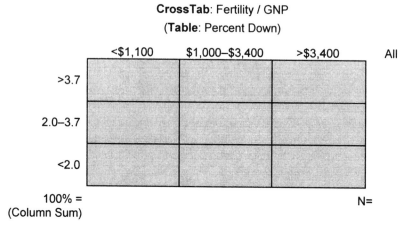

CrossTab: Fertility / GNP
(**Table**: Percent Down)

	<$1,100	$1,000–$3,400	>$3,400	All
>3.7				
2.0–3.7				
<2.0				
100% = (Column Sum)				N=

(Percentage difference between >$3,400 and <$1,100 for the ">3.7" row =   )

Prediction:

Finding:

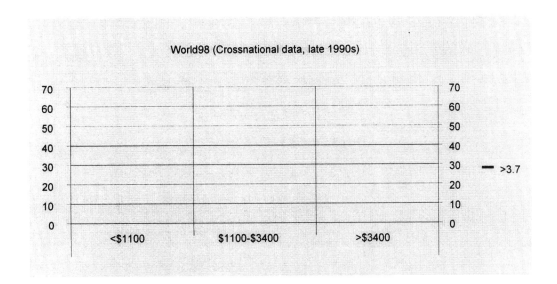

World98 (Crossnational data, late 1990s)

(b) Test the proposition that nations with high infant mortality rates will have to have high fertility rates if they are to reproduce themselves and keep their societies alive. Crosstab Fertility (Y) by InfDeath (X) ; also examine the relationship graphically (after doing the **CrossTab**, select the **Line** alternative for the **Plot** option under the **Table** command and highlight the "">3.7"" category). Does your finding confirm this proposition?

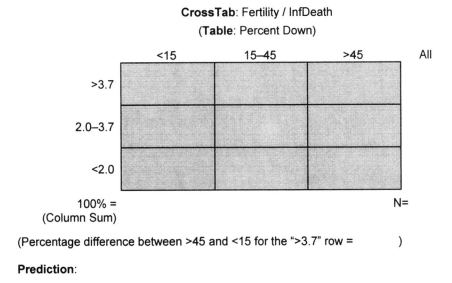

CrossTab: Fertility / InfDeath
(**Table**: Percent Down)

(Percentage difference between >45 and <15 for the ">3.7" row =   )

Prediction:

Finding:

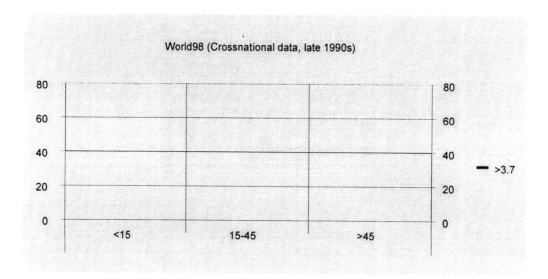

(c) Based on your findings in (3), (4a), and (4b), which causal order do you think best represents the truth: Fertility→Poverty, or, Poverty→Fertility? Discuss. (If possible, use your class notes and/or cite your textbook in support of your answer.)

Suggestions for Further Study

Joel F. Handler argues that trying to solve the problem of welfare dependency by requiring that welfare mothers go to work is doomed to failure. Structural changes in the economy have reduced the number of low-skill jobs, as well as their salaries. Job-training programs have a notorious record of failure, and the availability and costs of childcare are problems that those wanting welfare mothers to work usually ignore. Rising poverty rates are not a function of rising welfare rolls, rather it is the other way around. As a society, we should be concentrating our efforts on how to reduce poverty, not welfare benefits. See his classic essay "The Problem of Poverty, the Problem of Work," pp. 53–65 in Gregg Lee Carter (ed), *Perspectives on Current Social Problems* (Boston: Allyn & Bacon, 1997).

In another essay in *Perspectives on Current Social Problems* ("What the Minimum Wage Buys," pp. 67–71), Paula Mergenbagen demonstrates that America's poorest households often spend more than they have, and that their spending patterns are distinctive. Low-income Americans fall into three groups: the working poor, who spend on used cars and clothing; retired households, who spend on health care and personal care; and college students, who buy entertainment and education. All three groups spend a high share of their money on food and rent.

Perspectives on Current Social Problems also contains a United Nations report ("Hunger, Malnutrition and Food Supplies: The World Situation in the 1990s," pp. 359–368) revealing that many millions of people in the world go hungry, even though the global supply of food is sufficient to feed them adequately. Innovations such as the "green revolution," large investments in agricultural infrastructure and extension services, and improvements in markets, ensure a global output of food adequate to meet nutritional needs. However, the results of these initiatives have been uneven. Data in the report demonstrate that the nutritional situation has shown signs of improvement in Asia, long-term deterioration in Africa, and stagnation or some worsening in Latin America. Moreover, in the economies in transition (such as those nations belonging to the former Yugoslavia), the collapse of economic institutions has reduced output during the past several years.

Relevant World Wide Web Sites

The U.S. government has large amounts of U.S. and international data relevant to poverty, fertility, education, and other factors associated with material well-being at all levels of analysis (the individual, city, county, U.S. state, regional, and cross-national). Most importantly, see:

United States Census Bureau	www.census.gov
United States Department of Health & Human Services	www.dhhs.gov
National Center for Education Statistics	www.nces.ed.gov
Institute for Research on Poverty	www.ssc.wisc.edu/irp

For more survey data relevant to the "status attainment" model (e.g., income, education, race, family background), see the GSS and other related sources listed in the "Suggestions for Further Study" section in Chapter 1 (p. 64). The United Nations provides some on-line cross-national data: www.un.org. Finally, the Social Science Data Analysis Network at the University of Michigan has a treasure trove of U.S. census data related to poverty and surrounding issues: www.SSDAN.Net

Exploratory

I. Using any of the CHIP data files for this or the preceding chapter (*Equal98, Voter98, Status98,* or *World98*), state a hypothesis relating an X and a Y variable that have not already been analyzed together.

II. Sketch the bivariate model.

III. Give a brief interpretation of your hypothesis—that is, describe what is going on in the world such that we would expect to find data patterned in the way in which you have predicted.

IV. (a) Test your hypothesis with a **CrossTab**, putting your Y variable on the rows. Was your hypothesis confirmed? (Note: you may need to delete three columns; the following 3x6 table shell is simply a starting point.)

Original Table

CrossTab: _____(Y) /_____ (X)

(**Table**: Percent Down)

All

100% =   N=
(Column Sum)

(Percentage difference between the highest and lowest values of X on the highest value of Y =   )

Prediction:

Finding:

(b) Use **Plot** under the **Table** option to display the above relationship graphically. Feel free to be creative—trying out each of the plot types (line, bar, pie, stacked). Print out and attach the plot that you think best captures the relationship between your X and Y.

> **Do *either* parts V–VIII *or* parts IX–XII below.**

V. Perhaps the relationship you uncovered in #IV is spurious; that is, perhaps a third variable is predictive of both X and Y; if this is so, then the relationship between X and Y would exist **not** because X is causing Y, but simply because of their covariation with this third variable. If this third variable is held constant, then the relationship between X and Y will weaken greatly or disappear. Choose a third variable that might possibly be generating a spurious relationship between X and Y. Sketch the model showing the relationship between this third variable and X, and between this third variable and Y, as well as the lack of causal relationship between X and Y. Hint: refer back to the discussion on page 25 in the introductory chapter entitled "Elementary Data Analysis Tools Needed to Study Social Issues."

VI. A good social scientist does not choose just any variable to test for spuriosity. Just as you were able to defend the hypothesized relationship between X and Y in #III, develop a brief interpretation to defend the hypothesized relationship between Z and X, then between Z and Y.

(a) Interpretation of the Z–X relationship:

(b) Interpretation of the Z–Y relationship:

VII. Test the alternative model sketched in #V by crosstabbing Y by X and controlling for Z—using the appended table shells. (Note: you may need only 3 columns in each of these shells; also, you may not need all 6 of the partial tables provided; of course, you will need one partial table for each value of Z.)

VIII. What are your conclusions? For example, is the original X–Y relationship spurious? Is it nonspurious (i.e., causal)? Is a multivariable model evident?

IX. Examining all the variables in your data set, which one do you think might be serving as a causal mechanism connecting your X with your Y? In other words, which variable would you choose as "Z" in the following sketch: X→Z→Y? Hint: refer back to the discussion on page 26 in the introductory chapter entitled "Elementary Data Analysis Tools Needed to Study Social Issues."

X. A good social scientist does not choose just any variable to test as a causal mechanism (intervening variable). Just as you were able to defend the hypothesized relationship between X and Y in #III, develop a brief interpretation to defend the hypothesized relationship between X and Z, then between Z and Y.

  (a) Interpretation of the X–Z relationship:

  (b) Interpretation of the Z–Y relationship:

XI. Test the alternative model sketched in #IX by crosstabbing X and Y and controlling for Z—using the appended table shells. (Note: you may need only 3 columns in each of these shells; also, you may not need all 6 of the partial tables provided; of course, you will need one partial table for each value of Z.)

XII. What are your conclusions? Most importantly, do your findings support the notion that your Z is acting as an intervening variable (causal mechanism) connecting your X and your Y?

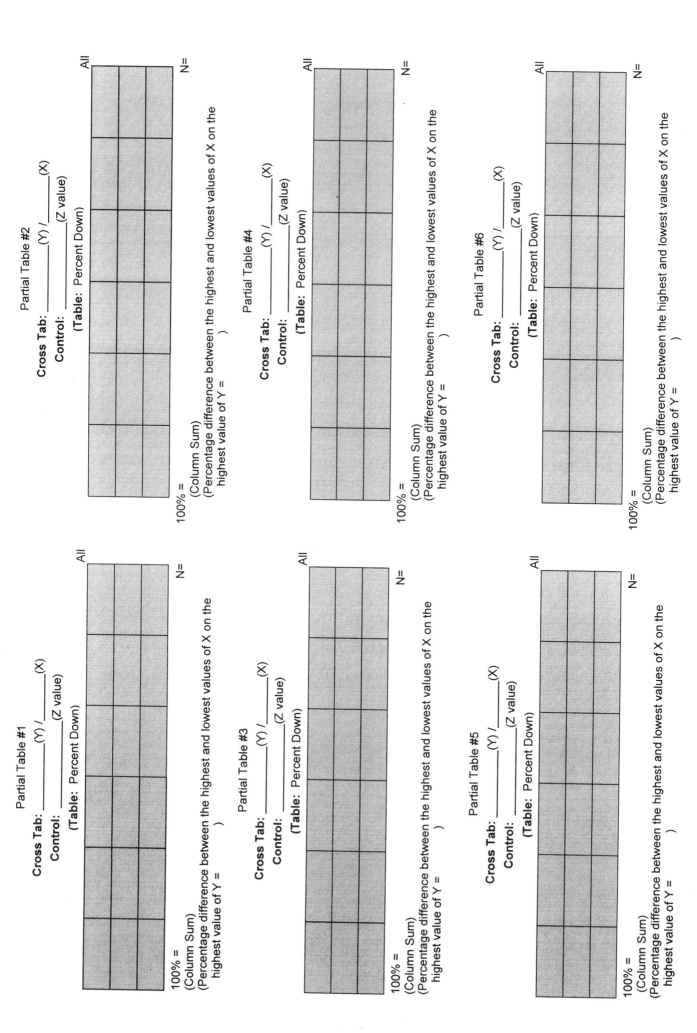

Partial Table #1

Cross Tab: _____ (Y) / _____ (X)

Control: _____ (Z value)

(Table: Percent Down)

All

N=

100% =
(Column Sum)
(Percentage difference between the highest and lowest values of X on the
highest value of Y =)

Partial Table #2

Cross Tab: _____ (Y) / _____ (X)

Control: _____ (Z value)

(Table: Percent Down)

All

N=

100% =
(Column Sum)
(Percentage difference between the highest and lowest values of X on the
highest value of Y =)

Partial Table #3

Cross Tab: _____ (Y) / _____ (X)

Control: _____ (Z value)

(Table: Percent Down)

All

N=

100% =
(Column Sum)
(Percentage difference between the highest and lowest values of X on the
highest value of Y =)

Partial Table #4

Cross Tab: _____ (Y) / _____ (X)

Control: _____ (Z value)

(Table: Percent Down)

All

N=

100% =
(Column Sum)
(Percentage difference between the highest and lowest values of X on the
highest value of Y =)

Partial Table #5

Cross Tab: _____ (Y) / _____ (X)

Control: _____ (Z value)

(Table: Percent Down)

All

N=

100% =
(Column Sum)
(Percentage difference between the highest and lowest values of X on the
highest value of Y =)

Partial Table #6

Cross Tab: _____ (Y) / _____ (X)

Control: _____ (Z value)

(Table: Percent Down)

All

N=

100% =
(Column Sum)
(Percentage difference between the highest and lowest values of X on the
highest value of Y =)

Chapter 4. Race and Ethnic Relations

Racial and ethnic differences among people would be of little interest to sociologists if it were not for the pervasive prejudice, discrimination, inequality, and conflict that are entwined with such differences. **Prejudice** is a mindset that involves invidious distinctions: *Those* people aren't like *us*—they're lazy; *they* aren't like *us*—they cheat one another; and so on. Prejudice provides a foundation for, but is not the same thing as, **discrimination**. While prejudice is a mindset, discrimination is *behavior* which favors one group over another for no objective reason. The potent combination of prejudice and discrimination generates inequalities between and among the more powerful and the less powerful racial and ethnic groups within a society.

Prejudice, discrimination, and inequality encourage conflict among groups. The conflict may be minor and subside if *assimilation* (the melding of two or more groups into one) occurs. It may be larger and result in a system of *accommodation* ("we'll live side-by-side, but will follow certain rules to make sure our groups don't mix too much, e.g., we'll live in separate neighborhoods"). The rules in such a case will, of course, be set by the more powerful of the groups. In its worst form, accommodation amounts to slavery; in its best form, it amounts to *cultural pluralism*—the acceptance of diversity by most members of a society, with few or no strings attached. Finally, the conflict may be enormous and result in the *banishment* or even the *annihilation* (i.e., *genocide*) of a weaker group.[1]

The computer exercises in Chapter 4 deal with race and ethnicity as they involve prejudice, discrimination, inequality, and conflict.

Race, Ethnicity, and Poverty—African-Americans, Latinos, Asians, and Whites

John D. Kasarda has demonstrated how the plight of many blacks in the United States has worsened in the past twenty years, despite tremendous reductions in discrimination.[2] His research helps us understand the underlying causes of the cataclysmic rioting in Los Angeles in the spring of 1992, as well as other inner-city riots that have occurred sporadically in the United States throughout the 1990s. Although Kasarda recognizes that there are many causes for the mounting impoverishment and forlornness of inner-city residents,[3] his main focus has been on the mismatch between the low education of many inner-

---

[1]One of the most extreme and infamous contemporary examples of genocide was "Adolph Hitler's Nazi Germany. In an attempt to establish an 'Aryan nation,' the Nazi regime systematically murdered more than six million Jews and other 'non-Aryan' people such as the Romany (commonly referred to as 'Gypsies') between 1933 and 1945. Genocide is not something that has happened only in faraway places. For example, the United States, during the California gold rush (1848–1873), the state government paid White settlers and prospectors for the heads of Indians, reimbursing individuals a total of about $1 million for the bullets they used. The Native American population in California declined from 150,000 to 30,000 during this period. More recent examples of genocide have occurred in the former Yugoslavia through 'ethnic cleansing' campaigns . . . and in Rwanda, where an estimated one million members of the Tutsi ethnic group have been killed by the rival Hutu ethnic group" (Daniel J. Curran and Claire M. Renzetti, *Social Problems: Society in Crisis*, 5th ed., Boston: Allyn & Bacon, 2000, p. 164). Other recent examples include "Pol Pot's Cambodia and Idi Amin's Uganda. Between 1975 and 1979, Pol Pot implemented his policies for the 'purification' of Cambodia that included the destruction of anything foreign, including any of his own people who spoke foreign languages. They were imprisoned and often beaten to death with sticks in a practice that one observer termed 'auto-genocide.' During Amin's presidency (1971–1979), 300,000 Ugandans—one in every forty—were killed. Thousands more were imprisoned as Amin attempted to eliminate almost every one who was not Moslem and a member of his own ethnic group, the Kakwas. The victims included Christians, Jews, and Asians, as well as rival ethnic groups" (see Curran and Renzetti's 3rd edition of their *Social Problems: Society in Crisis*, 1993, p. 237).

[2]See, for example, his "Urban Industrial Transition and the Underclass," *Annals of the American Academy of Political and Social Science*, v. 501 (January 1989), pp. 26–47.

[3]For example, Kasarda addresses the issue of why Asians and some Latino groups have fared fairly well in recent

city blacks and the high educational demands of current urban jobs, which are concentrated in white-collar service sectors. Loss of employment opportunities, in turn, has had devastating effects on African-American families—generating desertions, separations, out-of-wedlock births, single-parent homes, welfare dependency, and crime.

Kasarda's research meshes well with that of William Julius Wilson,[4] who emphasizes two causes of inner-city black impoverishment that are discrimination-related. First, even though they enjoy the protection of antidiscrimination laws, many African-Americans are suffering from the discrimination that their parents and grandparents endured. That is, their parents and grandparents were prevented from developing wealth and social connections that they could pass on to their children; such advantages can be crucial in obtaining a higher education, starting a family business, or landing a first job. Second, the lessening of housing discrimination has allowed an exodus of middle-class blacks from the ghetto. This exodus has two deleterious effects on poor black employment: First, many individuals hear about jobs and find work from those already in the labor market. With the employed minority middle classes leaving the ghetto, poor minorities are bereft of these job-landing networks. Second, the minority middle classes have traditionally provided mainstream role models that help to keep alive the perception that education is meaningful, that steady employment is a viable alternative to welfare, and that family stability is the norm, not the exception. What results is a vicious circle of poverty formation: As the black middle and working classes leave the ghetto, those left behind lose their job-finding networks and role models for working. As this happens, they fall into a lifestyle of unemployment, which, in turn, generates poverty, crime, poor schools, and other social problems. These problems encourage the middle classes all the more to flee the ghetto, and the vicious circle continues.

My own research empirically tests the thinking of Kasarda and Wilson with over-time census data on the inner-city neighborhood of "South Providence" in Providence, Rhode Island.[5] Indeed, South Providence largely confirms the thinking of Kasarda and Wilson. During the 1970s and 1980s, the American economy, in general, and the South Providence economy, in particular, were restructured drastically. Most significant for African-Americans was the deindustrialization of the urban economies in the Midwest and Northeast (including South Providence) and the massive loss of production jobs. Moreover, the restructuring occurred at the same time that a flood of immigrants was entering the workforce and competing with native African-Americans for low-skill and entry-level jobs in the urban economy.

The CHIP exercises that follow allow you to examine the various associations between and among race, ethnicity, education, household type, and income. The exercises include a test of Kasarda's fundamental hypothesis that low education accounts for much of the tendency for African-Americans to have lower incomes than their white counterparts.

---

years, while the situations of many blacks have worsened. His data reveal that many Asian and some Latino groups have carved out specialized economic enclaves (e.g., restauranting, laundering, green groceries). Importantly, the success of these enclaves is linked to ethnic social customs emphasizing mutual support. For example, many Asian small businesses do not have to rely on white banks to gain financing. Asian businessmen (and in a few instances businesswomen) pool their resources and lend to one another. Furthermore, ethnic-enclave establishments hire almost exclusively their own members, many of whom would likely face employment discrimination by firms outside their enclave. Kasarda proposes that such a system of mutual support would be an important means by which blacks could improve their collective lot.

[4]See, for example, Wilson's *The Truly Disadvantaged* (Chicago: University of Chicago Press, 1987), as well as his more recent *When Work Disappears: The World of the New Urban Poor* (New York: Alfred A. Knopf, 1996).

[5]Gregg Lee Carter, "Social Disintegration in Inner-City Black Neighborhoods of the Frostbelt: The Example of South Providence," *Research in Urban Economics* 9 (1993), pp. 115-140. reprinted in in Gregg Lee Carter (ed.), *Perspectives on Current Social Problems* (Boston: Allyn & Bacon, 1997), pp. 103–119.

File: **Voter98** (Social characteristics of voters and nonvoters. *Source*: 1993–98 cumulative GSS)

Info: Immigrant→Latino→RaceHH→Sex→Age→Ed→TypeHH→FamInc→Voter
  (2)   (2)   (4)   (2)   (3)   (3)   (5)   (3)   (2)

Immigrant	No, Yes
Latino	(Latino heritage) No, Yes (GSS coding for "Ethnicity" = 17, 22, 25, or 38)
RaceHH	(Race of household) White, Black, Asian, Other
Sex	Male, Female
Age	18–39, 40–64, 65+
Ed	<12yrs, 12yrs, 13–15yrs, 16+yrs
TypeHH	(Type of Household) Other (e.g., cohabitators, extended families, roommates), SingParent (Single Parent), SingAdult (Single Adult), MarrParent (Married-Couple with children), MarrNoKids (Married-Couple with no children)
FamInc	(Family Income) <$20K, $20K–$60K, $60K+
Voter	(Did you vote in the last presidential election?) No, Yes

Basic

1. Kasarda argues that many Asian immigrants and selected Latino groups have been able to use ethnic-based methods to assemble capital, establish internal markets, circumvent discrimination, and generate employment in their enclaves; such employment is relatively insulated from both swings in the national economy and urban structural transformation (from goods-producing to service industries). His contention implies that Latino and Asian rates of "low-income" (poverty) should be lower than the rate of African-Americans. Check out this hypothesis by crosstabbing (a) FamInc (Y) by RaceHH (X); and (b) FamInc (Y) by Latino (X). What did you find? (*Concentrate your discussion on the "low-income" – that is, <$20K – row.*)

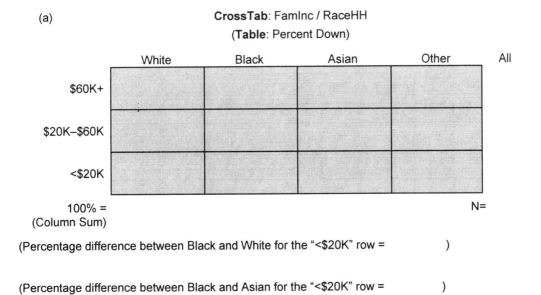

(a)   **CrossTab**: FamInc / RaceHH
              (**Table**: Percent Down)

(Percentage difference between Black and White for the "<$20K" row =   )

(Percentage difference between Black and Asian for the "<$20K" row =   )

(b)

CrossTab: FamInc / Latino
(**Table**: Percent Down)

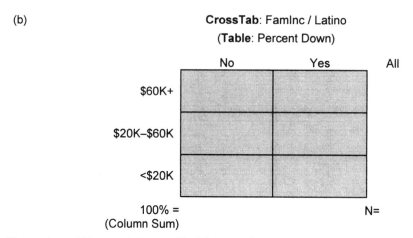

100% =
(Column Sum)   N=

(Percentage difference between *Black* in preceding crosstab and *Yes* in this crosstab for the "<$20K" row =   )

Answer/Discussion

2. Critical to Kasarda's explanation of African-American poverty is the argument that African-Americans have, on average, lower educational attainment than whites and other groups. Test this part of Kasarda's explanation by crosstabulating Ed (Y) by RaceHH (X). Is this piece of his explanation confirmed?

CrossTab: Ed / RaceHH
(**Table**: Percent Down)

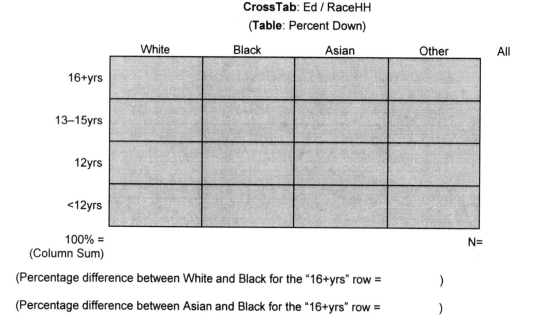

100% =
(Column Sum)   N=

(Percentage difference between White and Black for the "16+yrs" row =   )

(Percentage difference between Asian and Black for the "16+yrs" row =   )

Answer/Discussion

3. Kasarda points out that single-parent households (especially if they are mother-headed) are linked to lower education and higher poverty, which are in turn highly correlated. Test these links by crosstabulating:

   (a) Ed (Y) by TypeHH (X):

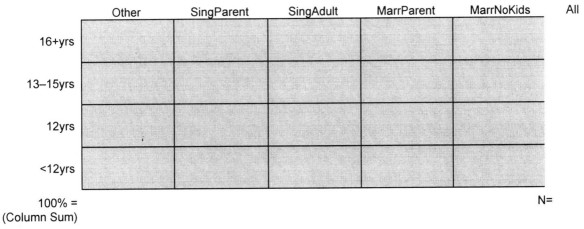

CrossTab: Ed / TypeHH
(**Table**: Percent Down)

	Other	SingParent	SingAdult	MarrParent	MarrNoKids	All
16+yrs						
13–15yrs						
12yrs						
<12yrs						
100% = (Column Sum)						N=

(Percentage difference between SingParent and MarrParent for "16+yrs" of education =   )

Prediction:

Finding:

(b) FamInc (Y) by TypeHH (X):

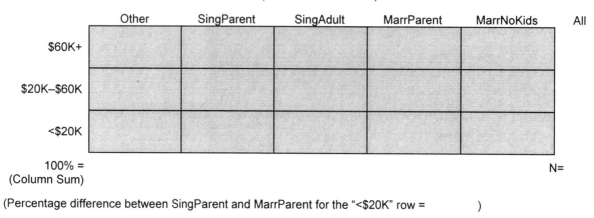

CrossTab: FamInc / TypeHH
(**Table**: Percent Down)

(Percentage difference between SingParent and MarrParent for the "<$20K" row =   )

Prediction:

Finding:

(c) FamInc (Y) by Ed (X):

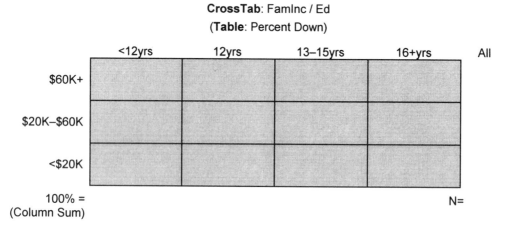

CrossTab: FamInc / Ed
(**Table**: Percent Down)

(Percentage difference between 16+yrs and <12yrs for the "$60K+" row =   )

Prediction:

Finding:

(d) Do we find all of the relationships that Kasarda has hypothesized? Would you say that his overall model for explaining poverty (low family income) has received generally strong confirmation? Discuss.

Advanced

4. The impact of race on poverty is probably a combination of direct and indirect effects. An example of an indirect effect would be that African-Americans face more discrimination in the work world than whites and, in turn, discrimination increases the odds of being out of work and poor. Another indirect effect would operate through education: African-Americans are less likely to get extra schooling, which, in turn increases their odds of being poor because schooling and employability are positively related. Because discrimination is almost always "unmeasured," its effect on income or poverty is usually taken as the direct effect of race on income or poverty after controlling for education (and other intervening variables). Considering both direct and indirect effects, we might sketch the relationship between race, education, and "low-income" (or "poverty") as follows:

(a) If this model is true, what will happen to the relationship between *Race* and *Low-Income* when *Education* is controlled for?

(b) Test your answer by crosstabbing FamInc (Y) by RaceHH (X) and control for Ed (Z). To simplify your analyses use the **Modify** command to **Omit** "Asians" and "Other" from RaceHH. Note that Student CHIP performs its modifications relatively slowly on this data file—so give it a few extra seconds to complete the task. To verify that you have properly executed this command, do an **Info** to confirm that RaceHH now has only 2 categories.

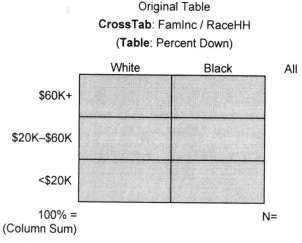

(Percentage difference between Black and White for the "$60K+" row =   )

Prediction:

Finding:

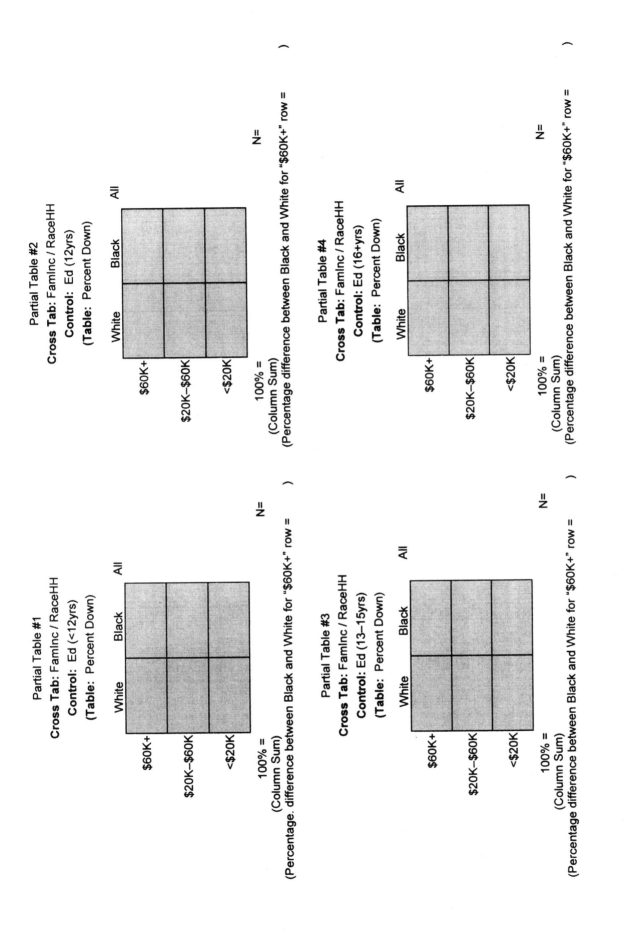

Partial Table #1

Cross Tab: FamInc / RaceHH

Control: Ed (<12yrs)

(Table: Percent Down)

	White	Black	All
$60K+			
$20K–$60K			
<$20K			
100% =(Column Sum)			
N=			

(Percentage. difference between Black and White for "$60K+" row =   )

Partial Table #2

Cross Tab: FamInc / RaceHH

Control: Ed (12yrs)

(Table: Percent Down)

	White	Black	All
$60K+			
$20K–$60K			
<$20K			
100% =(Column Sum)			
N=			

(Percentage difference between Black and White for "$60K+" row =   )

Partial Table #3

Cross Tab: FamInc / RaceHH

Control: Ed (13–15yrs)

(Table: Percent Down)

	White	Black	All
$60K+			
$20K–$60K			
<$20K			
100% =(Column Sum)			
N=			

(Percentage difference between Black and White for "$60K+" row =   )

Partial Table #4

Cross Tab: FamInc / RaceHH

Control: Ed (16+yrs)

(Table: Percent Down)

	White	Black	All
$60K+			
$20K–$60K			
<$20K			
100% =(Column Sum)			
N=			

(Percentage difference between Black and White for "$60K+" row =   )

(c) Do the partial tables support the model sketched above? What is happening in the partial tables that tells us that the model is (or is not) supported?

The International Scene: Ethnic Diversity and Civil War

Shirley M. Kolack's research on ethnic minorities in the former Soviet Union reveals the importance of ethnicity in understanding the upheavals in eastern Europe over the past several years.[6] Her particularized findings on the U.S.S.R. exemplify more general principles in this area of sociology: Ethnic pride fuels intra- and inter-societal conflict. Ethnic group membership partly determines how others treat you, as well as your chances for economic success. Ethnic group identification is strengthened when the group has a distinct language or dialect; when it experiences few inter-group marriages; when it is physically segregated (on a large scale, in its own province or territory; on a smaller scale, in its own neighborhood); and when its members are forced to rely on one another for material support due to discrimination against them on the part of society's dominant group. Such principles are as pertinent in understanding how ethnicity affects social and political affairs in the United States as in eastern Europe, Africa, and the rest the of the world.

As observed by Soroka and Bryjak, one advantage of the Cold War period (1946–1990) was that the "United States and the Soviet Union were able to keep their allies and subordinates (in the case of the Soviet Union) in check. However, now that the U.S.S.R. no longer exists and the chances of an East-versus-West nuclear confrontation has been drastically reduced . . . [there has been an] emergence of a multipolar Europe awash with tension and shifting alliances.".[7] In short, one consequence of the democratization of numerous societies that began in the 1980s in Europe, Asia, and Africa is an increase in political identification and action on the basis of in-group characteristics (ethnicity, religion, and common culture).

The CHIP data set *Revolt96* allows you to examine the connection between the heterogeneity of a nation and the odds of it experiencing a civil war (which are most often separatist movements, i.e., the desire for an ethnic group to form their own independent states or independent provinces within a larger country). The data set also allows you to investigate other contributing factors to civil war—including poverty, underdevelopment, and lack of political freedom.

File: **Revolt96** (Civil wars, 1990–96)[8]

Info: Region→Freedom→GNP→HDI→Farmers→Tongues→Revolt
     (6)   (3)   (3)   (3)   (3)   (2)   (2)

(Note: GNP, HDI, and Farmers are divided into three categories: bottom, middle, and top third.)

Region	(United Nations regional designation) Industrial, East-Europe, Africa-SubSaharan, Arab, Asia, Latin-America
Freedom	(Type of political regime) Not Free, Partly Free, Free
GNP	(Per capita GNP in 1997 U.S. dollars) <$1,100; $1,100–3,400; >$3,400
HDI	(United Nations "Human Development Index," combines measures of life expectancy, adult literacy, school enrollment, and per capita Gross Domestic Product; theoretically varying from 0 [lowest level of development] to 1 [highest]) <.700, .700–.800, >.800
Farmers	(Percentage of the workforce in agriculture) <14%, 14–40%, >40%
Tongues	(Number of different languages spoken in the nation) 1–2, 3+
Revolt	(Did nation experience a civil war during the 1990–1996 era?) No, Yes

---

[6]"Ethnic Minorities in the Soviet Union," *International Journal of Group Tension*, 21:3 (Fall, 1991), pp. 223–236.

[7]Michael P. Soroka and George J. Bryjak, *Social Problems: A World at Risk* 2nd ed. (Boston: Allyn & Bacon, 1999), p. 449.

[8]*Sources:* Central Intelligence Agency, *The World Factbook 1999* (Dulles, VA.: Brassey's Inc., 1999); Robert L. Bartley (ed.), *Freedom in the World: The Annual Survey of Political Rights and Civil Liberties, 1998-1999* (Piscataway, NJ: Transaction Publishers, 1999); Dan Smith, *The State of War and Peace Atlas, New Edition* (NY: Penguin USA, 1997);the United Nations' *Human Development Report 1999* (NY: Oxford University Press, 1999); and the *World Population Data Sheet*. (Washington, D.C.: Population Reference Bureau, 1999).

Country	Freedom	GNP	HDI	Farmers	Tongues	Revolt
Albania	Partly Free	360	.699	49.5	2	No
Algeria	Not Free	1,690	.665	22.0	3	Yes
Angola	Not Free	260	.398	85.0	3	Yes
Antigua and Barbuda	Partly Free	6,970	.828	11.0	1	No
Argentina	Free	8,060	.827	12.0	5	No
Armenia	Partly Free	670	.728	38.0	2	No
Australia	Free	17,980	.922	5.0	1	No
Austria	Free	24,950	.904	8.1	1	No
Azerbaijan	Partly Free	500	.695	32.0	3	No
Bahamas	Free	11,790	.851	5.0	2	No
Bahrain	Not Free	7,500	.832	1.0	4	No
Barbados	Free	6,530	.857	10.0	1	No
Belarus	Not Free	2,160	.763	19.0	2	No
Belgium	Free	22,920	.923	2.6	3	No
Belize	Free	2,550	.732	30.0	4	No
Brazil	Partly Free	3,370	.739	31.0	4	No
Brunei	Not Free	14,240	.878	4.0	3	No
Bulgaria	Free	1,160	.758	18.0	1	No
Cambodia	Not Free	300	.514	80.0	2	Yes
Cameroon	Not Free	680	.536	74.4	9	No
Canada	Free	19,570	.932	3.0	2	No
Cape Verde	Free	910	.677	57.0	2	No
Central African Republic	Partly Free	370	.378	85.0	5	No
Chile	Free	3,560	.844	19.2	1	No
China	Not Free	530	.701	50.0	9	No
Colombia	Partly Free	1,620	.768	30.0	1	Yes
Comoros	Partly Free	510	.506	80.0	3	No
Costa Rica	Free	2,380	.801	21.6	2	No
Cuba	Not Free	2,000	.765	20.0	1	No
Denmark	Free	28,110	.905	5.0	4	No
Dominica	Free	2,830	.776	40.0	2	No
Dominican Republic	Free	1,320	.726	50.0	1	No
Ecuador	Free	1,310	.747	29.0	2	No
Egypt	Not Free	710	.616	40.0	3	Yes
El Salvador	Free	1,480	.674	40.0	2	Yes
Estonia	Free	2,820	.773	11.0	5	No
Ethiopia	Partly Free	130	.298	80.0	7	Yes
Fiji	Partly Free	2,320	.763	67.0	3	No
Finland	Free	18,850	.913	8.6	4	No
France	Free	23,470	.918	5.0	1	No
Georgia	Partly Free	580	.729	25.0	4	Yes
Germany	Free	25,580	.906	2.7	1	No
Ghana	Partly Free	430	.544	61.0	5	Yes
Greece	Free	7,710	.867	19.8	3	No
Grenada	Free	2,620	.777	24.0	2	No
Guatemala	Partly Free	1,190	.624	58.0	9	Yes
Guyana	Free	530	.701	30.2	2	No
Haiti	Partly Free	220	.430	66.0	2	Yes
Honduras	Free	580	.641	37.0	2	No
Hungary	Free	3,840	.795	8.3	2	No
Iceland	Free	24,590	.919	5.1	1	No
India	Free	310	.545	67.0	9	Yes

Country	Freedom	GNP	HDI	Farmers	Tongues	Revolt
Indonesia	Partly Free	880	.681	41.0	4	Yes
Iran	Not Free	1,780	.715	33.0	7	Yes
Iraq	Not Free	1,940	.586	30.0	4	Yes
Ireland	Free	13,630	.900	10.0	2	No
Israel	Free	14,410	.883	2.6	3	Yes
Italy	Free	19,270	.900	7.0	4	No
Jamaica	Free	1,420	.734	22.5	2	No
Japan	Free	34,630	.924	6.0	1	No
Jordan	Partly Free	1,390	.715	7.4	2	No
Kazakhstan	Not Free	1,110	.740	23.0	2	No
Kenya	Not Free	260	.519	80.0	2	No
Kyrgyzstan	Partly Free	610	.702	40.0	2	No
Laos	Not Free	320	.491	80.0	3	Yes
Latvia	Free	2,290	.744	16.0	3	No
Lebanon	Not Free	3,350	.749	7.0	4	Yes
Liberia	Not Free	2,260	.239	70.0	9	Yes
Lithuania	Free	1,350	.761	20.0	3	No
Luxembourg	Free	39,850	.902	2.5	4	No
Malta	Free	7,970	.850	2.0	2	No
Mauritania	Not Free	480	.447	47.0	5	No
Mauritius	Free	3,180	.764	14.0	7	No
Mexico	Partly Free	4,010	.786	21.8	1	Yes
Moldova	Partly Free	870	.683	40.2	3	Yes
Morocco	Partly Free	1,150	.582	50.0	3	Yes
Mozambique	Partly Free	80	.341	80.0	1	Yes
Namibia	Free	2,030	.638	49.0	3	No
Nepal	Partly Free	200	.463	81.0	9	No
Netherlands	Free	21,970	.921	4.0	1	No
New Zealand	Free	13,190	.901	9.8	2	No
Nicaragua	Free	330	.616	31.0	2	Yes
Nigeria	Partly Free	280	.456	54.0	5	No
Norway	Free	26,480	.927	6.0	2	No
Pakistan	Partly Free	440	.508	47.0	7	Yes
Panama	Free	2,670	.791	26.8	2	No
Peru	Partly Free	1,890	.739	17.0	3	Yes
Philippines	Free	960	.740	39.8	2	Yes
Poland	Free	2,470	.802	26.0	1	No
Portugal	Free	9,370	.858	12.0	1	No
Romania	Free	1,230	.752	36.4	3	No
Russia	Partly Free	2,650	.747	20.0	9	Yes
Saudi Arabia	Not Free	7,240	.740	5.0	1	No
Seychelles	Partly Free	6,210	.755	10.0	3	No
Singapore	Partly Free	23,360	.888	11.4	4	No
South Africa	Free	3,010	.695	30.0	9	Yes
South Korea	Free	8,220	.852	21.0	2	No
Spain	Free	13,280	.894	8.0	4	Yes
Sri Lanka	Partly Free	640	.721	37.0	3	Yes
Sudan	Not Free	290	.475	80.0	7	Yes
Sweden	Free	23,630	.923	3.2	3	No
Switzerland	Free	37,180	.914	4.0	4	No
Syria	Not Free	1,120	.663	40.0	6	No
Tajikistan	Not Free	350	.665	52.0	2	Yes

Country	Freedom	GNP	HDI	Farmers	Tongues	Revolt
Thailand	Free	2,210	.753	54.0	2	No
Trinidad and Tobago	Free	3,740	.797	9.5	4	Yes
Tunisia	Not Free	1,800	.695	22.0	2	No
Turkey	Partly Free	2,450	.728	42.5	3	Yes
Turkmenistan	Not Free	640	.712	44.0	3	No
Ukraine	Partly Free	1,570	.721	24.0	5	No
United Kingdom	Free	18,410	.918	1.1	3	No
United States	Free	25,860	.927	2.7	2	No
Uruguay	Free	4,650	.826	11.0	1	No
Uzbekistan	Not Free	950	.720	44.0	4	No
Venezuela	Free	2,760	.792	13.0	1	Yes
Vietnam	Not Free	190	.664	65.0	6	No
Yemen	Partly Free	280	.449	92.0	1	Yes
Yugoslavia*	Not Free	1,100	.746	35.0	5	No
Zaire**	Not Free	110	.479	65.0	5	No
Zimbabwe	Partly Free	490	.560	74.0	3	No

*Republic of Macedonia; **Republic of Congo

Basic

(Note: for all the questions in this section, concentrate your answers on the "Yes" row of Revolt.)

1. Test the fundamental argument that heterogeneity—measured here by the number of languages spoken by a sizable portion of nation's population—encourages dissension by crosstabulating Revolt (Y) by Tongues; also examine the relationship graphically (after doing the **CrossTab**, select the **Line** alternative for the **Plot** option under the **Table** command and highlight the "Yes" category). Did you find the expected relationship?

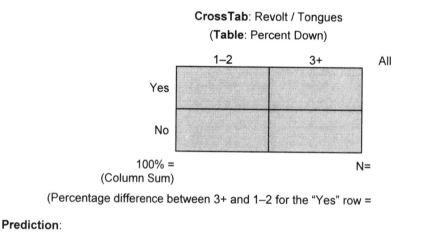

CrossTab: Revolt / Tongues
(**Table**: Percent Down)

(Percentage difference between 3+ and 1–2 for the "Yes" row =   )

Prediction:

Finding:

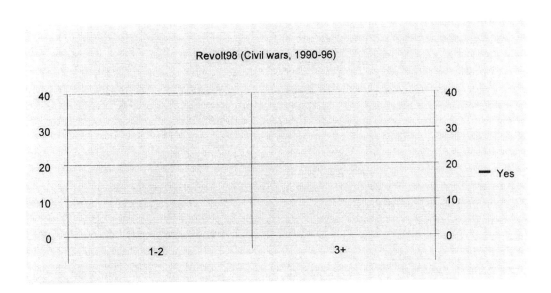

Revolt98 (Civil wars, 1990-96)

2. Glynn, Hohm, and Stewart point out that "most countries that depend on farming for the employ-
    ment of the majority of their people are very poor. One problem is that agricultural produce brings a
    low price relative to the prices of manufactured goods that must be imported . . . Often the best land
    in the country is owned by a small minority of people or by foreign corporations, and its products go
    to an overseas market, not the people themselves. Often only a minority can read or write, and poorly
    educated people are easily controlled by governments that do not represent their interests."[9] If gov-
    ernments are not open and democratic, we can expect the likelihood for rebellion to increase, as eth-
    nic minorities and other "subordinate groups . . . resort to violence when they have few other means
    of redressing grievances; . . . in fact, violence is an important mechanism for bringing about social
    change."[10]

    A number of hypotheses are implied by these observations about the relationships among the
    occupational structure, poverty, political freedom, ethnic diversity, and rebelliousness. Let's test out
    some of them:

    (a) You have just seen (#1 above) that highly heterogeneous nations—as measured by the number of
        different languages spoken—are more likely to incur civil wars; now test the notions that they are
        also more likely to be nonindustrial, poor, and to lack political freedom by filling in and complet-
        ing the following crosstabulations and plots. Are all of your findings confirmatory?

---

[9]James A. Glynn, Charles F. Hohm, and Elbert W. Stewart, *Global Social Problems* (NY: HarperCollins, 1996, pp. 237–38.

[10]Thomas J. Sullivan, Introduction to Social Problems, 5th ed. (Boston: Allyn & Bacon, 2000), p. 487.

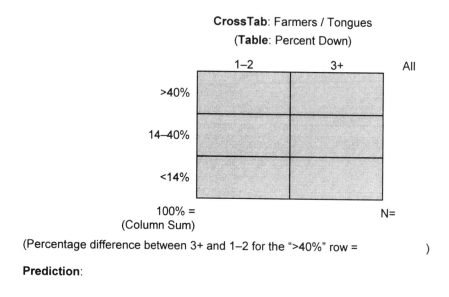

CrossTab: Farmers / Tongues
(**Table**: Percent Down)

(Percentage difference between 3+ and 1–2 for the ">40%" row =   )

Prediction:

Finding:

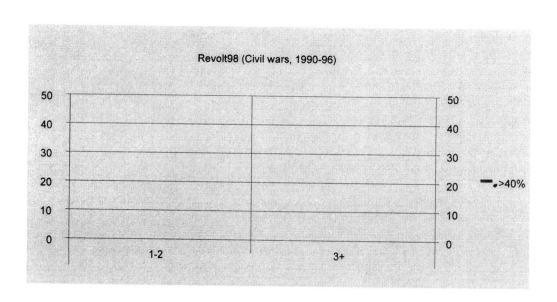

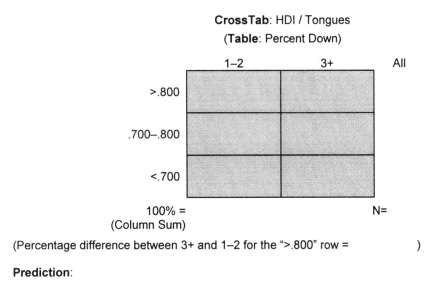

CrossTab: HDI / Tongues
(**Table**: Percent Down)

	1–2	3+	All
>.800			
.700–.800			
<.700			
100% = (Column Sum)			N=

(Percentage difference between 3+ and 1–2 for the ">.800" row =   )

Prediction:

Finding:

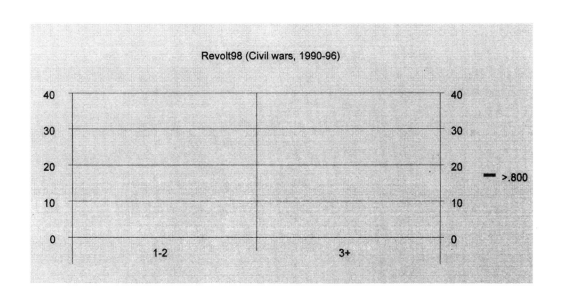

Revolt98 (Civil wars, 1990-96)

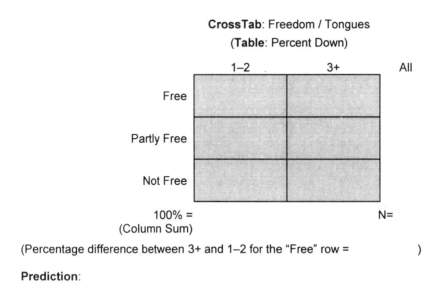

CrossTab: Freedom / Tongues
(**Table**: Percent Down)

(Percentage difference between 3+ and 1–2 for the "Free" row =   )

Prediction:

Finding:

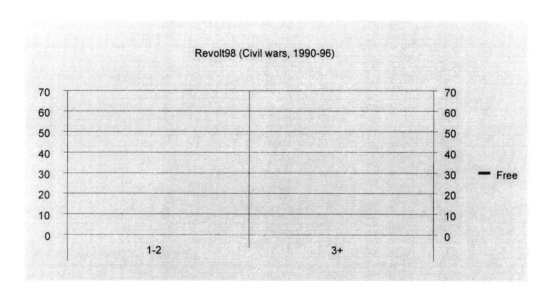

(b) Next, test the notions that nonindustrial, poor, and nondemocratic nations are more likely to incur civil wars by filling in and completing the following crosstabulations and plots. Are all of your findings confirmatory?

CrossTab: Revolt / Farmers
(**Table**: Percent Down)

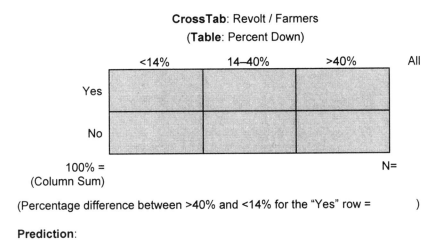

(Percentage difference between >40% and <14% for the "Yes" row =   )

Prediction:

Finding:

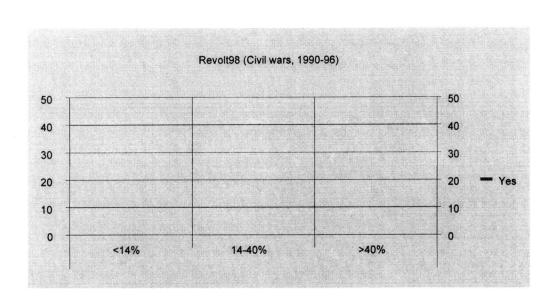

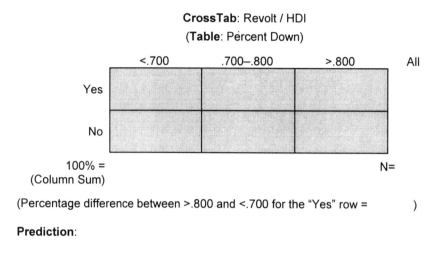

CrossTab: Revolt / HDI
(**Table**: Percent Down)

	<.700	.700–.800	>.800	All
Yes				
No				
100% = (Column Sum)				N=

(Percentage difference between >.800 and <.700 for the "Yes" row =   )

Prediction:

Finding:

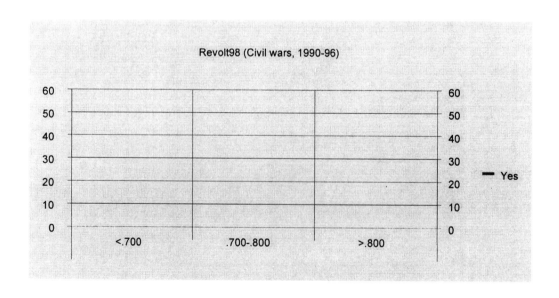

Revolt98 (Civil wars, 1990-96)

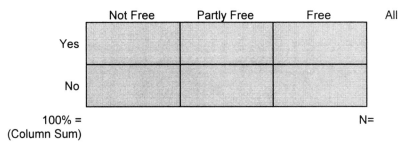

CrossTab: Revolt / Freedom
(**Table**: Percent Down)

	Not Free	Partly Free	Free	All
Yes				
No				

100% =
(Column Sum)   N=

(Percentage difference between Free and Not Free for the "Yes" row =   )

Prediction:

Finding:

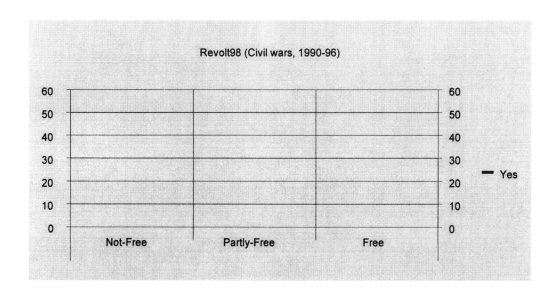

Revolt98 (Civil wars, 1990-96)

— Yes

(c) Examine closely your crosstabulation of Revolt by Freedom above. Why do you think the data are patterned in this way? That is, why do you think rebelliousness is highest for those nations that are "partly free" as opposed to those that are "not free?" Use your intuition, and, if possible, refer to your class notes and assigned readings.

Advanced

1. Perhaps the relationship found above between development (prosperity) and rebelliousness is spurious—due to the possibility that political freedom is correlated with development as well as with rebellion, and thus the association between development and rebellion is simply an artifact of their common relationship with political freedom. Sketch and defend the model that would show the relationship between HDI and Revolt as spurious, using Freedom as your antecedent variable. (Hint: you may want to review the section entitled "The Art of Reading Partial Tables" in your earlier chapter on *Elementary Data Analysis Tools Needed to Study Social Issues*.)

   (a) Model sketch:

   (b) Interpretation of the Freedom—HDI relationship:

   (c) Interpretation of the Freedom—Revolt relationship:

Original Table
CrossTab: Revolt / HDI
(**Table**: Percent Down)

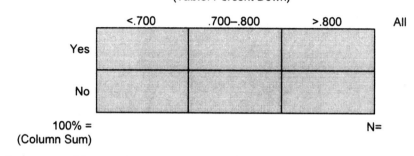

	<.700	.700–.800	>.800	All
Yes				
No				

100% =
(Column Sum)   N=

(Percentage difference between >.800 and <.700 for the "Yes" row =   )

Prediction:

Finding:

Partial Table #1
CrossTab: Revolt / HDI
Control: Freedom (Not Free)
(**Table**: Percent Down)

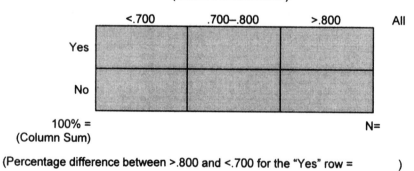

	<.700	.700–.800	>.800	All
Yes				
No				

100% =
(Column Sum)   N=

(Percentage difference between >.800 and <.700 for the "Yes" row =   )

Partial Table #2
CrossTab: Revolt / HDI
Control: Freedom (Partly Free)
(**Table**: Percent Down)

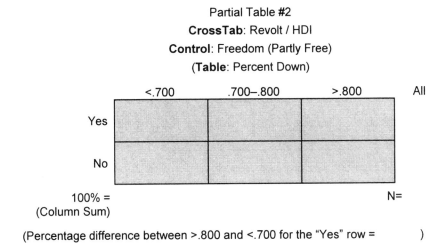

	<.700	.700–.800	>.800	All
Yes				
No				

100% =
(Column Sum)   N=

(Percentage difference between >.800 and <.700 for the "Yes" row =   )

Partial Table #3
CrossTab: Revolt / HDI
Control: Freedom (Free)
(**Table**: Percent Down)

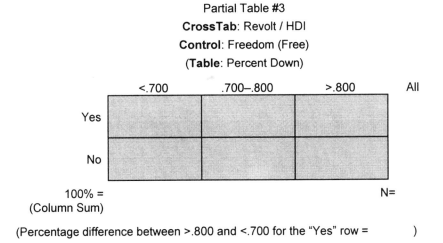

	<.700	.700–.800	>.800	All
Yes				
No				

100% =
(Column Sum)   N=

(Percentage difference between >.800 and <.700 for the "Yes" row =   )

(d) Was the original relationship spurious or nonspurious?

Suggestions for Further Study

In the 1960s sociologists developed an interpretation of the African-American experience that would make it fit the classic model of immigrant success: It was misleading to think of African Americans as having been in the United States since the 17th century; rather, they were in actuality a force in urban America only since World War II. By their third generation in the city, African Americans were expected to move steadily up the social class scale, with significantly fewer of them living in poverty. However, during the 1970s and 1980s the American economy restructured much more drastically than anticipated. Most significant for African Americans was the deindustrialization of urban economies in the Midwest and the Northeast and the massive loss of production jobs. Moreover, the restructuring occurred at the same time that a flood of immigrants was entering the workforce and competing with native African Americans for low-skill and entry-level jobs in the urban economy. Relying largely on 1970, 1980, and 1990 census data, I document how African Americans in one particular inner-city neighborhood—"South Providence" in Providence, Rhode Island—were adversely affected by the restructuring of the Northeast economy and, consequently, how for them socioeconomic success has not come with the passage of time. See "Social Disintegration in Inner-City Black Neighborhoods of the Frostbelt," pp. 103–119 in Gregg Lee Carter (ed.), *Perspectives on Current Social Problems* (Boston: Allyn & Bacon, 1997).

In another essay in *Perspectives on Current Social Problems* ("Black Ghettoization and Social Mobility," pp. 123–136), Norman Fainstein demonstrates that racial segregation has changed little in the U.S. over the past three decades. Further, he convincingly argues that residential segregation is the root of the "race problem" and that middle-class African Americans suffer under its yoke nearly as much as their poor counterparts. Fainstein's thesis runs counter to the more optimistic—and in vogue—view of many prominent social scientists (e.g., William Julius Wilson) that middle-class African Americans are escaping from the "ghetto" and that the race problem in the United States is becoming more and more restricted to poor, inner-city African-American neighborhoods

In a third essay in *Perspectives on Current Social Problems*, ("The United States and the Myth of Assimilation: Diversity and Alienation," pp. 137–149), Janet Mancini Billson argues that the idea of the United States having always been a "melting pot" is more myth than reality. The nation was born in diversity, has maintained its diversity, and is, indeed, becoming more diverse. Billson systematically details those forces that encourage pluralism as opposed to assimilation, finding that the forces encouraging diversity are often as powerful as the forces encouraging homogeneity.

In a fourth essay in *Perspectives on Current Social Problems*, ("The Bell Curve: Too Smooth to be True," pp. 161–168), Michael Nunley carefully reviews Richard J. Herrnstein and Charles Murray's *The Bell Curve: Intelligence and Class Structure in American Life*. This controversial book develops the thesis that intelligence is predictive of economic success in the U.S. and elsewhere and, further, that blacks tend to score lower on IQ tests, which can account, in part, for their lower odds of economic success compared to whites and Asians. Nunley assesses their evidence and concludes that it is filled with errors of both omission and commission. Given these errors, the book has needlessly confused the public and needlessly magnified interracial misunderstanding and tension. Nunley also discusses research—ignored by Murray and Herrnstein—that clearly shows no genetically-based differences in the IQs of "blacks" and "whites."

In a final essay in *Perspectives on Current Social Problems*, ("People Against States: Ethnopolitical Conflict and the Changing World System," pp. 33–50), Ted Robert Gurr demonstrates that the post-Cold War surge in "tribal" conflict is a continuation of a trend that began in the 1960s. The main issue of the fifty most serious current ethnopolitical conflicts is contention for state power among communal groups in the immediate aftermath of state formation, revolution, and efforts to democratize autocratic regimes. The end of the Cold War contributed to the long-term trend mainly by increasing the number of states with such power transitions. Communal conflicts across fault lines between civilizations and religious traditions are more intense than others but have not increased in relative frequency or severity since the end of the Cold War. Nor is there a strong global force leading toward the further fragmentation of the state system: since 1989 no serious new secessionist conflicts have begun outside the Soviet and Yugoslav successor states, and in 1993–94 the regional trend is toward accommodation. The most protracted and deadly ethnopolitical conflicts are likely to occur in poor, weak, heterogeneous states like those of Africa. They will continue to pose severe humanitarian problems but are foreseeable and, in principle, are capable of being contained and transformed through constructive regional and international action. Gurr identifies six general international strategies to restrain emerging ethnopolitical conflicts.

Relevant World Wide Web Sites

Both the United Nations and the U.S. government have large amounts of U.S. and international data relevant to race, ethnicity, and poverty at all levels of analysis (the individual, city, county, U.S. state, regional, and cross-national); see those web sites listed at the end of Chapter 3. In addition, see:

U.S. State Department	www.state.gov
Central Intelligence Agency	www.odci.gov
Population Reference Bureau	www.prb.org

Two important "all-purpose" sites that provide a host of links to locations dedicated to race and ethnicity are Inter-Links' "Resources for Diversity" (http://alabanza.com/kabacoff/Inter-Links/diversity.html) and Yahoo's "Society and Culture" (go to www.yahoo.com, then click on "Society and Culture," and then on "Cultures and Groups").

A host of individuals, as well as philanthropic and privately funded organizations dedicated to racial/ethnic equality, have web sites. Although the writing on these sites is sometimes very opinionated, they can be useful for the history of race/ethnic relations and for updates of political activities, court decisions, and other news on the racial or ethnic group at hand. Most importantly, see the National Urban League site listed at the end of Chapter 2 (p. 100), and:

Nat'l Assn. for the Advancement of Colored People	www.naacp.org
Minority Rights Group International	www.minorityrights.org
Eye on the Media	www.users.erols.com/eombr

Exploratory exercises for the *Revolt98 and Voter98* data files have been included with those for Chapter 5; see p. 177.

Chapter 5. Gender Inequality

Sex Differences in Income

In 1999, the median income for American males working year round and full-time was approximately $32,000; for females, it was about $24,700. Women's income is about three-quarters of men's income, and this ratio has risen only slightly over the past 25 years—despite the massive influx of women into the world of full-time work. Such gender inequality is found in virtually all nations, with women in Western Europe faring best by earning 85 percent of what men make, and doing worst in Latin America and Eastern Europe, where the same figure is about 65 percent; the percentage for African and Asian nations falls in between at about 75.[1]

The growing labor-force participation of women—in virtually all nations—brings into the limelight the problem of economic inequality between the sexes. In days gone by, when a woman's income was seen as a mere supplement to her husband's or to the overall family income, one might have used a convoluted model of fairness to justify men being paid more than women for the same work or job. However, such a model is clearly inappropriate today, when it is common for women to be heads of families (that is, raising children with no husband present), or live alone, or, if married, to be contributing heavily to family income and significantly defining the standard of living.

The CHIP exercises in this section allow you to discover to what degree sex differences in income are accountable by other factors—such as sex differences in educational attainment, occupational prestige, and family status. If controlling for these factors we still find significant differences in income between the sexes, then we must confront the high probability that what can account for such differences is, in part, one of the many faces of *sex discrimination.*[2]

File: **SexInc98** (Sex differences in income; *source:* '96 & '98 GSS; **Note:** *full-time workers < 50 only*)

Info: Region→Race→Sex→Age→Married→Kids→Ed→Prestige→Income
     (4)   (2) (2) (2)   (3)   (2)   (4)   (3)   (3)

Region	Northeast (CT, ME, MA, NH, NJ, NY, PA, RI, and VT) Midwest (IL, IN, IA, KS, MI, MN, MO, NE, ND, OH, SD, and WI) South (AL, AR, DE, FL, GA, KY, LS, MD, MS, NC, OK, SC, TN, TX, VA, and WV) West (AK, AZ, CA, CO, HI, ID, MT, NV, NM, OR, UT, WA, and WY)
Race	White, Black
Sex	Male, Female
Age	18–34, 35–49

---

[1]See Sharlene Hesse-Biber and Gregg Lee Carter, *Working Women in America: Split Dreams* (NY: Oxford University Press, 2000), Figure 3.7 on p. 63.

[2]For example, one "obstacle that women face in the occupational realm is that they tend to be saddled, more so than men, with familial obligations. Even when both spouses work, and even though men have taken on more responsibilities for these tasks in recent decades, women are still expected to take on more responsibility for raising the children, keeping up the home, and taking care of sick relatives"; see Thomas J. Sullivan, *Introduction to Social Problems*, 5th ed. (Boston: Allyn & Bacon, 2000), pp. 236–237. Dropping out of the workforce for one or more years to raise children or care for aging parents seriously hurts women economically when they return to their jobs—for example, they have lost seniority and opportunities for training and advancement that their male counterparts did not forfeit. If a society devotes very little of its resources to child-care facilities/support, then women are hurt more than men. Other faces of discrimination that haunt women more than men include being kept out of the "old-boy" network; tokenism; lack of "mentorism" (men are more likely to groom other men for promotion, likewise for women—but fewer women are in high-level positions); fewer opportunities for training and promotion because of actual or feared (by employers) child-care obligations; and sexual harassment.

Married   Never Married, DivSepWid (Divorced/Separated/Widowed), Married

Kids   (Does respondent have one or more children at home under the age of 18?) No, Yes

Ed   (Years of schooling) <12yrs, 12yrs, 13–15yrs, 16+yrs

Prestige   (Hodge-Segal-Rossi respondent's occupational prestige score) Low (17–35), Medium (36–49), High (50–86); for example, on this scale, Janitors=22, Cashiers=29, Apparel Sales Workers=30, Accountants=65, Architects=73, Teachers=74, Lawyers=75, Physicians=86

Income   (Respondent's individual income) <$17.5K, $17.5–$35K, $35K+

Basic

1. Test the fundamental proposition that full-time working women are less likely than their men counterparts to be high-income earners by crosstabulating Income (Y) by Sex (X); also examine the relationship graphically (after doing the **CrossTab**, select the **Line** alternative for the **Plot** option under the **Table** command and highlight the "$35K+" category). Does your finding confirm this proposition? *Concentrate your discussion on the "$35K+" row for all questions in this section.*

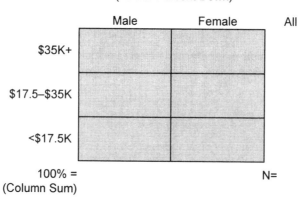

CrossTab: Income / Sex
(**Table**: Percent Down)

(Percentage difference between Females and Males for the "$35K+" row =   )

Prediction:

Finding:

2. Perhaps the income differences between men and women can be accounted for by their differences in education. (We have already standardized the data by age and working status.) It is well known that education is a powerful predictor of income (indeed, see your analyses of the *Status98* data set in Chapter 3!), and perhaps men are more likely to be high-income earners because they have more education. Test this possibility by crosstabulating Ed (Y) by Sex (X). What did you find?

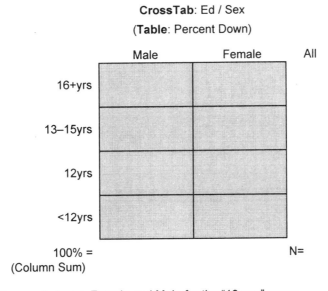

CrossTab: Ed / Sex
(**Table**: Percent Down)

(Percentage difference between Female and Male for the "16+yrs" row =   )

Prediction:

Finding:

3. Let us pursue the argument in #2. If the world truly does look like this: Sex→Ed→Income, then by controlling for education—that is, holding it constant—we should find the relationship between Sex and Income found in #1 above to disappear. (Think hard about this: If X influences Y via Z, and if we hold Z constant, then X will not be able to influence Y—empirically, we would find no relationship between X and Y—or more realistically because there are probably other "Z" factors (intervening variables), we would find a significantly weakened relationship. Here X=Sex; Y=Income; and Z=Ed.) Crosstab Income (Y) by Sex (X) and control for Ed (Z). What did you find? Did the relationship between Sex and Income weaken significantly (compare the average of the 4 "percentage-differences" from the partial tables with the original percentage-difference that you found in #1.)? Or did the relationship maintain itself—the average percentage-difference being similar to the original percentage-difference that was found in #1?

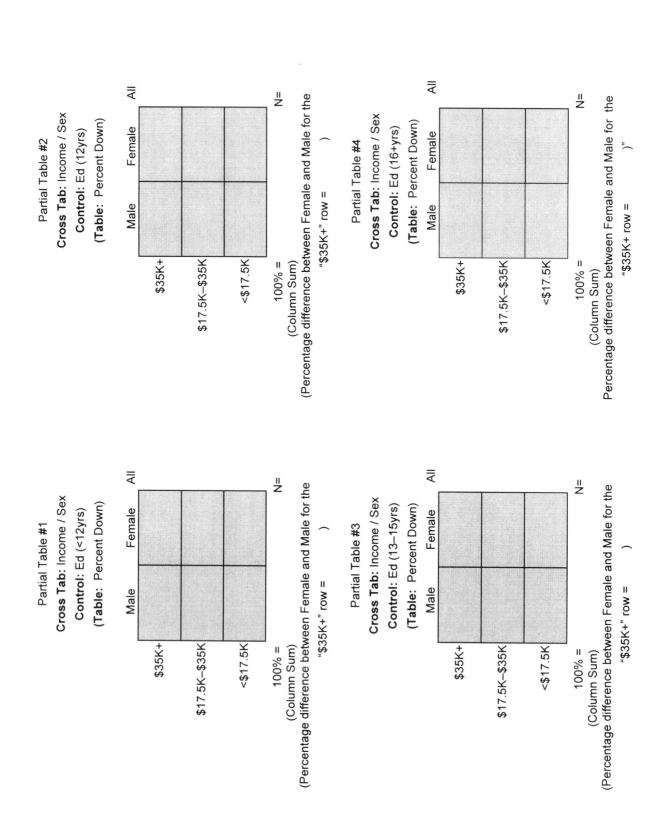

Partial Table #1

Cross Tab: Income / Sex

Control: Ed (<12yrs)

(Table: Percent Down)

	Male	Female	All
$35K+			
$17.5K–$35K			
<$17.5K			

100% =
(Column Sum)

N=

(Percentage difference between Female and Male for the
"$35K+" row =   )

Partial Table #2

Cross Tab: Income / Sex

Control: Ed (12yrs)

(Table: Percent Down)

	Male	Female	All
$35K+			
$17.5K–$35K			
<$17.5K			

100% =
(Column Sum)

N=

(Percentage difference between Female and Male for the
"$35K+" row =   )

Partial Table #3

Cross Tab: Income / Sex

Control: Ed (13–15yrs)

(Table: Percent Down)

	Male	Female	All
$35K+			
$17.5K–$35K			
<$17.5K			

100% =
(Column Sum)

N=

(Percentage difference between Female and Male for the
"$35K+" row =   )

Partial Table #4

Cross Tab: Income / Sex

Control: Ed (16+yrs)

(Table: Percent Down)

	Male	Female	All
$35K+			
$17.5K–$35K			
<$17.5K			

100% =
(Column Sum)

N=

Percentage difference between Female and Male for the
"$35K+ row =   )"

Answer/Discussion

4. Perhaps the income differences between men and women can be accounted for, in part, by their differences in occupational prestige. It is well known that occupational prestige is a significant predictor of income, and perhaps men are more likely to be high-income earners because they hold more prestigious jobs (e.g., college professors instead of preschool teachers; lawyers instead of legal aides). Test this possibility by crosstabulating Prestige (Y) by Sex (X). What did you find?

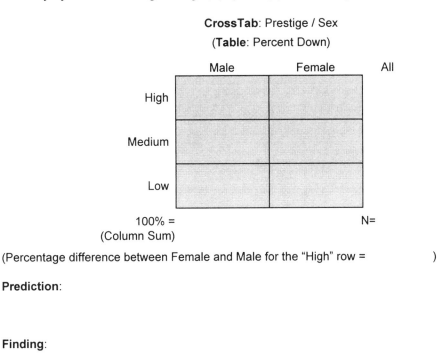

CrossTab: Prestige / Sex
(**Table**: Percent Down)

(Percentage difference between Female and Male for the "High" row =   )

Prediction:

Finding:

5. Let us pursue the argument in #4. If the world truly does look like this: Sex→Prestige→Income, then by controlling for occupational prestige—that is, holding it constant—we should find the relationship between Sex and Income found in #1 above to disappear. (Refer back to the discussion in question #3.) Crosstab Income (Y) by Sex (X) and control for Prestige (Z). What did you find? Did the average relationship between Sex and Income weaken across the three partial tables (again, compute the average percentage-difference for these tables)? Or, did the relationship maintain itself—the average percentage-difference being similar to the original percentage-difference that was found in #1?

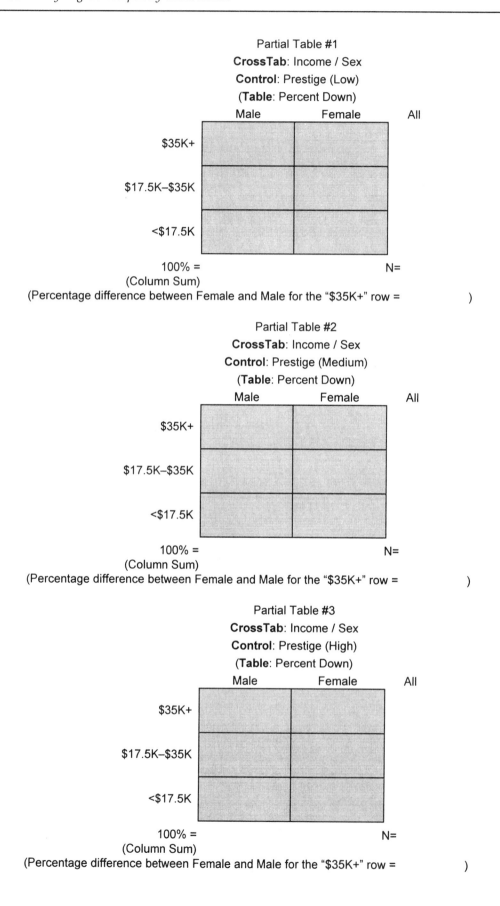

Partial Table #1
CrossTab: Income / Sex
Control: Prestige (Low)
(**Table**: Percent Down)

	Male	Female	All
$35K+			
$17.5K–$35K			
<$17.5K			

100% =   N=
(Column Sum)
(Percentage difference between Female and Male for the "$35K+" row =   )

Partial Table #2
CrossTab: Income / Sex
Control: Prestige (Medium)
(**Table**: Percent Down)

	Male	Female	All
$35K+			
$17.5K–$35K			
<$17.5K			

100% =   N=
(Column Sum)
(Percentage difference between Female and Male for the "$35K+" row =   )

Partial Table #3
CrossTab: Income / Sex
Control: Prestige (High)
(**Table**: Percent Down)

	Male	Female	All
$35K+			
$17.5K–$35K			
<$17.5K			

100% =   N=
(Column Sum)
(Percentage difference between Female and Male for the "$35K+" row =   )

Answer/Discussion

6. Ponder your findings in items 1–5 above. What are your key conclusions?

The Status of Women: Crossnational Comparisons

Medical scientists generally agree that part of the reason women tend to outlive men is genetic. Humans have twenty-three pairs of chromosomes, one of which determines sex. If an individual is male, his sex chromosomes are XY; a female has two X chromosomes. Scientists know that the X chromosome carries more genetic information than the Y, including some defects that can lead to physical abnormalities, but instead of making females more vulnerable to X-linked disorders, this seems to give them a genetic advantage. A female typically needs two defective X chromosomes for most genetically linked disorders to manifest themselves; otherwise, one healthy X chromosome can override the abnormal one. On the other hand, a male who has a defective X chromosome will have the genetically linked disease because that is the only X he has. This is thought to account for the higher number of miscarriages of male fetuses and the greater ratio of male to female infant deaths (146:100) and the deaths at all ages due to congenital abnormalities (120:100).

Hormonal differences also play a part in women's longevity. "In particular, the female sex hormones (the estrogens) seem to give women some protection against heart disease, the number one cause of death in" developed countries.[1]

However, this female advantage can be negated if she has too many children; the birthing process is risky for both mother and infant, and the more times the mother goes through it, the greater her odds of suffering an acute or delayed health calamity. Numerous pregnancies and their negative health consequences are much more likely to occur in the Third World: In most of the developing world, "people continue to have large families for a number of social, political, and religious reasons. Relatively early marriage and the almost immediate pregnancies that follow are intertwined with the roles of women. A World Fertility Survey found that approximately 30 percent of women in Latin America, 40 percent of women in Asia, and 50 percent of women in Africa are married by age 18. In Nigeria, girls marry as young as 11 or 12 years of age. In some cultures, a woman's value is directly related to how many children she produces (especially boys). For example, women are likely to be physically abused or abandoned if they do not deliver the expected (demanded by their husbands) number of offspring. Important religious rituals (including those rendered upon the death of a parent) can only be performed by sons, which means that a woman with two or more daughters will be under pressure to become pregnant as many times as necessary to produce a male child. Having many children within a short time period is unhealthy and greatly increases their likelihood of untimely death. With little if any political power in most poor countries, women do not have much of an opportunity to change a centuries-old way of existence that keeps them pregnant and bound to child care for most of their lives."[2]

Other customs concentrated in low-income nations reduce women's natural advantages over men in longevity. "For instance, in some societies women are prohibited by moral and religious teachings from being seen defecating, so they must wait until dark to relieve themselves. This can lead to constipation and other bowel and intestinal problems; it also increases women's risk of being assaulted."[3]

Such gender discrimination is common in much of North Africa, the Middle East, and South Asia. And it begins even before birth. For example, in China, especially in rural areas, many married couples "want sons so they can extend the male line into the future; some even believe they have dishonored their ancestors if they fail to do so. Female infanticide is a way to try again for a male child when the government strongly encourages one-child families. Information on the sex ratio in China supports the idea that some female infanticide is occurring. Biologically, in human populations, about 94 females are born for every 100 males. However, in recent years in China, as few as 85 to 89 females were reported born for each 100 males. Now, some of this involves families just not reporting a female birth to authorities so they can try again to have a

[1]Daniel J. Curran and Claire M. Renzetti, *Social Problems: Society in Crisis*, 5th ed. (Boston: Allyn & Bacon, 2000), p. 331; the preceding paragraph was excerpted from pp. 441–442 in the 3rd edition of this book.

[2]Michael P. Soroka and George J. Bryjak, *Social Problems: A World at Risk* 2nd (Boston: Allyn & Bacon, 1999), pp. 361–362.

[3]Curran and Renzetti, *op. cit.*, p. 332.

male. But some of it is undoubtedly due to infanticide."[4]

When female infants survive birth, they are often faced with a situation where nursing mothers are encouraged to breastfeed their sons much longer than their daughters. "Later, young girls eat only after their brothers have finished and have to make do with whatever food is left. As a result, most girls' nutritional needs go unmet, leading to undernourishment, chronic fatigue, and illness as they enter their reproductive years. These girls typically will experience a large number of pregnancies and (assuming they survive childbirth) will be expected to carry out demanding mothering roles with their children while still doing unpaid work in farming or other agricultural activities. The net result is greater fatigue, malnourishment, and severe health problems for the vast majority of women. If and when women in developing countries do have access to prenatal, childbirth, or reproductive health care, that care typically is less than adequate. Illnesses and diseases related to women's particular reproductive health needs remain major causes of female mortality in the developing world."[5]

In sum, the requirement that they play traditional family roles (mother and wife), their being denied a significant role in politics and the power such a role can engender, and their living in societies where the culture encourages gender discrimination, all result in poorer health and a shortened life expectancy for women in many developing countries. The following computer exercises below allow you to explore in greater detail the status of women as it relates to politics, education, fertility, and longevity at the cross-national level of analysis.

File: **Women98** (Cross-national data on the status of women in the late 1990s)

Info: Region→Freedom→GNP→FemRead→ReadIneq→WomInGov→SexRatio→Fertility→FemLife→FemAdv
 (6)   (3)   (3)   (3)   (3)   (3)   (3)   (3)   (3)   (3)

(Note: all variables, except Region and Freedom, are divided into 3 categories: bottom, middle, and top third.)

Region   (United Nations regional designation) Industrial, East-Europe, Africa-SubSaharan, Arab, Asia, Latin-America

Freedom   (Type of political regime) Not Free, Partly, Free

GNP   (Per capita GNP in 1997 U.S. dollars) <$875; $875–$2,625; >$2,625

FemRead   (Percentage of women that are literate) <72.5%, 72.5–95%, >95%

ReadIneq   ("Reading Inequality" = [Female Literacy Rate/Male Literacy Rate] x 100) <87.5%, 87.5–98%, >98%

WomInGov   ("Women in Government" = the percentage of top-level ["ministerial"] positions held by women) <3%, 3–7%, >7%

SexRatio   (Number of males per 100 females; "100" would equal a balanced sex ratio where the number of men was the same as the number of women) <97, 97–100, >100

Fertility (Total Fertility Rate, which is the number of children an adult woman, aged 15–44, can expect to have during her lifetime) <2.25, 2.25–4, >4

FemLife   (Female Life Expectancy) <68yrs, 68–74.5yrs, >74.5yrs

FemAdv   (Female Life Expectancy–Male Life Expectancy, i.e., "female advantage" over males in life expectancy) <3.9yrs, 3.9–5.9yrs, 6+yrs

---

[4]See Sullivan, *Introduction to Social Problems*, 5th ed., *op. cit.*, p. 423.

[5]See Soroka and George J. Bryjak, 2nd ed., *op. cit.*, pp. 125–126.

Country	Freedom	GNP	FemRead	ReadIneq	WomInGov	SexRatio	Fertility	FemLife	FemAdv
Algeria	Not Free	1,690	49.0	66.3	0	102	4.26	67.8	0.9
Angola	Not Free	260	28.0	50.0	10.7	101	6.48	48.0	4.0
Antig. & Barbuda	Partly	6,970	88.0	97.8	0	98	1.70	74.9	4.1
Argentina	Free	8,060	96.2	100.0	0	100	2.70	75.7	7.1
Armenia	Partly	670	98.0	99.0	0	95	1.70	74.4	6.5
Australia	Free	17,980	99.9	100.0	14.7	102	1.82	80.9	5.9
Azerbaijan	Partly	500	96.0	97.0	7.7	94	2.21	74.5	8.2
Bahamas	Free	11,790	98.0	99.5	18.8	96	1.91	75.3	7.0
Bahrain	Not Free	7,500	79.4	89.1	0	149	3.70	76.1	5.0
Barbados	Free	6,530	96.8	98.8	30.8	97	1.63	77.9	5.0
Belarus	Not Free	2,160	97.0	98.0	5.3	94	1.39	74.3	10.8
Belize	Free	2,550	70.3	100.0	0	103	4.50	74.1	4.1
Brazil	Partly	3,370	83.2	99.9	4.3	97	2.79	68.7	4.7
Brunei	Not Free	14,240	83.4	90.1	0	121	3.07	76.3	3.8
Bulgaria	Free	1,160	97.0	98.0	4.8	98	1.37	75.0	7.3
Cambodia	Not Free	300	22.0	45.8	0	87	5.81	50.8	3.0
Cameroon	Not Free	680	52.1	69.5	2.6	99	5.91	57.5	3.0
Cape Verde	Free	910	63.8	78.4	13.3	87	4.06	65.5	2.0
Cen. African Rep.	Partly	370	52.4	76.5	8.0	95	5.10	51.9	5.0
Chile	Free	3,560	95.0	99.6	14.3	99	2.54	75.6	7.1
China	Not Free	530	72.7	80.9	6.1	107	1.80	72.0	3.6
Colombia	Partly	1,620	91.4	100.2	12.5	95	3.00	72.3	5.9
Comoros	Partly	510	50.4	78.5	6.2	97	6.79	60.1	4.5
Costa Rica	Free	2,380	95.0	100.3	11.1	102	3.10	78.6	4.6
Cuba	Not Free	2,000	95.3	99.1	2.7	88	1.50	76.8	3.9
Dominica	Free	2,830	94.0	100.0	18.2	104	2.07	80.3	5.9
Dom. Republic	Free	1,320	82.2	100.2	4.0	103	3.31	70.6	4.4
Ecuador	Free	1,310	88.2	95.9	6.2	98	3.60	71.4	5.0
Egypt	Not Free	710	38.8	61.0	3.1	102	3.59	64.8	2.4
El Salvador	Free	1,480	69.8	95.0	6.2	84	3.80	70.4	5.3
Estonia	Free	2,820	99.9	100.0	0	92	1.38	75.0	10.9
Ethiopia	Partly	130	25.3	55.6	6.7	101	6.80	51.9	3.5
Fiji	Partly	2,320	89.3	95.2	4.8	100	3.00	65.2	3.9
France	Free	23,470	99.0	100.0	14.7	100	1.65	81.8	8.2
Georgia	Partly	580	98.0	98.0	0	92	1.29	76.1	7.4
Ghana	Partly	430	53.5	70.5	10.3	96	5.50	57.8	3.6
Greece	Free	7,710	93.0	94.9	0	100	1.34	79.9	5.0
Grenada	Free	2,620	98.0	100.0	21.4	115	3.82	73.3	5.0
Guatemala	Partly	1,190	48.6	77.8	13.3	100	5.10	67.3	4.9
Guyana	Free	530	97.5	98.9	5.6	101	2.55	68.0	5.6
Haiti	Partly	220	42.2	87.9	29.4	92	4.80	58.3	3.4
Honduras	Free	580	72.7	100.1	10.0	99	5.20	70.7	4.9
Hungary	Free	3,840	98.0	99.0	5.6	97	1.64	74.2	9.4
India	Free	310	37.7	57.6	3.2	108	3.40	59.3	1.0
Indonesia	Partly	880	78.0	87.1	3.6	99	2.85	64.9	3.7
Iran	Not Free	1,780	65.8	83.9	0	104	5.10	67.7	2.3
Iraq	Not Free	1,940	45.0	63.6	0	102	6.70	66.7	1.8
Israel	Free	14,410	93.0	95.9	13.0	100	2.88	78.5	3.4
Italy	Free	19,270	96.0	98.0	3.6	99	1.19	80.4	6.6
Jordan	Partly	1,390	79.4	85.0	6.1	105	4.60	70.0	4.0
Kazakhstan	Not Free	1,110	96.0	97.0	2.6	95	2.25	73.1	9.3

Country	Freedom	GNP	FemRead	ReadIneq	WomInGov	SexRatio	Fertility	FemLife	FemAdv
Kenya	Not Free	260	70.0	81.1	3.4	100	5.40	52.2	3.4
Kyrgyzstan	Partly	610	96.0	97.0	10.5	96	3.12	72.2	8.0
Laos	Not Free	320	48.0	68.6	0	95	6.07	53.3	3.1
Latvia	Free	2,290	99.0	99.0	11.1	90	1.25	72.9	12.2
Lebanon	Not Free	3,350	82.2	90.5	0	90	2.90	77.9	5.4
Lithuania	Free	1,350	98.0	99.0	0	93	1.54	74.9	12.1
Luxembourg	Free	39,850	99.9	100.0	28.6	104	1.72	79.1	6.5
Malta	Free	7,970	88.0	100.0	0	101	1.89	78.6	3.9
Mauritania	Not Free	480	26.3	53.0	3.6	94	5.01	53.1	3.2
Mauritius	Free	3,180	78.8	90.5	0	99	2.35	73.0	8.0
Mexico	Partly	4,010	87.4	95.2	15.8	95	3.10	75.5	6.0
Moldova	Partly	870	94.0	94.9	0	92	1.97	71.1	6.8
Morocco	Partly	1,150	31.0	54.8	0	98	4.04	70.2	3.8
Mozambique	Partly	80	23.3	40.4	4.0	95	6.50	48.0	3.1
Namibia	Free	2,030	31.0	68.9	8.7	97	5.40	60.0	2.5
Nepal	Partly	200	14.0	34.2	0	104	5.20	53.4	−2.5
Nigeria	Partly	280	47.3	70.3	7.7	103	6.00	57.6	2.6
Pakistan	Partly	440	24.4	48.8	4.0	105	5.60	60.6	−0.2
Panama	Free	2,670	90.2	98.7	16.7	103	2.96	75.0	4.1
Peru	Partly	1,890	83.0	87.8	5.6	101	3.54	67.9	3.8
Philippines	Free	960	94.3	99.3	4.5	98	4.09	66.4	3.6
Poland	Free	2,470	98.0	99.0	8.3	99	1.66	76.1	8.6
Portugal	Free	9,370	82.0	92.1	11.5	96	1.39	78.2	7.0
Romania	Free	1,230	95.0	96.9	0	98	1.35	73.3	7.4
Russia	Partly	2,650	97.0	97.0	2.4	93	1.36	71.1	13.6
Saudi Arabia	Not Free	7,240	50.2	70.2	0	146	5.50	72.3	3.4
Singapore	Partly	23,360	86.3	90.0	0	100	1.75	79.0	5.0
South Africa	Free	3,010	81.7	99.8	1.0	98	4.11	68.0	5.0
South Korea	Free	8,220	96.7	97.4	3.0	103	1.73	75.7	8.0
Spain	Free	13,280	94.0	95.9	16.7	100	1.22	80.9	7.6
Sri Lanka	Partly	640	87.2	93.4	13.0	96	2.28	74.8	4.7
Sudan	Not Free	290	34.6	60.0	2.4	100	6.09	55.2	1.8
Syria	Not Free	1,120	55.8	65.1	6.8	104	6.90	67.4	2.5
Tajikistan	Not Free	350	97.0	98.0	3.7	98	3.66	71.1	5.7
Thailand	Free	2,210	91.6	95.4	0	97	2.20	72.0	4.0
Trinidad &Tobago	Free	3,740	97.0	98.2	16.0	108	2.19	73.2	5.2
Tunisia	Not Free	1,800	54.6	69.5	2.9	100	3.36	68.7	1.8
Turkey	Partly	2,450	72.4	79.0	2.9	103	2.69	70.0	4.6
Turkmenistan	Not Free	640	97.0	98.0	3.1	96	3.87	69.3	7.0
Ukraine	Partly	1,570	97.0	97.0	0	92	1.50	73.2	10.4
United States	Free	25,860	97.0	100.0	14.3	99	2.00	79.0	6.7
Uruguay	Free	4,650	97.7	100.8	6.7	97	2.34	75.7	6.4
Uzbekistan	Not Free	950	99.0	100.0	2.6	98	3.55	72.4	6.3
Venezuela	Free	2,760	90.3	98.4	11.1	101	3.10	74.7	5.8
Vietnam	Not Free	190	91.2	94.5	7.0	94	3.73	67.3	4.4
Yemen	Partly	280	26.0	49.1	0	104	7.70	52.9	2.3
Zaire*	Not Free	110	67.7	78.2	8.0	95	6.64	49.6	3.8
Zimbabwe	Partly	490	80.0	88.9	8.3	97	4.40	62	1.0

*(Republic of Congo)

Basic

1. Let us test out the basic model developed above that economic prosperity decreases fertility (as more infants survive in richer countries, where healthcare, sanitation services, and food supplies are more plentiful), which in turn increases the longevity of women. Using the variables in the *Womand98* data file, we can sketch this model as follows: GNP→Fertility→FemLife. Three fundamental relationships are implied here: (a) GNP should correlate negatively with Fertility; (b) GNP should correlate positively with FemLife; and (c) Fertility should correlate negatively with FemLife; moreover, if part of the influence of GNP on FemLife is transmitted via Fertility then (d) holding this variable "constant" should reduce the strength of the original relationship between GNP and FemLife. (Again, put on your analytical-thinking- skills cap: if X causes Z to vary, which in turn causes Y to vary, and if we do not let Z vary, then X will lose its effect on Y. Right?! Here, GNP=X, Fertility=Z, and FemLife=Y.)

(a) Crosstabulate Fertility (Y) by GNP (X); also examine the relationship graphically (after doing the **CrossTab**, select the **Line** alternative for the **Plot** option under the **Table** command and highlight the ">4" category). Did you find the expected relationship? (*Concentrate your discussion on the ">4" row of Fertility.*)

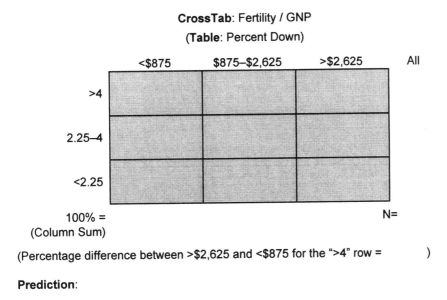

CrossTab: Fertility / GNP
(**Table**: Percent Down)

	<$875	$875–$2,625	>$2,625	All
>4				
2.25–4				
<2.25				
100% = (Column Sum)				N=

(Percentage difference between >$2,625 and <$875 for the ">4" row =   )

Prediction:

Finding:

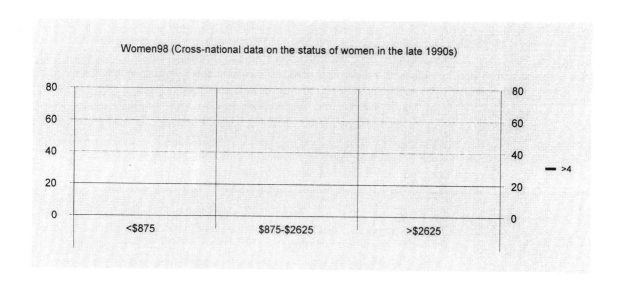

Women98 (Cross-national data on the status of women in the late 1990s)

(b) Crosstabulate FemLife (Y) by GNP (X); also examine the relationship graphically (after doing the **CrossTab**, select the **Line** alternative for the **Plot** option under the **Table** command and highlight the ">74.5yrs" category). Did you find the expected relationship? (*Concentrate your discussion on the ">74.5yrs" row of FemLife.*)

CrossTab: FemLife / GNP

(**Table**: Percent Down)

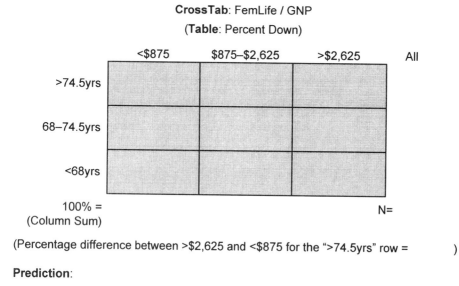

(Percentage difference between >$2,625 and <$875 for the ">74.5yrs" row =   )

Prediction:

Finding:

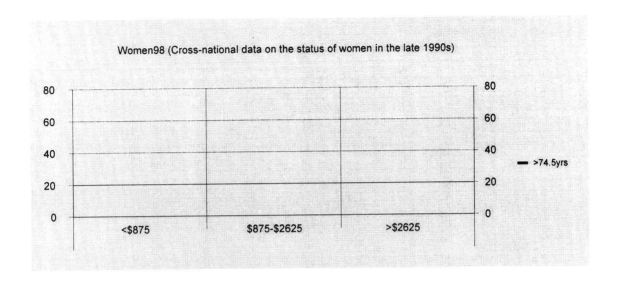

(c) Crosstabulate FemLife (Y) by Fertility (X); also examine the relationship graphically (after doing the **CrossTab**, select the **Line** alternative for the **Plot** option under the **Table** command and highlight the ">74.5yrs" category). Did you find the expected relationship? (*Concentrate your discussion on the ">74.5yrs" row of FemLife.*)

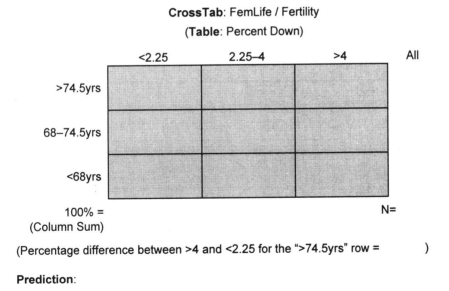

(Percentage difference between >4 and <2.25 for the ">74.5yrs" row =   )

Prediction:

Finding:

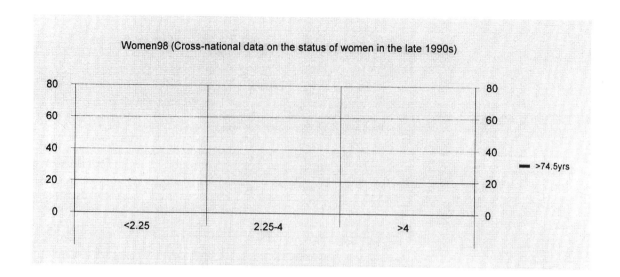

Women98 (Cross-national data on the status of women in the late 1990s)

(d) Crosstabulate FemLife (Y) by GNP (X), then control for Fertility (Z). What did you find? Did the relationship between GNP and FemLife weaken significantly? (You will need to compare the average of the 3 "percentage-differences" from the partial tables with the original percentage-difference that you found in [b].) Or did the relationship maintain itself—the average percentage-difference being similar to the original percentage-difference that was found in (b)?

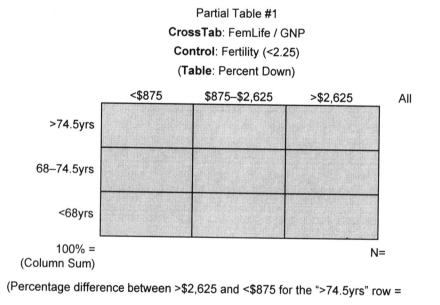

Partial Table #1
CrossTab: FemLife / GNP
Control: Fertility (<2.25)
(**Table**: Percent Down)

	<$875	$875–$2,625	>$2,625	All
>74.5yrs				
68–74.5yrs				
<68yrs				
100% = (Column Sum)				N=

(Percentage difference between >$2,625 and <$875 for the ">74.5yrs" row =   )

Partial Table #2
CrossTab: FemLife / GNP
Control: Fertility (2.25–4)
(**Table**: Percent Down)

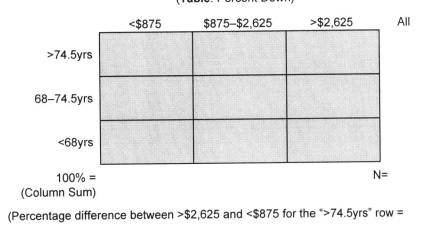

	<$875	$875–$2,625	>$2,625	All
>74.5yrs				
68–74.5yrs				
<68yrs				

100% =
(Column Sum)   N=

(Percentage difference between >$2,625 and <$875 for the ">74.5yrs" row =   )

Partial Table #3
CrossTab: FemLife / GNP
Control: Fertility (>4)
(**Table**: Percent Down)

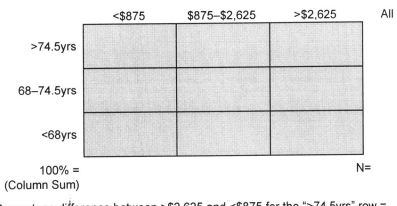

	<$875	$875–$2,625	>$2,625	All
>74.5yrs				
68–74.5yrs				
<68yrs				

100% =
(Column Sum)   N=

(Percentage difference between >$2,625 and <$875 for the ">74.5yrs" row =   )

Answer/Discussion

2. The introductory comments to this section implied that women in poorer countries are denied high levels of education to conform with the cultural demand to be family-oriented (wives and mothers). Further, it was observed that women lacked the political power to change this situation. Test out these hypotheses by crosstabulating (a) ReadIneq (Y) by GNP (X), and (b) WomInGov (Y) by GNP (X); also examine the relationships graphically (after doing the first **CrossTab**, select the **Line** alternative for the **Plot** option under the **Table** command and highlight the "<87.5%" category; after the second **CrossTab**, select the same option and highlight ">7%"). Did you find the expected relationships?

(a) ReadIneq (Y) by GNP (X).

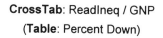

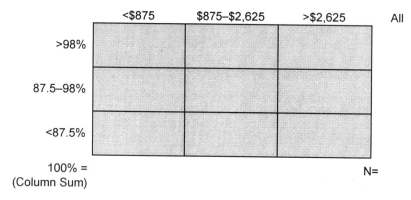

(Percentage difference between >$2,625 and <$875 for the "<87.5%" row =)
Prediction:

Finding:

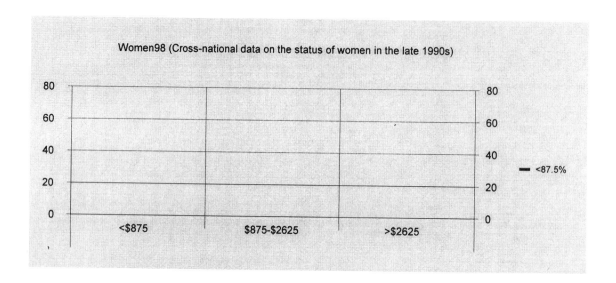

(b) WomInGov (Y) by GNP (X).

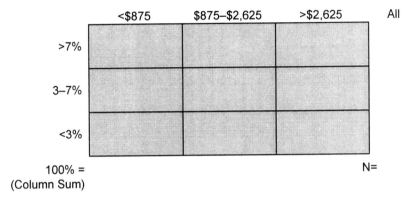

(Percentage difference between >$2,625 and <$875 for the ">7%" row =   )

Prediction:

Finding:

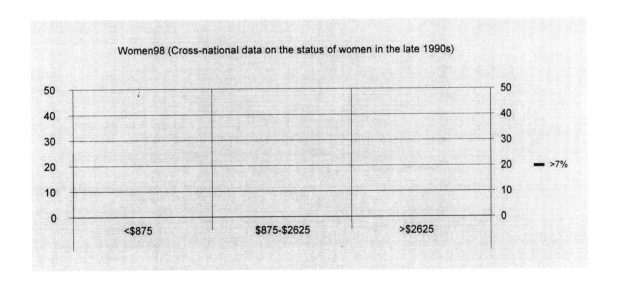

Suggestions for Further Study

Sharlene Hesse-Biber argues that the current outbreak of eating disorders and weight obsession among women is part of a larger historical transformation of women's bodies into commodities through a "marriage" between capitalistic and patriarchal interests. These interests have transformed women's body images increasingly toward an ultra-slender ideal. She explores the relationship between eating disorders and ultra-slenderness by focusing on the eating habits and attitudes of a sample of college students. Her results indicate that women were more likely than men to follow an ultra-slender "cultural" model of ideal weight. Women who follow this cultural model were three times more likely to score abnormally high on a standard measure of eating disorders than women who follow a less stringent "medical" model of ideal weight. This has serious, negative impacts on gender inequality. More specifically, women's spending an enormous amount of time, emotional energy, and money attempting to attain the ultra-slender ideal drain economic and emotional capital away from other investments they might make in, for example, political activity, education, and career advancement—activities that would promote their empowerment and increase their financial standing vis-à-vis men. See "Women, Thinness and Eating Disorders: A Sociocultural Problem," pp. 197–208 in Gregg Lee Carter (ed.), *Perspectives on Current Social Problems* (Boston: Allyn & Bacon, 1997).

In another essay in *Perspectives on Current Social Problems* ("Gender Equity in Athletics," pp. 209–218), Michael Malec examines the history of the exclusion of women from sport and looks at the changes that have occurred since 1972, when the laws that effectively excluded women from sport were revoked. The recent change in girls' sports participation is more important than the average person might think. Social scientists have long contended that team sports provide boys with valuable learning environments that have an impact on future economic success. Team sports cultivate social skills: learning to deal with diversity in memberships where each person is doing a special task; learning to coordinate actions and maintain cohesiveness among group members; learning to cope with impersonal rules; learning to work for collective as well as personal goals; developing one's strategic thinking; gaining experience in leadership positions; learning to deal with interpersonal competition in a forthright manner; experiencing face-to-face confrontations—often involving a close friend—and learning how to depersonalize the attack; learning self-control and keeping one's "cool" under fire. Despite the revolution in girls' sports participation, they are still only about two-thirds as likely as boys to participate in school sports programs.

In a third essay in *Perspectives on Current Social Problems*, ("Sexual Harassment Stories of College Women: From Insults to Assault," pp. 219–225), Kathleen McKinney reports her findings on college women alleging to have been victims of sexual harassment. She elicited information on the interviewees' definitions of sexual harassment, details of the incidents, responses to the harassment, and views of the institution's role in cases of sexual harassment. Most of the women discussed harassment by male peers that occurred on campus. The harassment was usually verbal, but several women reported unwanted touching and pressure for sex. In general, the women had negative emotional reactions, but did not file formal complaints—expressing pessimism about doing so. Such an attitude can carry over into the world of work and hurt women financially, but it is also one with some justification. Indeed, a New York task force on the issue concluded that the "filing of a sexual harassment complaint often is a form of career suicide."[6]

Relevant World Wide Web Sites

The web sites listed at the end of Chapter 3 (p. 133) offer plenty of data relevant to gender inequality. Many women's organizations offer current and historical information on the economic, political, and social progress of women. The most important of these are National Organization for Women (which focuses mainly on the U.S.: www.now.org) and the more internationally oriented Feminist Majority Foundation Online (www.feminist.org). Both of these sites provide links to a wide variety of government and private organizations concerned with gender equality across a broad range of concerns (e.g., politics, education, family life, sports, the media, the business world).

---

[6]As quoted in Hesse-Biber and Carter, *op. cit.*, p. 121.

Exploratory

I. Using any of the CHIP data files for this or the preceding chapter (*Revolt98, Voter98, SexInc98,* or *Women98*), state a hypothesis relating an X and a Y variable that have not already been analyzed together.

II. Sketch the bivariate model.

III. Give a brief interpretation of your hypothesis—that is, describe what is going on in the world such that we would expect to find data patterned in the way in which you have predicted.

IV. (a) Test your hypothesis with a **CrossTab**, putting your Y variable on the rows. Was your hypothesis confirmed? (Note: you may need to delete one to three columns; the following 3x6 table shell is simply a starting point.)

Original Table

CrossTab: _____(Y) /_____ (X)

(**Table**: Percent Down)

All

100% =   N=
(Column Sum)

(Percentage difference between the highest and lowest values of X on the highest value of Y =   )

Prediction:

Finding:

(b) Use **Plot** under the **Table** option to display the above relationship graphically. Feel free to be creative—trying out each of the plot types (line, bar, pie, stacked). Print out and attach the plot that you think best captures the relationship between your X and Y.

> **Do *either* parts V–VIII *or* parts IX–XII below.**

V. Perhaps the relationship you uncovered in #IV is spurious; that is, perhaps a third variable is predictive of both X and Y; if this is so, then the relationship between X and Y would exist **not** because X is causing Y, but simply because of their covariation with this third variable. If this third variable is held constant, then the relationship between X and Y will weaken greatly or disappear. Choose a third variable that might possibly be generating a spurious relationship between X and Y. Sketch the model showing the relationship between this third variable and X, and between this third variable and Y, as well as the lack of causal relationship between X and Y. Hint: refer back to the discussion on page 25 in the introductory chapter entitled "Elementary Data Analysis Tools Needed to Study Social Issues."

VI. A good social scientist does not choose just any variable to test for spuriosity. Just as you were able to defend the hypothesized relationship between X and Y in #III, develop a brief interpretation to defend the hypothesized relationship between Z and X, then between Z and Y.

(a) Interpretation of the Z–X relationship:

(b) Interpretation of the Z–Y relationship:

VII. Test the alternative model sketched in #V by crosstabbing Y by X and controlling for Z—using the appended table shells. (Note: you may need only 3 columns in each of these shells; also, you may not need all 6 of the partial tables provided; of course, you will need one partial table for each value of Z.)

need all 6 of the partial tables provided; of course, you will need one partial table for each value of Z.)

VIII. What are your conclusions? For example, is the original X–Y relationship spurious? Is it nonspurious (i.e., causal)? Is a multivariable model evident?

IX. Examining all the variables in your data set, which one do you think might be serving as a causal mechanism connecting your X with your Y? In other words, which variable would you choose as "Z" in the following sketch: X→Z→Y? Hint: refer back to the discussion on page 26 in the introductory chapter entitled "Elementary Data Analysis Tools Needed to Study Social Issues."

X. A good social scientist does not choose just any variable to test as a causal mechanism (intervening variable). Just as you were able to defend the hypothesized relationship between X and Y in #III, develop a brief interpretation to defend the hypothesized relationship between X and Z, then between Z and Y.

(a) Interpretation of the X–Z relationship:

(b) Interpretation of the Z–Y relationship:

XI. Test the alternative model sketched in #IX by crosstabbing X and Y and controlling for Z—using the appended table shells. (Note: you may need only 3 columns in each of these shells; also, you may not need all 6 of the partial tables provided; of course, you will need one partial table for each value of Z.)

XII. What are your conclusions? Most importantly, do your findings support the notion that your Z is acting as an intervening variable (causal mechanism) connecting your X and your Y?

Partial Table #1

Cross Tab: _____ (Y) / _____ (X)

Control: _____ (Z value)

(Table: Percent Down)

All

N=

100% = _____
(Column Sum)
(Percentage difference between the highest and lowest values of X on the
highest value of Y =)

Partial Table #2

Cross Tab: _____ (Y) / _____ (X)

Control: _____ (Z value)

(Table: Percent Down)

All

N=

100% = _____
(Column Sum)
(Percentage difference between the highest and lowest values of X on the
highest value of Y =)

Partial Table #3

Cross Tab: _____ (Y) / _____ (X)

Control: _____ (Z value)

(Table: Percent Down)

All

N=

100% = _____
(Column Sum)
(Percentage difference between the highest and lowest values of X on the
highest value of Y =)

Partial Table #4

Cross Tab: _____ (Y) / _____ (X)

Control: _____ (Z value)

(Table: Percent Down)

All

N=

100% = _____
(Column Sum)
(Percentage difference between the highest and lowest values of X on the
highest value of Y =)

Partial Table #5

Cross Tab: _____ (Y) / _____ (X)

Control: _____ (Z value)

(Table: Percent Down)

All

N=

100% = _____
(Column Sum)
(Percentage difference between the highest and lowest values of X on the
highest value of Y =)

Partial Table #6

Cross Tab: _____ (Y) / _____ (X)

Control: _____ (Z value)

(Table: Percent Down)

All

N=

100% = _____
(Column Sum)
(Percentage difference between the highest and lowest values of X on the
highest value of Y =)

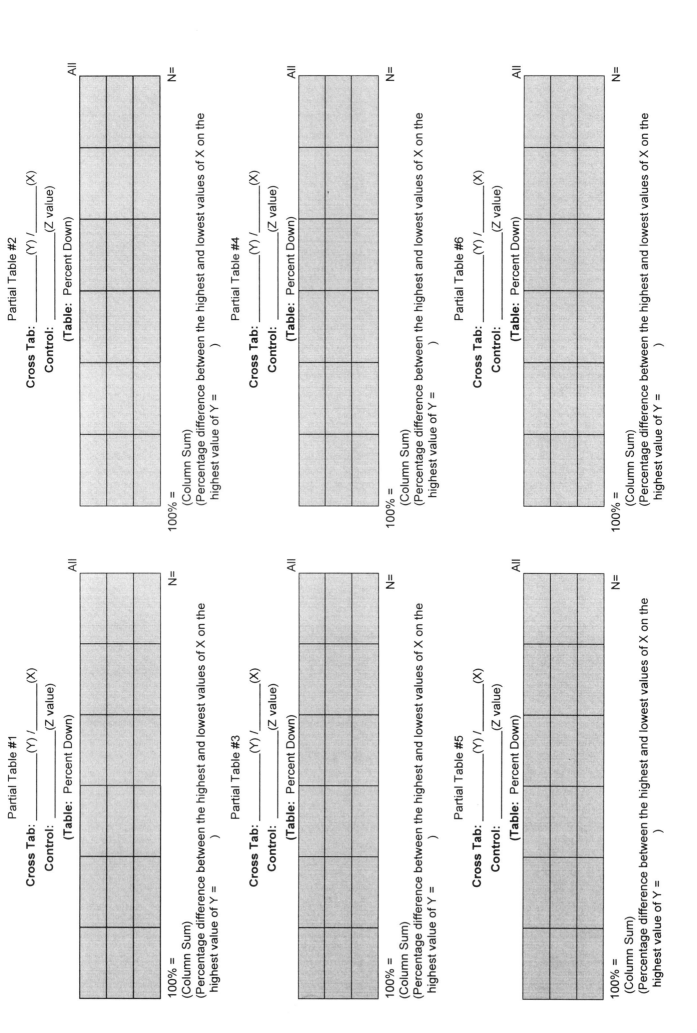

Chapter 6. Aging Issues

Health, Poverty, and Social Interaction

Aging issues are of growing importance in U.S. society and economy — and will become ever more so as the 70+ million "baby boomers" (born between 1946 and 1964) grow old. They are the "pig in the python" (imagine a python that has swallowed a small pig; as time goes by the shape of the python will change to accommodate the piglet: first the snake's neck will bulge, then its midsection, and finally its tail; in like fashion, the shape of U.S. society at any particular time is determined, to a great extent, by the age of the baby boomers). They disrupted the educational system when they were young. To confront the fierce competition they faced for jobs, they swamped the nation's colleges and universities when they reached late adolescence. In their late adolescence and early adult years, they made the crime rate skyrocket (youth and crime are highly correlated). As they got married and began their families, they inflated housing costs in the 1980s. In the 1990s, in their 40s, they bloated the stock market. Now reaching their 50s, they are beginning to overwhelm the health-care system. When they retire, the Social Security system will strain under the weight of their huge numbers.

Of the many aging issues explored in standard sociology textbooks, three stand out: (a) the psychological, social, and financial costs of declining health; (b) the loss of income due to retirement and other reasons for withdrawing from the workforce; and (c) the social isolation of the elderly as they lose friends and relatives to death and debilitation, and as they become more fearful of leaving their houses (e.g., because they can no longer drive; e.g., because they are more fearful of crime).

Health: Most older people (65+) are in reasonably good health. Of all age groups, however, the elderly are the most affected by ill health. Although the elderly comprised just 13 percent of the U.S. population in the late 1990s, they consumed more than one-third of all health care. Prescription drugs represent the largest out-of-pocket healthcare expense for 75 percent of older people — and the costs of these drugs are rising much faster than inflation. Although Medicare helps with the medical costs of the aged, they still pay a quarter of these costs themselves. Moreover, because the elderly face such severe health problems — and because our culture places such value on youthfulness and physical fitness — the elderly are especial-ly susceptible to quackery that promises to alleviate their pain and improve their functioning. The elderly are the victims of 60 percent of all health-care frauds and are cheated out of billions of dollars each year.[1]

Income: A commonly held belief about the elderly is that most of them live in abject poverty. However, this is more myth than truth: The economic condition of elderly people has improved in both absolute and relative terms over the past three decades — especially because Social Security benefits have risen in line with inflation and because retirees today are "more likely to be covered by private pension plans and to have dividend and interest income from accumulated assets. Finally, the elderly are more likely than the young to be homeowners. Buying a home is a primary means of amassing and retaining wealth."[2] The upshot is that in the late 1990s, the poverty rate of those over age 65 is lower than that of the general population (10.5% vs 12.7%). However, all of this said, the annual income of a family headed by a person sixty-five years of age or older is still considerably less than that of other families (by about almost one-half: $21,729 vs $38,886),[3] Moreover, some groups

---

[1]See D. Stanley Eitzen and Maxine Baca Zinn, *Social Problems*, 8th ed. (Boston: Allyn & Bacon, 2000), p. 130; and Thomas J. Sullivan, *Introduction to Social Problems*, 5th ed. (Boston: Allyn & Bacon, 2000), p. 272.

[2]Daniel J. Curran and Claire M. Renzetti, *Social Problems: Society in Crisis*, 5th ed. (Boston: Allyn & Bacon, 2000), p. 276.

[3]The latest statistics on poverty and income can be found at the U.S. Census Bureau's web site: www.census.gov.

among the elderly are not doing so well: **Women** — almost three quarters of the poor among the elderly are women, and women constitute over 80 percent of the elderly poor who live alone (the "old, rich widow" is truly a myth).[4] **African-Americans** and **Latinos** — Individual and institutional sources of discrimination coalesce to make these people's lives especially miserable and problematic. One-fourth of the black and Latino elderly are poor compared to less than 10 percent for whites over the age of 65. "The higher probability of older African Americans being poor is a direct consequence of their relatively low status throughout life. With average incomes only about 60 percent of those of Whites, they have little chance of building a nest egg to supplement their pension incomes. African Americans are also more likely than Whites to have worked at jobs that do not qualify for Social Security. And if they have worked at jobs qualifying for Social Security, minority members usually are eligible only for lower benefits because of their lower wages."[5]

Social Interaction: Another commonly held belief about the elderly is that they are isolated, neglected, and miserable. However, this is also more myth than truth: Studies using large and representative samples of older people find that these individuals typically do not become isolated and neglected by their families and friends. Even if they are living alone, relatively few of them are lonely and desolate. Those elderly most likely to undergo social isolation are of advanced old age (75+), suffer from serious physical ailments, or are very poor. "It is these elderly who are least likely to visit friends, go to the library, or attend social events." However, older people as a group are much more likely to fear crime and to stay within the confines of their homes because of this fear. Indeed, some surveys have shown that the elderly consider crime to be a more severe problem than health, poverty, or loneliness.[6]

The CHIP data set *Aging95* will allow you to investigate the preceding aging issues in greater detail and to uncover the relationships "age" has with health, income, social interaction, and fear of crime; you will also be able to explore how gender and race influence these relationships.

File: **Aging95** (Aging issues; *source*: 1991–1994 GSS)

    Info: Race→Sex→Age→Married→Ed→FamInc→SatFF→FearWalk→Happy→Health
       (2)   (2)   (3)   (4)   (4)   (3)   (3)   (2)   (3)   (3)

Race	White, Black
Sex	Male, Female
Age	18–39, 40–64, 65+
Married	Never Married, Div/Sep, Widowed, Married
Ed	(Years of schooling) <12yrs, 12yrs, 13–15yrs, 16+yrs
FamInc	(Family Income) <$20K, $20K–$50K, $50K+
SatFF	(*Satisfaction with family life and friends.* Sum of A and B, where: A= "How much satisfaction do you get from your family life": 6=very great, 5=great, 4=quite a lot, 3=fair, 2=some, 1=little, 0=none; B= "How much satisfaction do you get from your friendships": 6=very great, 5=great, 4=quite a lot, 3=fair, 2=some, 1=little, 0=none) So–so (0–9), Good (10–11), Excellent (12)

[4]See Curran and Renzetti, p. 277; Eitzen and Zinn, p. 123; Sullivan, p. 269.

[5]Eitzen and Zinn, p. 124.

[6]Sullivan, pp. 271–272; also see Curran and Renzetti, pp. 271–272.

FearWalk ("Is there any area right around here—that is, within a mile—where you would be afraid to walk alone at night?") No, Yes

Happy ("Taken all together, how would you say things are these days; would you say that you are very happy, pretty happy, not too happy?") Not Too Happy, Pretty Happy, Very Happy

Health ("Would you say your own health, in general, is . . .") Poor/Fair, Good, Excellent

Basic

1. Are older people more likely to suffer poor health? Answer this question by crosstabulating Health (Y) by Age (X); also examine the relationship graphically (after doing the **CrossTab**, select the **Line** alternative for the **Plot** option under the **Table** command and highlight the "Poor/Fair" category). Did you find what you expected? (*Concentrate your discussion on the "Poor/Fair" row of Health.*)

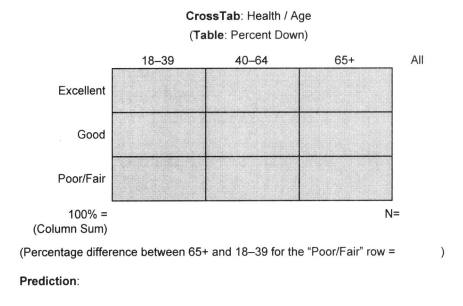

CrossTab: Health / Age
(**Table**: Percent Down)

	18–39	40–64	65+	All
Excellent				
Good				
Poor/Fair				
100% = (Column Sum)				N=

(Percentage difference between 65+ and 18–39 for the "Poor/Fair" row =)

Prediction:

Finding:

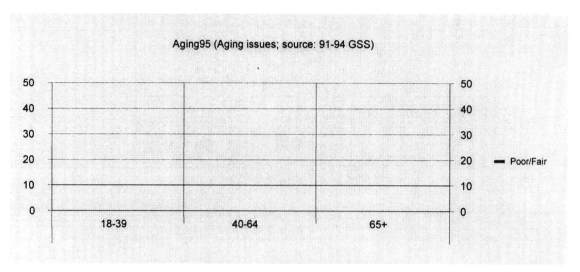

Answer/Discussion

2. Are older people more likely to have "low" incomes? Answer this question by crosstabulating FamInc (Y) by Age (X); also examine the relationship graphically (after doing the **CrossTab**, select the **Line** alternative for the **Plot** option under the **Table** command and highlight the "<$20K" category). Did you find what you expected? (*Focus your comments on the "<$20K" row.*)

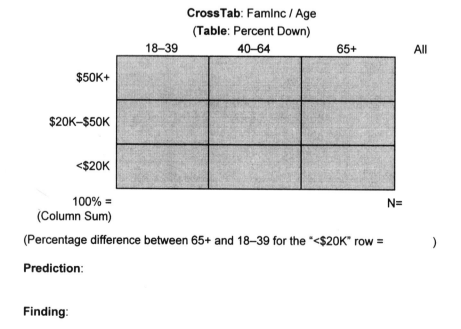

(Percentage difference between 65+ and 18–39 for the "<$20K" row =   )

Prediction:

Finding:

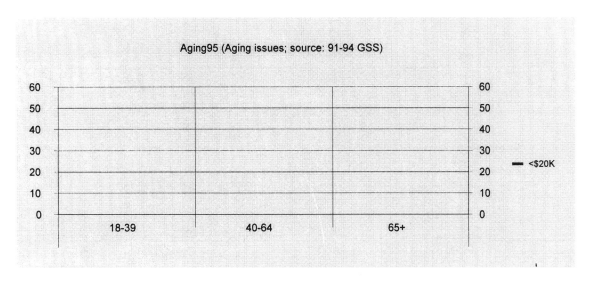

Aging95 (Aging issues; source: 91-94 GSS)

Answer/Discussion

3. Do older people suffer from reduced social interaction? For example, are older people more likely to be fearful to walk about their neighborhoods after dark (which would curtail the quantity of their social interactions)? Do older people complain more than their younger counterparts that the quality of their social relationships with friends and family is not so great? (Or is this a myth, as partly contended in the introductory comments to this chapter—see the comments under the subheading **Social Interaction**). Answer these questions by doing the following:

   (a) Crosstabulate FearWalk (Y) by Age (X); also examine the relationship graphically (after doing the **CrossTab**, select the **Line** alternative for the **Plot** option under the **Table** command and highlight the "Yes" category). Did you find what you expected? (*Focus your comments on the "Yes" row.*)

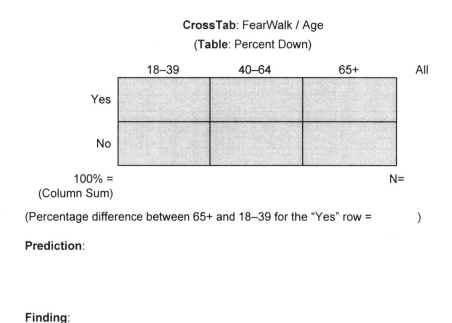

CrossTab: FearWalk / Age
(**Table**: Percent Down)

(Percentage difference between 65+ and 18–39 for the "Yes" row =   )

Prediction:

Finding:

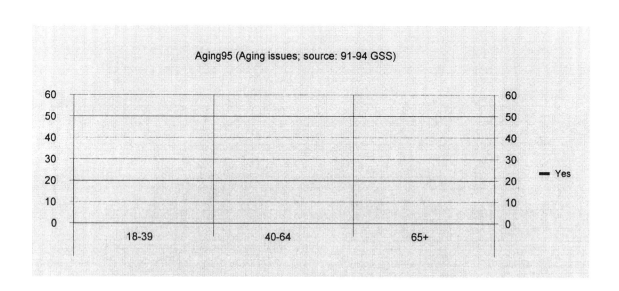

(b) Crosstabulate SatFF (Y) by Age (X); also examine the relationship graphically (after doing the **Cross-Tab**, select the **Line** alternative for the **Plot** option under the **Table** command and highlight the "So-so" category). Did you find what you expected? (*Focus your comments on the "So-so" row.*)

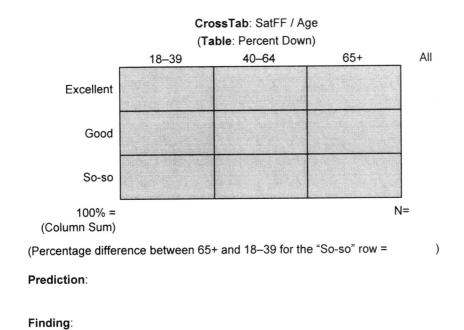

CrossTab: SatFF / Age
(**Table**: Percent Down)

	18–39	40–64	65+	All
Excellent				
Good				
So-so				

100% =
(Column Sum)   N=

(Percentage difference between 65+ and 18–39 for the "So-so" row =   )

Prediction:

Finding:

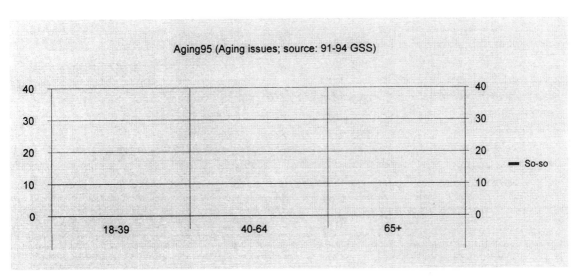

Aging95 (Aging issues; source: 91-94 GSS)

Answer/Discussion

4. According to sociology textbook writers—and as presented in the introduction to this chapter—the problems of old age are magnified for women and for those individuals with a minority heritage (especially African-American or Latino). Explore the interactions between age and gender, and between age and minority background by doing the following:

(a) Crosstab FamInc (Y) by Sex (X) and **control** for Age (Z). In which column (Male or Female), in which partial table (18-39, 40-64, or 65+) do we find those individuals with the greatest odds of having family incomes under 20 thousand dollars per year? Does this confirm what sociology textbook authors say about old age and gender?

Partial Table #1

CrossTab: FamInc / Sex

Control: Age (18–39)

(**Table**: Percent Down)

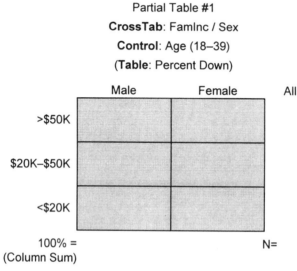

	Male	Female	All
>$50K			
$20K–$50K			
<$20K			
100% = (Column Sum)			N=

(Percentage difference between Female and Male for the "<$20K" row =   )

Partial Table #2

CrossTab: FamInc / Sex

Control: Age (40–64)

(**Table**: Percent Down)

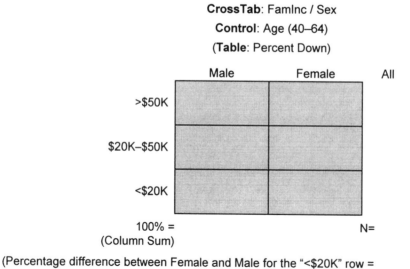

	Male	Female	All
>$50K			
$20K–$50K			
<$20K			
100% = (Column Sum)			N=

(Percentage difference between Female and Male for the "<$20K" row =   )

Partial Table #3
CrossTab: FamInc / Sex
Control: Age (65+)
(**Table**: Percent Down)

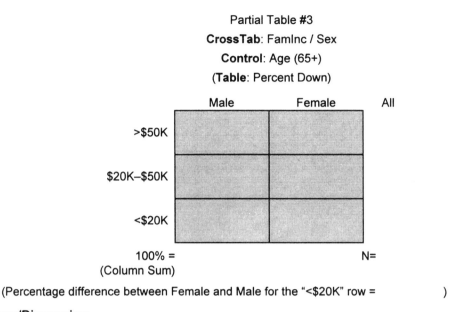

(Percentage difference between Female and Male for the "<$20K" row =   )

Answer/Discussion

(b) Crosstab FamInc (Y) by Race (X) and **control** for Age (Z). In which column (White or Black), in which partial table (18–39, 40–64, or 65+) do we find those individuals with the greatest odds of having family incomes under 20 thousand dollars per year? Does this confirm what sociology textbook authors say about old age and minority status?

Partial Table #1
CrossTab: FamInc / Race
Control: Age (18–39)
(**Table**: Percent Down)

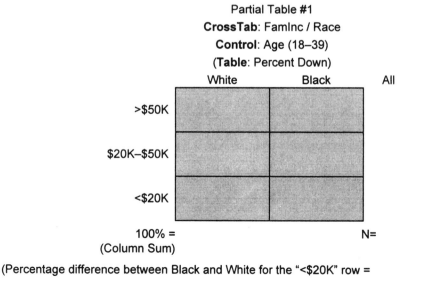

(Percentage difference between Black and White for the "<$20K" row =   )

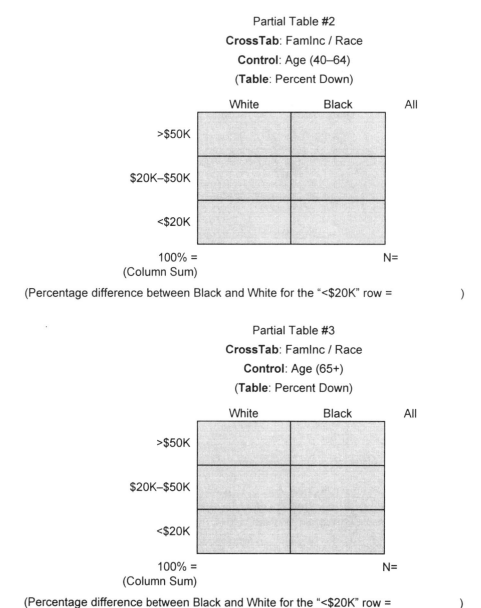

Partial Table #2

CrossTab: FamInc / Race

Control: Age (40–64)

(**Table**: Percent Down)

	White	Black	All
>$50K			
$20K–$50K			
<$20K			
100% = (Column Sum)			N=

(Percentage difference between Black and White for the "<$20K" row =   )

Partial Table #3

CrossTab: FamInc / Race

Control: Age (65+)

(**Table**: Percent Down)

	White	Black	All
>$50K			
$20K–$50K			
<$20K			
100% = (Column Sum)			N=

(Percentage difference between Black and White for the "<$20K" row =   )

Answer/Discussion

Advanced

5. Perhaps the relationship between Age and FearWalk found in #3(a) is spurious. More specifically, perhaps both variables are dependent upon the antecedent variable "sex." Sketch the model that would show the relationship between these two variables as spurious, using Sex as your control variable. Defend this alternative model.

   (a) Model sketch:

   (b) Interpretation of the Sex–Age relationship:

   (c) Interpretation of the Sex–FearWalk relationship:

6. Let's check out the empirical validity of the model you've sketched above: crosstabulate FearWalk (Y) by Age (X) and control for Sex (Z). Does the relationship between Age and FearWalk maintain itself? Is there a multivariable model evident? That is, do both Age and Sex have independent effects on Fear-Walk? Defend your answer by referring to the correct percentage-differences.

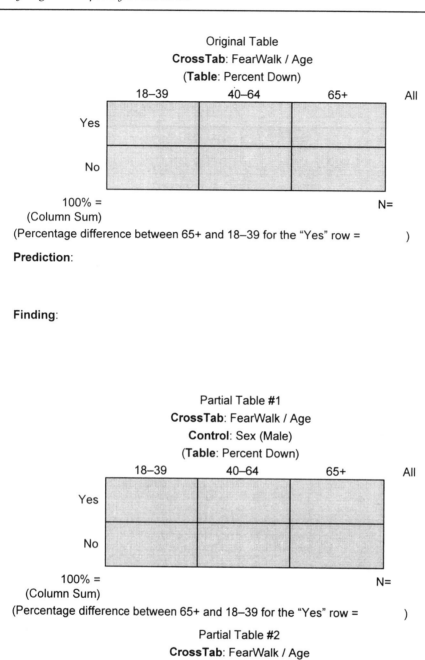

Original Table
CrossTab: FearWalk / Age
(**Table**: Percent Down)

100% =
(Column Sum)

(Percentage difference between 65+ and 18–39 for the "Yes" row =   )

Prediction:

Finding:

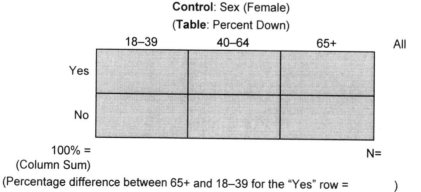

Partial Table #1
CrossTab: FearWalk / Age
Control: Sex (Male)
(**Table**: Percent Down)

100% =
(Column Sum)

(Percentage difference between 65+ and 18–39 for the "Yes" row =   )

Partial Table #2
CrossTab: FearWalk / Age
Control: Sex (Female)
(**Table**: Percent Down)

100% =
(Column Sum)

(Percentage difference between 65+ and 18–39 for the "Yes" row =   )

Answer/Discussion

Suggestions for Further Study

Jan Larson uses Bureau of Labor Statistics data to demonstrate that outsourcing is one of the hottest branches of the labor force. "Contingent workers" enjoy variety and flexibility, but they usually earn lower pay and benefits. Indeed, most would prefer "regular" jobs, but employers are not hiring. The result is unmet demand for health insurance and other necessities of modern life that temps lack. However, because workers over 65 have Social Security and Medicare benefits, the temporary workforce is becoming especially appealing to both them and their prospective employers. From ages 25 to 64 most workers are not contingent, but temporary workers outnumber their non-temporary counterparts for those under the age of 25, as well as those over 65. See Larson's "Temporary Workers Are Here to Stay," pp. 85–90 in Gregg Lee Carter (ed.), *Perspectives on Current Social Problems* (Boston: Allyn & Bacon, 1997).

The Administration on Aging of the U.S. Department of Health & Human Services and the American Association of Retired People (AARP) annually publish one of the best reference volumes about older Americans. *Profile of Older Americans* is a concise, compact, and comprehensive collection of facts and figures about the 34.4 million people in the U.S. who are age 65 and older. Topics include health, life expectancy, marital status, living arrangements, geographic distribution, racial/ethnic composition, economic status, employment, and education. See their web site: http://research.aarp.org/general/profile99.html

Relevant World Wide Web Sites

The General Social Survey — the source of the *Aging95* data file used in this chapter — is available on the Web. Simple analyses may be done on-line, but data may also be downloaded for investigation with SPSS or similar statistical analysis software: http://www.icpsr.umich.edu/gss.

The government web sites cited at the end of earlier chapters also contain large amounts of useful data on the problems of the aged; see especially the Census Bureau (www.census.gov), and the Administration on Aging links listed at the Department of Health and Human Services site (http://www.dhhs.gov).

A number of professional and special-interest groups represent older Americans. Although the writing on their web sites is sometimes highly opinionated, they are useful for updates of political activities, court decisions, and other news on the issues confronting the aged. Most importantly, see:

American Association of Retired Persons	www.aarp.org
The Gray Panthers	www.graypanthers.org
The Gerontological Society of America	www.geron.org

Exploratory exercises for the *Aging95* data file have been included with those for the Chapter 8; see page 221.

Chapter 7. Crime, Deviance, and Social Control

Anomie Theory, Control Theory, and Understanding Deviance

Robert K. Merton's classic essay on the causes of crime and deviance emphasizes that a society's cultural goals may not be accompanied by realistic means for attaining them – at least not for everyone.[1] Those who want the accepted goals but do not have ready access to the accepted means to attain them may "innovate" and come up with their own means. Thus, for example, the inner-city adolescent whose family has few resources to send him to private school or to help him get a job or to start a career and who attends a school where the majority of students will drop out may well find himself out on the streets as a young man with few prospects. From the popular culture – television, movies, magazines – and from his friends and family he has absorbed the cultural goal of material success. Unable to achieve it by conventional means – that is, by getting an education and using his networks to get a good first job – he "innovates" and tries to reach it through criminal means (he steals, sells drugs, or whatever).

We tend to associate crime with poor, minority-group neighborhoods. Given this association, Merton's argument has great intuitive appeal. However, it has not stood up well to the test of empirical confirmation.[2] The argument implies an inverse relationship between social class and crime. In studies of street crime (muggings, robberies, assaults, murders), the relationship can be confirmed; but when crime is defined more broadly, to include white-collar and business crimes, and when crime is measured by indicators other than official police reports (e.g., by self-report), the relationship is weak and inconsistent.

Merton's theory of crime and deviance has become known as "anomie theory" in sociological jargon. He adopted the concept of "anomie" from Durkheim's writings.[3] *Anomie* means being without norms or in a state of normative confusion; it can be used to characterize individuals, groups, or societies. Whereas Merton viewed anomie as arising from blocked opportunity, Durkheim saw it more as a product of the weakening of the quality and quantity of social ties – which may be caused by rapid social change, divorce, and other threats to the solidarity of the groups to which individuals belong.

Following in the footsteps of Durkheim, Travis Hirschi (see footnote #2 below) demonstrated the importance of an individual's attachment to the group in keeping the individual in check, i.e., in line with normative expectations for behavior. Hirschi emphasizes that the key question in the study of deviance is *not* "Why do individuals commit deviant acts?" but rather, "Why don't individuals commit deviant acts?" His answer is founded on a fundamental principle of human reality: People like being liked and like being accepted; to achieve these aims they conform to expectations of those whom they want to like and accept them. Thus, Hirschi found that adolescents who had strong ties to their families and to their schools were less likely to commit delinquent acts – because such acts are frowned upon by these two groups. Hirschi's interpretation of Durkheim has become known as "control theory" in sociological jargon, implying that individuals with strong attachments to mainstream groups (e.g., family, school, church) are held in check, or *controlled*, from committing deviant acts.

---

[1] *Social Theory and Social Structure: Enlarged Edition* (New York: Free Press, 1968), Chapter 6.

[2] See, for example, Travis Hirschi, *Causes of Delinquency* (Berkeley: University of California Press, 1969), key portions of which are reprinted in Part 8 of Gregg Lee Carter, *Empirical Approaches to Sociology*, 3rd edition (Boston: Allyn & Bacon, 2001); Rodney Stark, *Sociology*, 5/e (Belmont, CA: Wadsworth Publishing Company, 1994), p. 189; Charles R. Tittle, *et al.*, "The Myth of Social Class and Criminality: An Empirical Assessment of the Empirical Evidence," *American Sociological Review* 43:5 (October 1978), pp. 643–656; and Charles R. Tittle and Robert F. Meier, "Specifying the SES/Delinquency Relationship," *Criminology* 28 (1990), pp. 271–299.

[3] Émile Durkheim, *Suicide: A Study in Sociology* (New York: Free Press, 1951 [org. 1897]); key portions of which are reprinted in Part 1 of Carter, *Ibid.*

The CHIP files *Arrested* and *Div72_98* allow you to assess the social class→deviance relationship by examining the empirical associations between social class and crime, and between social class and divorce. The data files also allow you to examine the same dependent variables from a *control theory* perspective (which we might schematicize as: social integration→deviance). The patterns in your findings should prod you to begin thinking about the true nature of deviance as it relates to social class and social integration.

File: **Arrested** (Who gets arrested? *Source:* 1973–86 GSS)

Info: Race→Sex→Ed→Prestige→Attend→SatFamily→Arrested
    (2)   (2)   (4)   (3)   (3)   (3)   (2)

Race	White, Black
Sex	Male, Female
Ed	(Years of schooling) <12yrs, 12yrs, 13–15yrs, 16+yrs
Prestige	(Hodge-Segal-Rossi occupational prestige scores) 12–32 (=Low), 33–46 (=Medium), 47+ (=High)
Attend	(How often do you attend religious services?) Yearly (or less), Monthly, Weekly
SatFamily	*(Satisfaction with family life.* How much satisfaction do you get from your family life: 6=very great, 5=great, 4=quite a lot, 3=fair, 2=some, 1=little, 0=none) Low (0–2), Medium (3–4), High (5–6)
Arrested	(Have you ever been picked up, or charged, by the police for any reason other than a parking or traffic violation, whether or not you were guilty?) No, Yes

File: **Div72_98** (Who's most likely to divorce? 72–74, 85–86, and 96–98 GSS; does not include respondents who have never married)

Info: Era→ Region→Race→Sex→Age→Ed→Attend→Divorced
    (3)   (4)   (2) (2) (3) (4)   (4)   (2)

Era	72–74, 85–86, 96–98
Region	Northeast (CT, ME, MA, NH, NJ, NY, PA, RI, and VT) Midwest (IL, IN, IA, KS, MI, MN, MO, NE, ND, OH, SD, and WI) South (AL, AR, DE, FL, GA, KY, LS, MD, MS, NC, OK, SC, TN, TX, VA, and WV) West (AK, AZ, CA, CO, HI, ID, MT, NV, NM, OR, UT, WA, and WY)
Race	White, Black
Sex	Male, Female
Age	18–39, 40–64, 65+
Ed	<12yrs, 12yrs, 13–15yrs, 16+yrs
Attend	(How often do you attend religious services? [respondents were given a 9-point scale ranging from: (0) Never . . . to (8) Several Times a Week; these were recoded as follows]) Never, Yearly, Monthly, Weekly
Divorced	("Have your ever been divorced or legally separated?") No, Yes

Social Class and Deviance

Basic

1. In his writings on anomie, Merton contends that those without a great deal of opportunity to achieve the "American dream" (material success) — that is, the uneducated and the poor — would be most motivated to steal and commit street crime. Let's examine the social class→crime relationship at the individ-

ual level of analysis, using education and job prestige as measurements for the social class standing of an individual. **Open** the *Arrested* file and crosstabulate Arrested (Y) by Ed (X); also examine the relationship graphically (after doing the **CrossTab**, select the **Line** alternative for the **Plot** option under the **Table** command and highlight the "Yes" category). Note that the "arrest" might have been for any kind of offense, not just street crime. What did you find? Does the relationship seem strong and inverse (as predicted by Merton), or does it seem weak and inconsistent (as described in the introduction to this chapter)? (*Focus your answer on the "Yes" row.*)

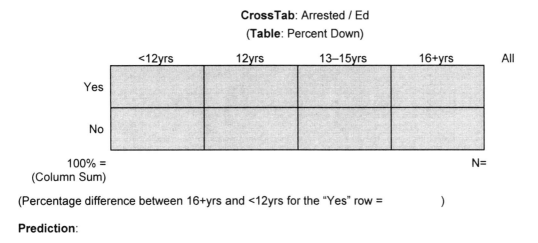

CrossTab: Arrested / Ed
(**Table**: Percent Down)

	<12yrs	12yrs	13–15yrs	16+yrs	All
Yes					
No					

100% =
(Column Sum)

N=

(Percentage difference between 16+yrs and <12yrs for the "Yes" row =   )

Prediction:

Finding:

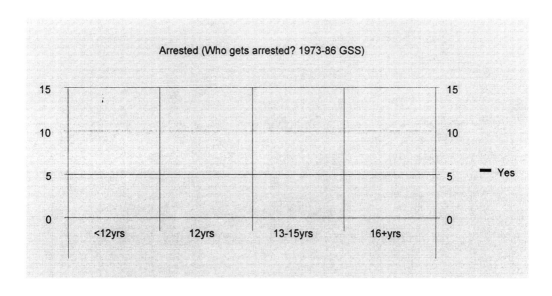

Arrested (Who gets arrested? 1973-86 GSS)

Answer/Discussion

2. Repeat #(1), but let X=Prestige.

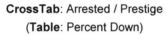

CrossTab: Arrested / Prestige
(**Table**: Percent Down)

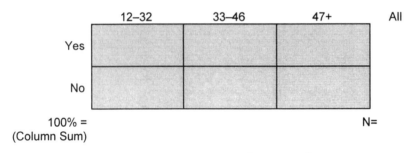

	12–32	33–46	47+	All
Yes				
No				

100% =
(Column Sum)   N=

(Percentage difference between 47+ and 12–32 for the "Yes" row =   )

Prediction:

Finding:

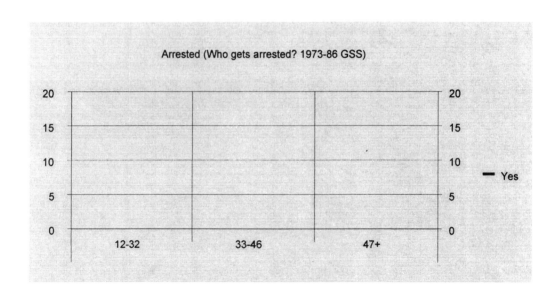

Answer/Discussion

3. Jeffrey Reiman has persuasively demonstrated that, all things equal, individuals from the bottom half of the social class system are much more likely to be arrested and sent to jail than those from the top half.[4] Why do you think this is so?

4. Given Reiman's findings, should we be convinced, or not convinced, that the weak negative association between social class and arrest-probability found in #(1) and #(2) is truly reflecting that the poor are more criminally prone? Why?

5. We would expect social class and divorce to be negatively related: Poorer people experience more strains on their relationships (lack of money is a constant source of tension); moreover, divorce typically lowers the income of women. Let's examine the social class→divorce relationship at the individual level of analysis, using education as a measurement for the social class standing of an individual. **Open** the *Div72_98* file and crosstabulate Divorced (Y) by Ed (X); also examine the relationship graphically (after doing the **CrossTab**, select the **Line** alternative for the **Plot** option under the **Table** command and highlight the "Yes" category). What did you find? (*Focus your answer on the "Yes" row.*)

---

[4]*The Rich Get Richer and the Poor Get Prison:* 4th ed. (Boston: Allyn & Bacon, 1995); see especially Chapter 6; reprinted in Gregg Lee Carter, *Perspectives on Current Social Problems* (Boston: Allyn & Bacon, 1997).

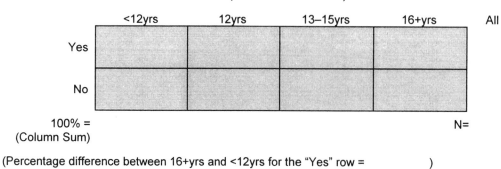

CrossTab: Divorced / Ed
(**Table**: Percent Down)

	<12yrs	12yrs	13–15yrs	16+yrs	All
Yes					
No					

100% =   N=
(Column Sum)

(Percentage difference between 16+yrs and <12yrs for the "Yes" row =   )

Prediction:

Finding:

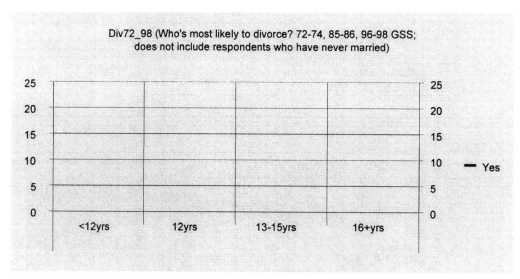

Div72_98 (Who's most likely to divorce? 72-74, 85-86, 96-98 GSS;
does not include respondents who have never married)

Answer/Discussion

Social Integration and Deviance

Basic

1. Let's pursue the Durkheim/Hirschi/Control Theory of crime and deviance at the individual level of analysis. Re-**Open** the *Arrested* file. According to *control theory*, we would anticipate individuals with strong social attachments to conventional groups (e.g., the family; church) to deviate less from expected (socially acceptable) behaviors. Test this prediction by crosstabbing Arrested (Y) by SatFamily (X); also examine the relationship graphically (after doing the **CrossTab**, select the **Line** alternative for the **Plot** option under the **Table** command and highlight the "Yes" category). What did you find? (*Focus your comments on the "Yes" column.*)

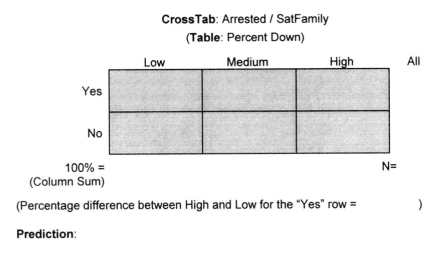

CrossTab: Arrested / SatFamily
(**Table**: Percent Down)

(Percentage difference between High and Low for the "Yes" row =   )

Prediction:

Finding:

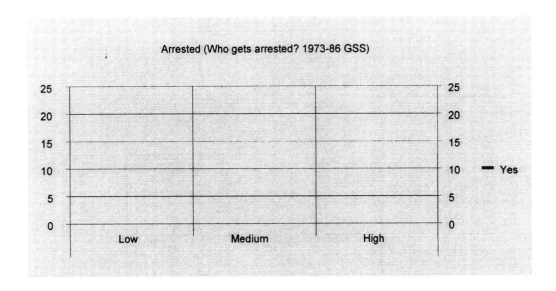

Answer/Discussion

2. Repeat #(1), but let X=Attend.

CrossTab: Arrested / Attend
(**Table**: Percent Down)

	Yearly	Monthly	Weekly	All
Yes				
No				

100% =
(Column Sum)   N=

(Percentage difference between Weekly and Yearly for the "Yes" row =   )

Prediction:

Finding:

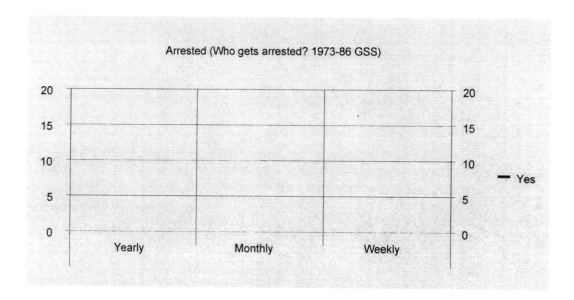

Answer/Discussion

3. According to your understanding of *control theory*, who would be more "deviant" — a poor person with strong social ties to his or her friends, family, church, and job . . . or a prosperous person lacking such strong ties? Test this prediction by crosstabulating Arrested (Y) by Prestige (X) and control for SatFamily (Z). (Hint: Examine the "Yes" row for the low prestige column for the crosstab where SatFamily is "High" and compare it to the "Yes" row for the high prestige column for SatFamily = "Low.")

(a) **Your prediction and defense of it:**

(b) **Complete the crosstabulations below to arrive at your findings:**

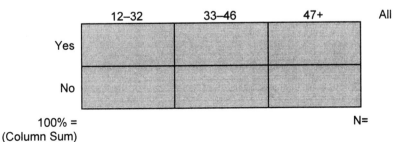

CrossTab: Arrested / Prestige
Control: SatFamily (Low)
(Table: Percent Down)

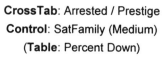

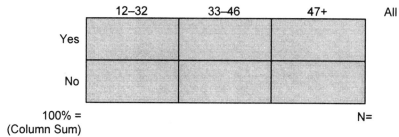

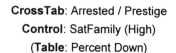

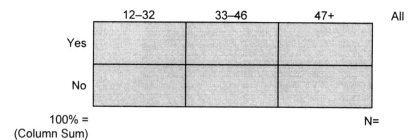

Answer/Discussion

4. We would expect church attendance and divorce to be negatively related: Fellow church-goers can offer social and material support during times of marital stress. Moreover, per the assumptions of *control theory*, people like being liked and like being accepted; to achieve these aims they conform to expectations of those whom they want to like and accept them. Thus, those with strong ties to their churches would be less likely to commit deviant acts—including adultery—because such acts are frowned upon

by this group. In short, *control theory* predicts that individuals with strong attachments to mainstream groups (e.g., family, school, church) are held in check, or *controlled*, from committing deviant acts. Let's examine the social integration→divorce relationship at the individual level of analysis, using church attendance as an indicator of the degree to which an individual is socially integrated into a mainstream group. **Open** the *Div72_98* file and crosstabulate Divorced (Y) by Attend (X); also examine the relationship graphically (after doing the **CrossTab**, select the **Line** alternative for the **Plot** option under the **Table** command and highlight the "Yes" category). What did you find? (*Focus your answer on the "Yes" row.*)

CrossTab: Divorced / Attend
(**Table**: Percent Down)

	Never	Yearly	Monthly	Weekly	All
Yes					
No					

100% =   N=
(Column Sum)

(Percentage difference between Weekly and Never for the "Yes" row =   )

Prediction:

Finding:

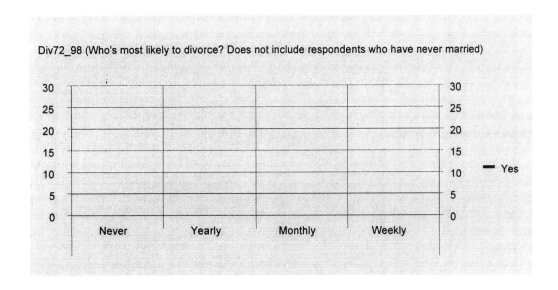

Div72_98 (Who's most likely to divorce? Does not include respondents who have never married)

Answer/Discussion

Advanced

5. Re-examine the tables you constructed in #(3b). Is a multivariable model evident? That is, do both Prestige and SatFamily have independent effects on the odds of having been arrested? Refer to the correct percentage-differences in support of your answer.

6. Perhaps the relationship between SatFamily and Arrested found in #(1) is spurious: Perhaps — compared to women — men are more likely to commit crime and less likely be involved with their families. If this is so, controlling for Sex might make the SatFamily→Arrested association disappear.

   (a) Sketch this alternative model — that is, that Arrested and SatFamily are only related because of their common association with Sex.

   (b) Test this alternative model by crosstabulating Arrested (Y) by SatFamily (X) and control for Sex (Z).

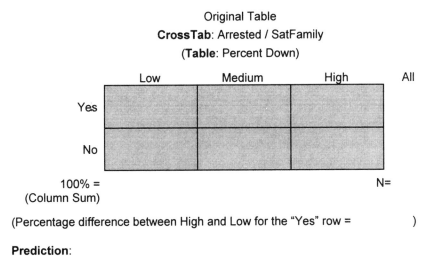

Original Table
CrossTab: Arrested / SatFamily
(**Table**: Percent Down)

(Percentage difference between High and Low for the "Yes" row =   )

Prediction:

Finding:

Partial Table #1
CrossTab: Arrested / SatFamily
Control: Sex (Male)
(**Table**: Percent Down)

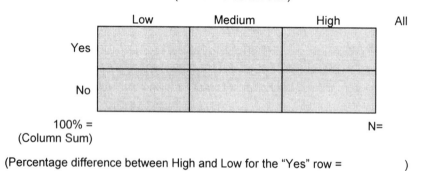

	Low	Medium	High	All
Yes				
No				

100% =
(Column Sum)   N=

(Percentage difference between High and Low for the "Yes" row =   )

Partial Table #2
CrossTab: Arrested / SatFamily
Control: Sex (Female)
(**Table**: Percent Down)

	Low	Medium	High	All
Yes				
No				

100% =
(Column Sum)   N=

(Percentage difference between High and Low for the "Yes" row =   )

(c) Was the original Arrested/SatFamily relationship spurious? That is, did the relationship maintain itself or did it disappear?

(d) Is a multivariable model apparent—that is, do both SatFamily and Sex have independent effects on the odds of having been arrested? Refer to the correct percentage-differences to support your answer.

Suggestions for Further Study

Jeffrey Reiman demonstrates that the criminal justice system has built-in biases that greatly increase the odds of a poor person ending up in jail, while at the same time greatly reducing the odds for a prosperous individual. These biases also ensure that the system will discriminate against African Americans, who are disproportionately poor. More specifically, Reiman shows that (a) the decisions of police and prosecutors on whom to arrest or charge do not reflect the only or the most dangerous behaviors legally defined as "criminal"; (b) the decisions of juries and judges regarding criminal convictions do not reflect the only or the most dangerous individuals among those arrested and charged; and (c) the decisions of sentencing judges do not reflect the goal of protecting society from the only or the most dangerous of those convicted by meting out punishments proportionate to the harmfulness of the crime committed. See his classic essay "And the Poor Get Prison," pp. 269–301 in Gregg Lee Carter (ed.), *Perspectives on Current Social Problems* (Boston: Allyn & Bacon, 1997).

In a second essay in *Perspectives on Current Social Problems* ("The Relationship Between Legal Gambling and Local Crime," pp. 229–238), Lori M. Hunter observes that the nationwide spread of gambling has produced a popular fear of negative social impacts. However, whether this fear is justified—that is, whether legalized gambling truly comes bundled with a rise in social problems—has been little studied. Hunter finds a slight rise in crime after gambling was legalized in two of three regions examined in her essay. Her findings would indicate that the public concerns over gambling are not unjustified, or at the very least that indicators of social well-being (e.g., crime and divorce rates) in casino areas should be monitored closely.

In a third essay in *Perspectives on Current Social Problems* ("Kids, Crack, and Crime," pp. 239–249), James A. Inciardi and Anne E. Pottieger empirically test the popular notion that the infiltration of crack cocaine into the inner-cities of America was a prime cause of the rising rate of violent crimes among youth. Their intensive study of "seriously delinquent" teens in Miami largely confirms this notion: the more a teen is involved in the crack trade, the more likely he or she is to be involved in violent crime.

In a final essay in *Perspectives on Current Social Problems* ("Guns and Violence: Cross-national Comparisons," pp. 251–267), I demonstrate that the correlation between gun prevalence and gun violence is strong when cross-national comparisons are made. I further demonstrate that compared to its socioeconomic peer nations, the United States has very weak gun-control laws. The data analyses in this essay imply that one tactic the U.S. might use in controlling its violent crime rate is to enact gun laws on par with its counterpart nations in Europe and Canada.

Relevant World Wide Web Sites

The General Social Survey contains many items relevant to individual attitudes and behaviors on a variety of "deviance" and crime-related issues—including alcohol and drug use, gun control, sexual orientation, and capital punishment (www.icpsr.umich.edu/gss); also see the other public opinion data repositories cited at the end of Chapter 1.

The Center on Juvenile and Criminal Justice is a private, non-profit organization whose mission is to reduce society's reliance on the use of incarceration as a solution to social problems; see their web site for a number of statistical reports on crime and punishment: www.cjcj.org.

The federal government maintains a host of on-line reports and data files on crime. Most importantly, see:

Bureau of Justice Statistics	www.ojp.usdoj.gov/bjs
Federal Bureau of Investigation	www.fbi.gov
Federal Bureau of Prisons	www.bop.gov
Office of Juvenile Justice and Delinquency Prevention	www.ojjdp.ncjrs.org/facts/facts.html
Drug Enforcement Administration	www.usdoj.gov/dea
National Institute of Justice's Arrestee Drug Abuse Monitoring Program	www.adam-nij.net/adam

Finally, for international crime and deviance data, see:

United Nations Crime and Justice Information	www.uncjin.org
Bureau of Justice Statistics (International Statistics) "Links Page"	www.ojp.usdoj.gov/bjs/otherscr.htm

Exploratory exercises for *Arrested* and *Div72_98* have been included with those for the next chapter; see page 221.

Chapter 8. The Family and Intimate Relationships

Who's Most Likely To Be Divorced?

Despite the rise of nontraditional family forms in recent years—e.g., single-parent, nonmarital cohabitation, and married gay households—most Americans still aspire to form traditional families: to be "married with children." Indeed, by age thirty-five, 94 percent of men and 96 percent of women have married in the United States. However, many marriages do not last. Between the late 1940s and mid-1970s, divorce rates rose dramatically and then leveled off. Recent divorce rates reveal that the chances of a first marriage ending in divorce are about one in two.[1] To put this statistic in perspective, this rate was 25 percent in the 1940s, and 10 percent in the early 1900s.

Many sociological reasons can account for the dramatic rise in divorce in the 20th century. Among the most important are the increased social and financial independence of women, greater tolerance of divorce by religious groups, and the relaxing of divorce laws. Of great importance, too, is the loss of many of the family's functions: In the past, unhappy couples "might have remained married because neither spouse felt he or she could raise the children alone or he or she needed the family for support in old age. Today, single parents are better prepared to raise a child, and most people are supported by retirement plans in their old age. In fact, the high levels of affluence afforded by industrialization have made people less dependent on kinship ties for support, with consequent changes in the family as an institution."[2]

Despite the relatively high rate of divorce in contemporary society, marital dissolution is not evenly distributed throughout the population. Certain social and economic characteristics are correlated with divorce, and in most cases the correlations can be considered causal in nature—with divorce as the dependent variable. The CHIP exercises below allow you to examine some of these correlations and to explore interpretations of them.

File: **Divorc98** (Who's most likely to divorce? *Source:* 1993–98 GSS)

Info: Immigrant→Latino→Race→Sex→Age→Ed→FamInc→Attend→Strayed→Married
      (2)   (2)   (4)   (2)   (3) (4)   (3)   (4)   (2)   (2)

Immigrant	No, Yes
Latino	(Latino Heritage) No, Yes (GSS coding for "Ethnicity" = 17, 22, 25, or 38)
Race	White, Black, Asian, Other
Sex	Male, Female
Age	18–39, 40–64, 65+
Ed	<12yrs, 12yrs, 13–15yrs, 16+yrs
FamInc	(Family income) <$20K, $20K–$60K, >$60K
Attend	(How often do you attend religious services?: Respondents were given a 9-point scale ranging from: [0] Never . . . to [8] Several Times a Week; these were recoded as follows) Never, Yearly, Monthly, Weekly

---

[1]D. Stanley Eitzen and Maxine Baca Zinn, *Social Problems*, 8th ed. (Boston: Allyn & Bacon, 2000), pp. 364–65; Michael P. Soroka and George J. Bryjak, *Social Problems: A World at Risk* 2nd ed. (Boston: Allyn & Bacon, 1999), pp. 60–65; Thomas J. Sullivan, *Introduction to Social Problems*, 5th ed. (Boston: Allyn & Bacon, 2000), pp. 83–85.

[2]Sullivan, p. 85. Note that most industrial nations have experienced a dramatic rise in divorce rates in recent decades. For example, since the mid-1960s divorce rates have more than doubled in each of the following countries: Canada, England, France, Germany, and Sweden. The most notable exception is Japan, where divorce is still strongly discouraged. Japan's very low divorce rate is a consequence of it being a very group-oriented society, where nonconformity is greatly frowned upon. In addition, the media foster the belief that divorced women are a disgrace to their families. Finally, "because of wage discrimination against women in general, and older women in particular, it is difficult for divorced women to earn an adequate living" (see Soroka and Bryjak, *ibid.*, p. 61).

Strayed   (Have you ever had sex with someone other than you husband or wife while you were married?) No, Yes

Married   (Marital status) Married, Divorced (includes "divorced" and "separated")

Basic

1. Social class has been found to correlate strongly with divorce. State a hypothesis on the relationship between these two variables (would poorer individuals be more—or less—likely to be divorced?). Defend your hypothesis (what's going on in the world that would encourage individuals from one end of the social class spectrum to have a greater likelihood to divorce?). If possible, cite your class notes and textbook in support of your interpretation.

    Prediction and defense of it:

2. Check to see if your prediction was correct by crosstabulating Married (Y) by FamInc (X); also examine the relationship graphically (after doing the **CrossTab**, select the **Line** alternative for the **Plot** option under the **Table** command and highlight the "Divorced" category). What did you find? Was your prediction realized? Or, were you wrong? If you were wrong, why do you think the relationship comes out the way that it actually does? (*Focus your answer on the "**Divorced**" row throughout this section.*)

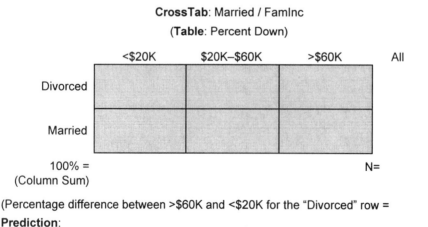

CrossTab: Married / FamInc
(**Table**: Percent Down)

(Percentage difference between >$60K and <$20K for the "Divorced" row =   )
Prediction:

Finding:

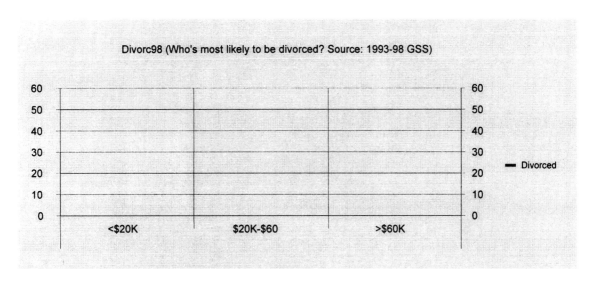

Divorc98 (Who's most likely to be divorced? Source: 1993-98 GSS)

Answer/Discussion

3. Do you think that a highly educated man (16 or more years of schooling) or a highly educated woman would be most likely to be divorced? Why? If possible, cite your class notes and textbook in support of your interpretation.

    Prediction and defense of it:

4. See if the data verify your thinking by crosstabulating Married (Y) by Ed (X), then control for Sex (Z). What did you find? Was your prediction realized? Or, were you wrong? If you were wrong, why do you think the data come out the way that they actually do?

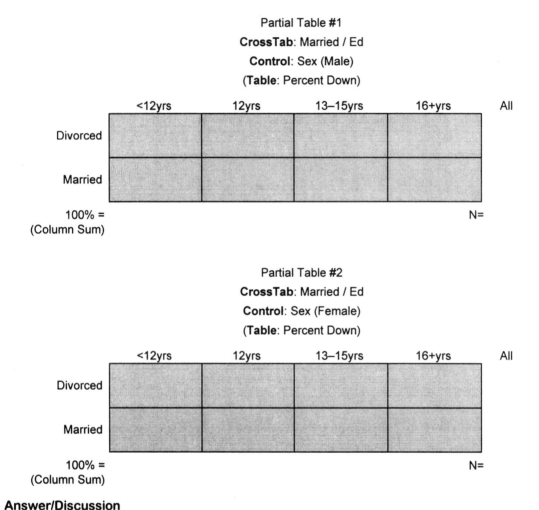

Partial Table #1

CrossTab: Married / Ed

Control: Sex (Male)

(**Table**: Percent Down)

Partial Table #2

CrossTab: Married / Ed

Control: Sex (Female)

(**Table**: Percent Down)

Answer/Discussion

5. Since 1960, African Americans have had a divorce rate almost double that of whites. This correlation (between race and divorce) has been explained, in part, by higher rates of African-American teenage and premarital pregnancies. Women whose first birth is out-of-wedlock are more likely to separate than those whose initial birth is after marriage. Another explanation points to the disproportionate number of African Americans who are poor: The frustration and tension resulting from a chronic shortage of money places a tremendous strain on individuals and often leads to divorce.[3] The relationship between

[3]Soroka and Bryjak, *op. cit.*, p. 65.

race, income, and divorce can be sketched as follows: Race→Income→Divorce. Let's examine this model empirically:

(a) Verify that African Americans have a greater likelihood of experiencing divorce by crosstabulating Married (Y) by Race (X). What did you find?

CrossTab: Married / Race

(**Table**: Percent Down)

	White	Black	Asian	Other	All
Divorced					
Married					

100% =   N=
(Column Sum)

(Percentage difference between Black and White for the "Divorced" row =   )

Prediction:

Finding:

(b) Verify that African Americans have a greater likelihood of being poor by crosstabulating FamInc (Y) by Race (X). What did you find? (*Concentrate your answer on the ">$60K" row.*)

CrossTab: FamInc / Race

(**Table**: Percent Down)

	White	Black	Asian	Other	All
>$60K					
$20–$60K					
<$20K					

100% =   N=
(Column Sum)

(Percentage difference between Black and White for the ">$60K" row =   )
Prediction:

Finding:

(c) Put on your thinking cap: Analytically, the model diagrammed above reads: "A change in X (race) produces a change in Z (family income), which, in turn, produces a change in Y (divorce)." One implication of such an analytical scheme is that X and Y will be correlated (as we have just seen in part [a]). But there is a more critical implication that you must be able to recognize: if this X–Z–Y model is true, then what will happen to the relationship between X and Y when we control for Z?

6. Verify your answer in (c) above by crosstabulating Married (Y) by Race (X), and then control for FamInc (Z). What did you find? (*Hint*: Compare your original percentage-difference in crosstabulation [5a] above to the average of the percentage-differences you found in the three partial tables below. What happened? Is this what we expected to happen?)

Partial Table #1

CrossTab: Married / Race

Control: FamInc (<$20K)

(**Table**: Percent Down)

	White	Black	Asian	Other	All
Divorced					
Married					

100% =   N=
(Column Sum)

(Percentage difference between Black and White for the "Divorced" row =   )

Partial Table #2

CrossTab: Married / Race

Control: FamInc ($20K–$60K)

(**Table**: Percent Down)

	White	Black	Asian	Other	All
Divorced					
Married					

100% =   N=
(Column Sum)

(Percentage difference between Black and White for the "Divorced" row =   )

Partial Table #3

CrossTab: Married / Race

Control: FamInc (>$60K)

(**Table**: Percent Down)

	White	Black	Asian	Other	All
Divorced					
Married					

100% =   N=

(Column Sum)

(Percentage difference between Black and White for the "Divorced" row =   )

Answer/Discussion

7. According to the "control" theory of deviance explored in Chapter 7, individuals with strong attachments to conventional groups (e.g., family; church) will be less likely to engage in behavior that deviates from idealized societal norms. Thus, for example, an individual who goes to church often and has many friends or family members there will be less likely to break up his or her marriage because (a) the loss of face or embarrassment he or she would feel (doing something so contrary to what a "religious" man or women would do); and, (b) fellow church members offer emotional, social, and/or financial support during times of distress (such as experienced by those having trouble in their marriages). Does the CHIP data file *Divorc98* offer any empirical support of control theory? To answer this question, crosstabulate Married (Y) by Attend (X); also examine the relationship graphically (after doing the **CrossTab**, select the **Line** alternative for the **Plot** option under the **Table** command and highlight the "Divorced" category).

CrossTab: Married / Attend
(**Table**: Percent Down)

	Never	Yearly	Monthly	Weekly	All
Divorced					
Married					

100% =
(Column Sum)   N=

(Percentage difference between Weekly and Never for the "Divorced" row =   )

Prediction:

Finding:

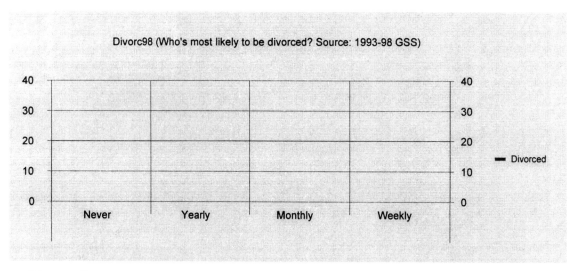

Divorc98 (Who's most likely to be divorced? Source: 1993-98 GSS)

Answer/Discussion

8. State a hypothesis on the relationship between "Strayed" and "Married" (would those individuals admitting having strayed from marital vows be more—or less—likely to be divorced?). Defend your hypothesis (what's going on in the world that would encourage individuals who answered the "have-you-ever-strayed?" question one way, versus the other, to have a greater likelihood to report being divorced?).

Prediction and defense of it:

9. Check to see if your prediction was correct by crosstabulating Married (Y) by Strayed (X). What did you find?

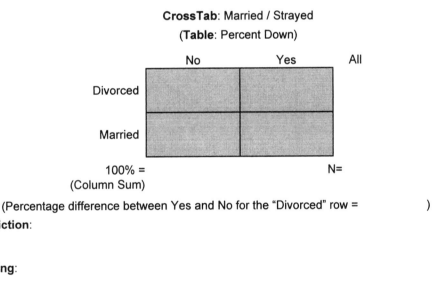

CrossTab: Married / Strayed
(**Table**: Percent Down)

(Percentage difference between Yes and No for the "Divorced" row =   )

Prediction:

Finding:

Answer/Discussion

Suggestions for Further Study

Jerri Schneider Shevlin observes that wife abuse is positively correlated with the odds of a family being broken apart by divorce or separation. She also observes that such abuse is both poorly measured and poorly understood, even though it is pervasive in contemporary American society. She notes that many local and state governments are trying to improve upon their measurements and responses to the problem. In "Wife Abuse: Its Magnitude and One Jurisdiction's Response" (pp. 305–323 in Gregg Lee Carter (ed.), *Perspectives on Current Social Problems* [Boston: Allyn & Bacon, 1997]), she closely examines one such effort, in Fairfax, Virginia. She finds that its newly implemented pro-arrest and pro-prosecution policies have resulted in increased charges and convictions for spousal assaults. But, it remains to be proven if they will reduce male assaults on their female intimate partners.

In another essay in *Perspectives on Current Social Problems* ("Single-Parent Families, Blended Families, and the Academic Achievement of Adolescents," pp. 325–336), Michael Fraleigh demonstrates one risk incurred by children when their families break apart: poorer academic performance. Fraleigh argues that single-parent families are not pathological, but nonetheless are more likely to face challenges that make successful parenting more difficult, often including a scarcity of parental resources such as time, money, and the emotional strength to deal with psychological stress. With the continuing trend toward single-parent families that is expected well into the 21st century, the academic achievement of poor adolescents will undoubtedly grow as a social problem.

Relevant World Wide Web Sites

The General Social Survey contains many items relevant to individual attitudes and behaviors regarding divorce, family violence, adultery, and family relationships (www.icpsr.umich.edu/gss); also see the other public opinion data repositories cited at the end of Chapter 1.

The federal government maintains a host of on-line reports and data files on divorce and its effects. Most importantly, see the web sites of the Administration for Children and Families (www.acf.dhhs.gov/), the National Center for Health Statistics (www.cdc.gov/nchs), and the Census Bureau (www.census.gov). International data and reports can be found at the United Nations Commission on the Status of Women (www.un.org/womenwatch/daw/csw). Two other important sites containing a large number of reports and relevant data on the family, including divorce, include:

Penn State University "Family Relations" web site	www.personal.psu.edu/faculty/n/x/nxd10/family3.htm
Online Concepts' "Divorce Central"	www.divorcecentral.com

Exploratory

I. Using any of the CHIP data files for this or the preceding two chapters (*Aging95, Arrested, Div72_98*, or *Divorc98*), state a hypothesis relating an X and a Y variable that have not already been analyzed together.

II. Sketch the bivariate model.

III. Give a brief interpretation of your hypothesis—that is, describe what is going on in the world such that we would expect to find data patterned in the way in which you have predicted.

IV. (a) Test your hypothesis with a **CrossTab**, putting your Y variable on the rows. Was your hypothesis confirmed? (Note: you may need to delete one or two rows and/or one or two columns; the following 4x4 table shell is simply a starting point.)

Original Table

CrossTab: _____(Y) /_____ (X)

(**Table**: Percent Down)

All

100% =   N=
(Column Sum)

(Percentage difference between the highest and lowest values of X on the highest value of Y =   )

Prediction:

Finding:

(b) Use **Plot** under the **Table** option to display the above relationship graphically. Feel free to be creative—trying out each of the plot types (line, bar, pie, stacked). Print out and attach the plot that you think best captures the relationship between your X and Y.

> **Do *either* parts V–VIII *or* parts IX–XII below.**

V. Perhaps the relationship you uncovered in #IV is spurious; that is, perhaps a third variable is predictive of both X and Y; if this is so, then the relationship between X and Y would exist **not** because X is causing Y, but simply because of their covariation with this third variable. If this third variable is held constant, then the relationship between X and Y will weaken greatly or disappear. Choose a third variable that might possibly be generating a spurious relationship between X and Y. Sketch the model showing the relationship between this third variable and X, and between this third variable and Y, as well as the lack of causal relationship between X and Y. Hint: refer back to the discussion on page 25 in the introductory chapter entitled "Elementary Data Analysis Needed to Study Social Issues."

VI. A good social scientist does not choose just any variable to test for spuriosity. Just as you were able to defend the hypothesized relationship between X and Y in #III, develop a brief interpretation to defend the hypothesized relationship between Z and X, then between Z and Y.

(a) Interpretation of the Z–X relationship:

(b) Interpretation of the Z–Y relationship:

VII. Test the alternative model sketched in #V by crosstabbing Y by X and controlling for Z—using the appended table shells.

VIII. What are your conclusions? For example, is the original X–Y relationship spurious? Is it nonspurious (i.e., causal)? Is a multivariable model evident?

IX. Examining all the variables in your data set, which one do you think might be serving as a causal mechanism connecting your X with your Y? In other words, which variable would you choose as "Z" in the following sketch: X→Z→Y? Hint: refer back to the discussion on page 26 in the introductory chapter entitled "Elementary Data Analysis Tools Needed to Study Social Issues."

X. A good social scientist does not choose just any variable to test as a causal mechanism (intervening variable). Just as you were able to defend the hypothesized relationship between X and Y in #III, develop a brief interpretation to defend the hypothesized relationship between X and Z, then between Z and Y.

(a) Interpretation of the X–Z relationship:

(b) Interpretation of the Z–Y relationship:

XI. Test the alternative model sketched in #IX by crosstabbing X and Y and controlling for Z—using the appended table shells. (Note: you may need more than the four partial tables provided; of course, you will need one partial table for each value of Z.)

XII. What are your conclusions? Most importantly, do your findings support the notion that your Z is acting as an intervening variable (causal mechanism) connecting your X and your Y?

Use the following 4x4 table shells to record your findings from *either* VII *or* XI above. Note: you may need fewer partial tables; you will need one partial table for each value of Z. Also, you may need to delete 1 or 2 rows and/or 1 or 2 columns. The appended shells simply provide you with a starting point.

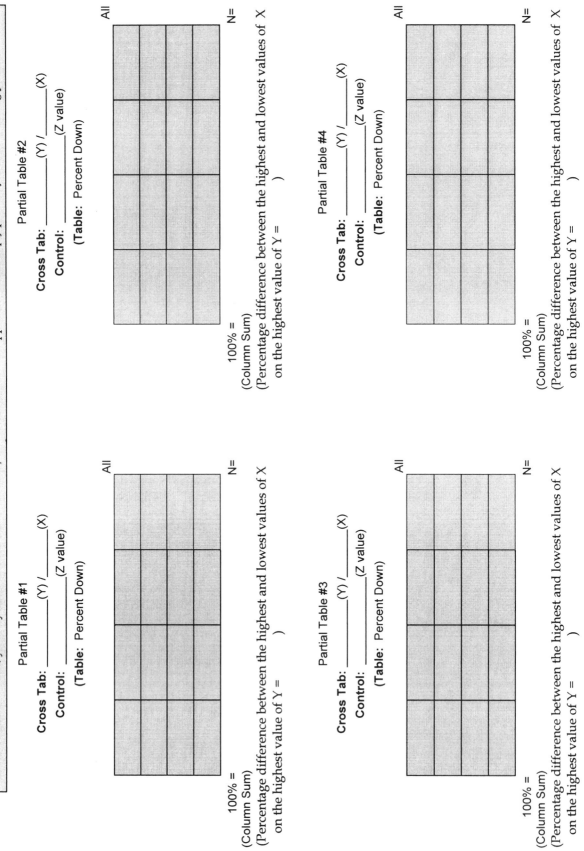

Partial Table #1

Cross Tab: _____ (Y) / _____ (X)

Control: _____ (Z value)

(**Table:** Percent Down)

                                                              All

                                                              N=

100% =
(Column Sum)
(Percentage difference between the highest and lowest values of X
on the highest value of Y =   )

Partial Table #2

Cross Tab: _____ (Y) / _____ (X)

Control: _____ (Z value)

(**Table:** Percent Down)

                                                              All

                                                              N=

100% =
(Column Sum)
(Percentage difference between the highest and lowest values of X
on the highest value of Y =   )

Partial Table #3

Cross Tab: _____ (Y) / _____ (X)

Control: _____ (Z value)

(**Table:** Percent Down)

                                                              All

                                                              N=

100% =
(Column Sum)
(Percentage difference between the highest and lowest values of X
on the highest value of Y =   )

Partial Table #4

Cross Tab: _____ (Y) / _____ (X)

Control: _____ (Z value)

(**Table:** Percent Down)

                                                              All

                                                              N=

100% =
(Column Sum)
(Percentage difference between the highest and lowest values of X
on the highest value of Y =   )

Chapter 9. Health Issues

Social Class and Health

Without even examining the data, we might assume that prosperity and health would be inversely correlated. The social and environmental context of the lives of low-income individuals make them more susceptible to illness and disease: "They live under less sanitary conditions, have less nutritious diets, and are less likely to take preventative health actions such as obtaining routine physical examinations." Poor women are less likely to have prenatal checkups and more likely to have poor diets; the result is an increased probability of having low birth-weight infants, who are at a greater risk of dying or surviving with mental or physical imperfections. Moreover, "despite the considerable advances brought about by Medicare and Medicaid, many poor people are not covered by these programs, and some health care still depends on out-of-pocket costs, which the poor usually cannot afford. Finally, the care that poorer individuals receive is more likely to be of a lower quality: They are more likely to be treated in a hospital outpatient clinic or emergency room, where the continuity of care, follow-up treatment, and patient education are less common than in a physician's office[1].

The CHIP exercises below allow you to explore the relationship between socioeconomic location in society and health status.

File: **Health95** (Quality of social ties and health/happiness; *source:* 1991–1994 GSS)

Info: Race→Sex→Age→Married→ Ed→FamInc→SatFF→Health→Happy
    (2)   (2)   (3)   (4)   (4)   (3)   (3)   (3)   (3)

Race	White, Black
Sex	Male, Female
Age	18–39, 40–64, 65+
Married	Never Married, Div/Sep, Widowed, Married
Ed	(Years of schooling) <12yrs, 12yrs, 13–15yrs, 16+yrs
FamInc	(Family Income) <$20K, $20K–$50K, $50K+
SatFF	*(Satisfaction with family life and friends.* Sum of A and B, where: A= "How much satisfaction do you get from your family life": 6=very great, 5=great, 4=quite a lot, 3=fair, 2=some, 1=little, 0=none; B= "How much satisfaction do you get from your friendships": 6=very great, 5=great, 4=quite a lot, 3=fair, 2=some, 1=little, 0=none) So-so (0–9), Good (10–11), Excellent (12)
Health	("Would you say your own health, in general, is . . .") Poor/Fair, Good, Excellent
Happy	("Taken all together, how would you say things are these days; would you say that you are very happy, pretty happy, not too happy?") Not Too Happy, Pretty Happy, Very Happy

Basic

1. Are poorer people, compared to their more prosperous counterparts, more likely to report being in poor health? Answer this question by crosstabulating Health (Y) by FamInc (X); also examine the relationship

---

[1]Thomas J. Sullivan, *Introduction to Social Problems,* 5th ed. (Boston: Allyn & Bacon, 2000), pp. 123–124. Compare: Daniel J. Curran and Claire M. Renzetti, *Social Problems: Society in Crisis,* 5th ed. (Boston: Allyn & Bacon, 2000), pp. 335–337; D. Stanley Eitzen and Maxine Baca Zinn, *Social Problems,* 8th ed. (Boston: Allyn & Bacon, 2000), pp. 412–417; Michael P. Soroka and George J. Bryjak, *Social Problems: A World at Risk* 2nd ed. (Boston: Allyn & Bacon, 1999), pp. 141–143; and Vincent N. Parrillo, John Stimson, and Ardyth Stimson, *Contemporary Social Problems* 4th ed. (Boston: Allyn & Bacon, 1999), p. 379.

graphically (after doing the **CrossTab**, select the **Line** alternative for the **Plot** option under the **Table** command and highlight the "Poor/Fair" category). What did you find? (*Focus your comments on the "Poor/Fair" column for all questions in this section.*)

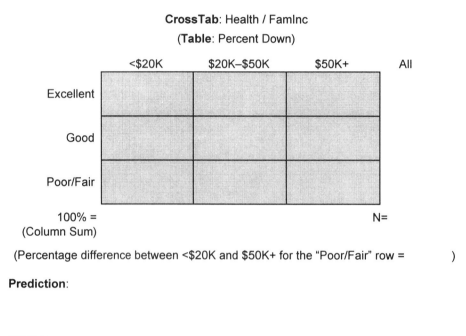

CrossTab: Health / FamInc

(**Table**: Percent Down)

(Percentage difference between <$20K and $50K+ for the "Poor/Fair" row =   )

Prediction:

Finding:

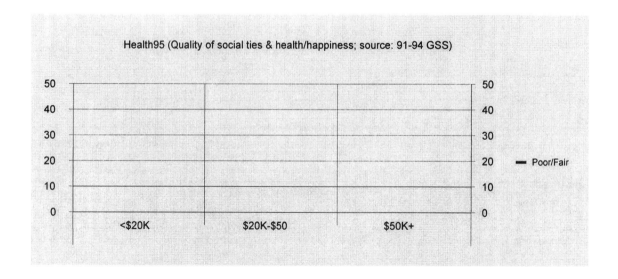

2.   African Americans have higher death rates, shorter life expectancies, and more serious life-threatening

health conditions — such as high blood pressure and diabetes — than do whites.[2] As is common knowledge, and as we discovered in Chapter 4 in this workbook, race and social class are strongly correlated in the United States. Are African Americans more likely to report being in poor health than are whites? Answer this question by crosstabulating Health (Y) by Race (X). What did you find?

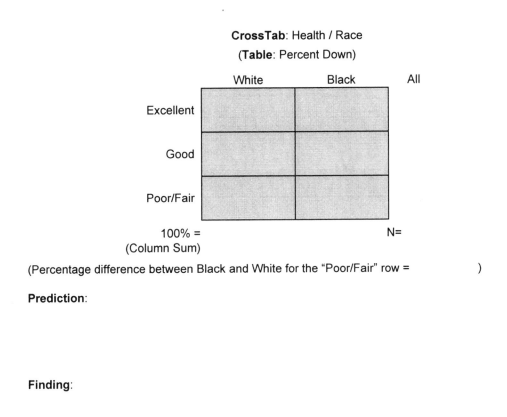

CrossTab: Health / Race
(**Table**: Percent Down)

(Percentage difference between Black and White for the "Poor/Fair" row =   )

Prediction:

Finding:

3. The relationship between race, income, and health implied in #2 can be sketched as follows: Race→ FamInc→Health. Let's examine this model empirically:

   (a) We have already verified that income and health are positively related (in #1), and that African Americans have a greater likelihood of experiencing poor health (in #2). Now verify that race and income are correlated by crosstabulating FamInc (Y) by Race (X). What did you find?

---

[2]Sullivan, p. 125. Compare: Curran and Renzetti, pp. 334–335, and Eitzen and Baca Zinn, pp. 417–421.

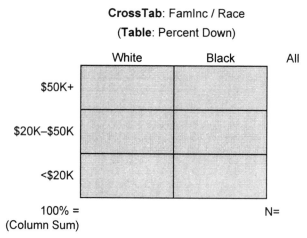

CrossTab: FamInc / Race

(**Table**: Percent Down)

(Percentage difference between Black and White for the "$50K+" row =   )

Prediction:

Finding:

(b) Put on your thinking cap: Analytically, the model diagrammed above reads: "A change in X (race) produces a change in Z (family income), which, in turn, produces a change in Y (health). One implication of such an analytical scheme is that X and Y will be correlated (as we saw in #2). If this X–Z–Y model is true, then what will happen to the relationship between X and Y when we control for Z?

4. Verify your answer in (b) above by crosstabulating Health (Y) by Race (X), and then control for FamInc (Z). What did you find? (*Hint*: Compare your original percentage-difference in crosstabulation [2] above to the average of the percentage-differences you found in the three partial tables below. What happened? Is this what we expected to happen?)

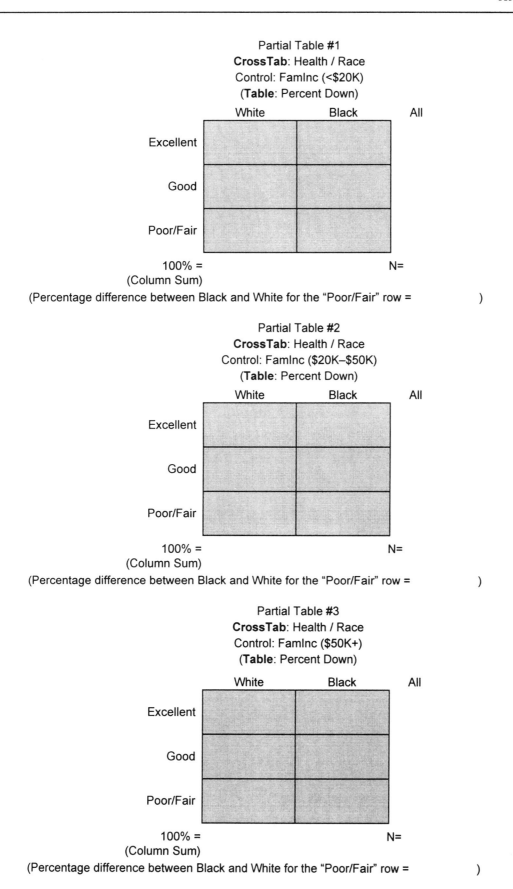

Partial Table #1
CrossTab: Health / Race
Control: FamInc (<$20K)
(**Table**: Percent Down)

	White	Black	All
Excellent			
Good			
Poor/Fair			

100% =   N=
(Column Sum)

(Percentage difference between Black and White for the "Poor/Fair" row =   )

Partial Table #2
CrossTab: Health / Race
Control: FamInc ($20K–$50K)
(**Table**: Percent Down)

	White	Black	All
Excellent			
Good			
Poor/Fair			

100% =   N=
(Column Sum)

(Percentage difference between Black and White for the "Poor/Fair" row =   )

Partial Table #3
CrossTab: Health / Race
Control: FamInc ($50K+)
(**Table**: Percent Down)

	White	Black	All
Excellent			
Good			
Poor/Fair			

100% =   N=
(Column Sum)

(Percentage difference between Black and White for the "Poor/Fair" row =   )

Answer/Discussion

5. Does the relationship between FamInc and Health hold up fairly well across the ages? Answer this question by crosstabulating Health (Y) by FamInc (X) and then control for Age (Z). What did you find?

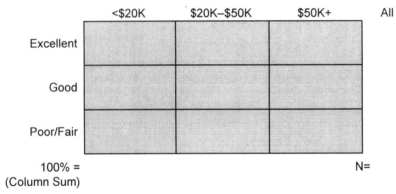

Partial Table #1
CrossTab: Health / FamInc
Control: Age (18–39)
(**Table**: Percent Down)

(Percentage difference between <$20K and $50K+ for the "Poor/Fair" row =   )

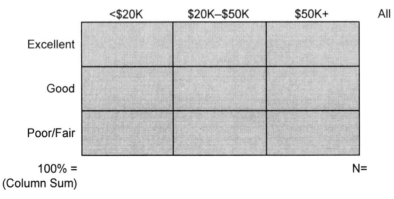

Partial Table #2
CrossTab: Health / FamInc
Control: Age (40–64)
(**Table**: Percent Down)

(Percentage difference between <$20K and $50K+ for the "Poor/Fair" row =   )

Partial Table #3
CrossTab: Health / FamInc
Control: Age (65+)
(**Table**: Percent Down)

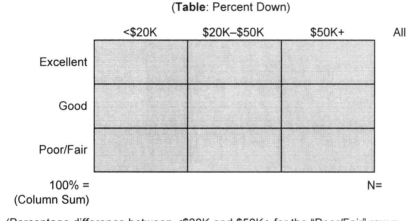

100% =
(Column Sum)   N=

(Percentage difference between <$20K and $50K+ for the "Poor/Fair" row =   )

Answer/Discussion

6. Does the relationship between FamInc and Health hold up fairly well across the races? Answer this question by crosstabulating Health by FamInc (X) and then control for Race (Z). What did you find?

Partial Table #1
CrossTab: Health / FamInc
Control: Race (White)
(**Table**: Percent Down)

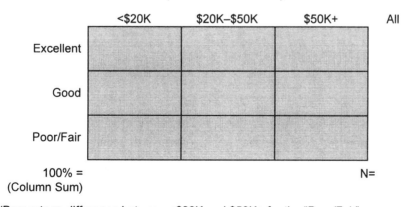

100% =
(Column Sum)   N=

(Percentage difference between <$20K and $50K+ for the "Poor/Fair" row =   )

Partial Table #2
CrossTab: Health / FamInc
Control: Race (Black)
(**Table**: Percent Down)

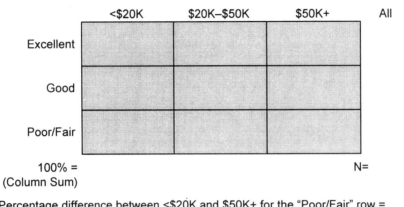

	<$20K	$20K–$50K	$50K+	All
Excellent				
Good				
Poor/Fair				

100% =
(Column Sum)   N=

(Percentage difference between <$20K and $50K+ for the "Poor/Fair" row =   )

Answer/Discussion

7. Does the relationship between FamInc and Health hold up fairly well across the sexes? Answer this question by crosstabulating Health (Y) by FamInc (X) and then control for Sex (Z). What did you find?

Partial Table #1
CrossTab: Health / FamInc
Control: Sex (Male)
(**Table**: Percent Down)

	<$20K	$20K–$50K	$50K+	All
Excellent				
Good				
Poor/Fair				

100% =
(Column Sum)   N=

(Percentage difference between <$20K and $50K+ for the "Poor/Fair" row =   )

Partial Table #2
CrossTab: Health / FamInc
Control: Sex (Female)
(**Table**: Percent Down)

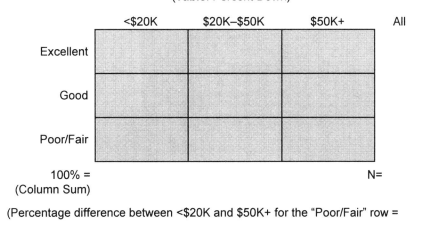

	<$20K	$20K–$50K	$50K+	All
Excellent				
Good				
Poor/Fair				

100% =
(Column Sum)   N=

(Percentage difference between <$20K and $50K+ for the "Poor/Fair" row =   )

Answer/Discussion

8. Consider your findings in #1 and in #s 5–7. What is your fundamental conclusion concerning the relationship between income and health?

Advanced

9. Examine the partial tables in #5. Is a multivariable model evident? That is, do both FamInc and Age have independent effects on Health? Refer to the correct percentage differences in defense of your answer.

10. Examine the partial tables in #6. Is a multivariable model evident? That is, do both FamInc and Race have independent effects on Health? Refer to the correct percentage differences in defense of your answer.

AIDS— A Crossnational Examination

AIDS (acquired immune deficiency syndrome) is a communicable disease contracted by one individual from another either directly through sexual activity or indirectly by contact with infected blood (usually through a transfusion or intravenous drug use). Pregnant women who are infected can also transmit the disease to their babies. Unless they have access to a variety of expensive and high-tech drugs (usually reserved for individuals residing in wealthy nations such as the United States), people suffering AIDS typically die within a few years of the onset of symptoms (e.g., pneumonia, tuberculosis, or Kaposi's sarcoma), and the mortality rate in developing nations is almost 100 percent.[3]

The precursor to AIDS is the HIV virus. As of the summer of 1999, in the U.S., there were approximately 384,000 confirmed cases of full-blown AIDS, and about 47,000 new cases appearing each year (down from a rate of 70,000 cases per year in the early 1990s). Although both the incidence rate (number of new cases each year) and the death rate for AIDS have been declining since 1996 in the United States, the situation is dramatically different for the world as a whole, where two-thirds of all countries have a per capita GNP under $3,000, and half under $2,000 (note that the combination drug therapies used in the U.S. and other developed nations of the world have a per-patient cost of $12,000 per year). Worldwide, there were about some 42 million cases of HIV/AIDS, with 5.8 million new cases each year (more than 16,000 per day) — and this incidence rate is predicted to rise steadily for decades. Some 1,600 babies are infected each day (either at birth or from breast-feeding).[4] In the U.S., the most common transmission pattern has been via male homosexual contact (accounting for 54% of all cases) and illegal intravenous drug use (26% of all cases).[5] However, in developing countries, AIDS is spreading rapidly through heterosexual intercourse, with initial outbreaks in an area often propelled forward by truck drivers who have come in contact with prostitutes (especially in sub-Saharan Africa and India[6]).

As is the case at the individual level of analysis (see preceding section), prosperity and the ability to deal with disease are strongly correlated. Developing nations lack the economic, public health, and medical-care resources to fight the spread of the HIV virus and AIDS. Moreover, the cultures of many developing nations aggravate the situation. For example, in the developing countries of Africa, AIDS infection among women has skyrocketed and heterosexual contact is the key means of transmission. "Long-standing traditions have made women completely subordinate to men, so that they have no say in their marital sexual relations. In Africa, husbands infected by prostitutes or through casual extramarital sex have spread AIDS to their wives and children, causing millions of children and monogamous married women to come down with the disease. Inasmuch as they are completely dependent on their husbands for financial support, women who fear infections nonetheless cannot refuse their husbands sex, out of fear of being abandoned or punished for not fulfilling their marital obligations. In this case, the women's low social status is literally killing them."[7]

Developed countries must take much more than a casual interest in the spread of AIDS in the Third World. On every continent, millions of migrant laborers wash across boundaries like tidal waves. Today's workers flee poverty in their homelands. The increasing interconnectedness of economies and peoples means that we

---

[3]Soroka and Bryjak, p. 128; also see Curran and Renzetti, pp. 335–337.

[4]U.S. figures taken from *HIV/AIDS Surveillance Report*, vol. 11, #1 (Atlanta: Centers for Disease Control, December, 1999); world data are from the CDC's publication "CDC's International Activities Support Global HIV Prevention Efforts" (November, 1999), and the *Report on the Global HIV/AIDS Epidemic* (NY: United Nations, June 1998). These documents, and many others related to HIV/AIDS, are most readily obtained at the CDC's web site: www.cdc.gov.

[5]However, dynamic growth in AIDS prevalence is being fueled by contact and by low-income African Americans and Latinos. African Americans make up 12% of the U.S. population, but 37% of all AIDS cases; Latinos represent 13% of the population (including Puerto Rico), but 20% of the AIDS cases; see the CDC reports "HIV/AIDS Among African Americans" (August, 1999), and "HIV/AIDS Among Hispanics in the United States" (August, 1999).

[6]Soroka and Bryjak, p. 129.

[7]Soroka and Bryjak, p. 131.

can no longer fence out problems. Indeed, North America's experience with migration from Mexico and Central American shows that quotas and boundary checks are ineffective dams to the flow of motivated migrants.[8]

The CHIP exercises below allow you to become familiar with the distribution of AIDS in both developed and developing countries, and with the kinds of social, economic, and political variables that are correlated with the prevalence of the disease.

File: **AIDS98** (Crossnational data on AIDS prevalence, 1998)[9]

Region→Muslims→Freedom→Farmers→Literate→GNP→Doctors→Calories→AIDS→InfDeath→LifeExp
  (6)   (3)   (3)   (3)   (3)   (3)   (3)   (3)   (3)   (3)   (3)

(Note: all variables, except Region, Muslims, and Freedom, are divided into three categories: bottom, middle, and top third.)

Region	(United Nations regional designation) Industrial, East-Europe, Africa-SubSaharan, Arab, Asia, Latin-America
Muslims	(Percentage of population that is Muslim) 0% (less than 0.5%), 1%–25%, >25%
Freedom	(Type of political regime) Not Free, Partly Free, Free
Farmers	(Percentage of the workforce in agriculture) <12%, 12–39%, >40%+
Literate	(% of pop. literate) <85%, 85–97%, >97%
GNP	(Per capita GNP in 1997 U.S. dollars) <$1,160; $1,160–$3,900; >$3,900
Doctors	(Number of M.D.s per 100,000 population) <85, 85–245, >245
Calories	(Average calories consumed per day) <2,500; 2,500–3,000; >3,000
AIDS	(Number of AIDS cases per 100,000 population) <2, 2–30, >30
InfDeath	(Infant deaths per 1,000 births) <14, 14–42, >42
LifeExp	(Life Expectancy) <66.7yrs, 66.7–72.5yrs, >72.5yrs

Country	Muslims	Freedom	Farmers	Literate	GNP	Doctors	Calories	AIDS	InfDeath	LifeExp
Albania	70	Partly	49.5	93.0	360	141	2,523	0.3	33.2	72.5
Algeria	99	Not Free	22.0	61.6	1,690	83	3,020	1.1	55.0	67.3
Angola	0	Not Free	85.0	42.0	260	13	1,983	11.2	137.0	46.0
Argentina	0	Free	12.0	96.2	8,060	268	3,136	29.9	22.9	72.1
Armenia	0	Partly	38.0	99.0	670	312	2,147	0.2	15.1	71.2
Australia	0	Free	5.0	100.0	17,980	245	3,001	40.5	5.8	78.0
Austria	0	Free	8.1	99.0	24,950	327	3,343	21.7	5.5	76.6
Azerbaijan	93	Partly	32.0	97.0	500	390	2,139	0.1	25.2	70.5
Bahamas	0	Free	5.0	98.2	11,790	141	2,443	891.3	23.8	71.8
Bahrain	100	Not Free	1.0	85.2	7,500	11	3,054	6.4	19.4	73.2
Barbados	0	Free	10.0	97.4	6,530	113	3,207	290.8	9.1	75.5
Belarus	5	Not Free	19.0	98.0	2,160	379	3,101	0.2	12.9	69.3
Belgium	0	Free	2.6	99.0	22,920	365	3,543	23.7	7.6	76.5
Belize	0	Free	30.0	70.3	2,550	47	2,862	88.4	34.0	72.1
Brazil	0	Partly	31.0	83.3	3,370	134	2,938	69.4	58.0	66.4

---

[8]See Robert Searles Walker, *AIDS: Today, Tomorrow* (Atlantic Heights, NJ: Humanities Press International, 1991), p. 167.

[9]*Sources*: Central Intelligence Agency, *The World Factbook 1999* (Dulles, VA.: Brassey's Inc., 1999); Robert L. Bartley (ed.), *Freedom in the World: The Annual Survey of Political Rights and Civil Liberties, 1998-1999* (Piscataway, NJ: Transaction Publishers, 1999); and *Human Development Report 1999* (NY: Oxford University Press, 1999).

Country	Muslims	Freedom	Farmers	Literate	GNP	Doctors	Calories	AIDS	InfDeath	LifeExp
Bulgaria	13	Free	18.0	98.0	1,160	333	2,756	0.6	15.5	71.4
Cameroon	16	Not Free	74.4	63.4	680	7	2,175	69.1	65.0	56.0
Canada	0	Free	3.0	97.0	19,570	221	3,056	50.4	6.2	77.8
Cen. Afr. Rep	15	Partly	85.0	60.0	370	6	1,938	205.4	97.0	49.4
Chile	0	Free	19.2	95.2	3,560	108	2,810	13.4	13.1	72.1
Colombia	0	Partly	30.0	91.3	1,620	105	2,800	21.5	28.0	69.4
Comoros	86	Partly	80.0	57.3	510	10	1,824	2.8	80.0	57.8
Costa Rica	0	Free	21.6	94.8	2,380	126	2,822	32.8	13.0	76.3
Cuba	0	Not Free	20.0	95.7	2,000	518	2,357	5.4	9.4	74.8
Denmark	0	Free	5.0	99.0	28,110	283	3,808	40.1	5.4	75.2
Dominic. Rep.	0	Free	50.0	82.1	1,320	77	2,316	48.7	51.5	68.4
Ecuador	0	Free	29.0	90.1	1,310	111	2,592	5.2	40.0	68.9
Egypt	94	Not Free	40.0	51.4	710	202	3,289	0.2	62.0	63.6
El Salvador	0	Free	40.0	71.5	1,480	91	2,515	34.1	41.0	67.8
Estonia	0	Free	11.0	100.0	2,820	312	3,004	1.2	14.5	69.9
Ethiopia	50	Partly	80.0	35.5	130	4	1,845	35.9	120.0	50.2
Fiji	8	Partly	67.0	91.6	2,320	38	3,038	1	19.0	63.2
Finland	0	Free	8.6	100.0	18,850	269	2,916	5.2	4.7	76.6
France	1	Free	5.0	99.0	23,470	280	3,551	81	6.1	77.8
Georgia	11	Partly	25.0	99.0	580	436	2,184	0.4	18.3	72.6
Germany	2	Free	2.7	99.0	25,580	319	3,330	20.7	5.5	75.8
Ghana	30	Partly	61.0	64.5	430	4	2,560	102.1	66.0	56.0
Greece	1	Free	19.8	95.0	7,710	387	3,575	16.5	8.3	77.4
Guatemala	0	Partly	58.0	55.6	1,190	90	2,191	17.9	51.0	64.8
Guyana	9	Free	30.2	98.1	530	33	2,392	99.4	48.0	65.2
Haiti	0	Partly	66.0	45.0	220	16	1,855	67.2	74.0	56.6
Honduras	0	Free	37.0	72.7	580	22	2,368	107.1	50.0	68.2
Hungary	0	Free	8.3	99.0	3,840	337	3,402	2.8	11.5	69.7
Iceland	0	Free	5.1	100.0	24,590	230	3,104	15.7	3.4	78.8
Iraq	97	Not Free	30.0	58.0	1,940	51	2,252	0.5	67.0	65.8
Ireland	0	Free	10.0	98.0	13,630	167	3,636	17.1	5.9	76.3
Israel	15	Free	2.6	95.0	14,410	459	3,272	8.1	6.9	76.8
Italy	0	Free	7.0	97.0	19,270	292	3,504	71.5	8.3	77.2
Jamaica	0	Free	22.5	85.0	1,420	57	2,575	86.8	24.0	73.6
Japan	0	Free	6.0	99.0	34,630	177	2,905	1.2	4.2	79.8
Jordan	96	Partly	7.4	86.6	1,390	158	2,681	0.9	34.0	67.9
Kazakhstan	47	Not Free	23.0	98.0	1,110	360	3,007	0.1	27.4	68.6
Kenya	7	Not Free	80.0	78.1	260	15	1,971	263.1	62.0	50.5
Kyrgyzstan	75	Partly	40.0	97.0	610	310	2,489	0	29.1	68.3
Laos	0	Not Free	80.0	60.0	320	19	2,143	1.3	102.0	51.7
Latvia	0	Free	16.0	100.0	2,290	303	2,861	0.8	18.8	67.2
Lebanon	70	Not Free	7.0	86.4	3,350	191	3,279	3.1	28.0	75.2
Lithuania	0	Free	20.0	98.0	1,350	399	2,805	0.3	14.1	69.2
Luxembourg	0	Free	2.5	100.0	39,850	213	3,485	29.3	5.3	75.9
Malta	0	Free	2.0	88.0	7,970	250	3,417	11.6	9.1	76.7
Mauritania	100	Not Free	47.0	37.7	480	11	2,653	6.7	101.0	51.5
Mauritius	17	Free	14.0	82.9	3,180	85	2,952	3.8	18.1	69.3
Mexico	0	Partly	21.8	89.6	4,010	107	3,137	34.3	33.9	72.5
Moldova	0	Partly	40.2	96.0	870	356	2,562	0.4	22.6	67.9
Morocco	99	Partly	50.0	43.7	1,150	34	3,244	1.4	57.0	68.2
Mozambique	20	Partly	80.0	40.1	80	1	1,799	33.5	148.0	46.4
Namibia	0	Free	49.0	38.0	2,030	23	2,168	420.6	57.0	58.8

Country	Muslims	Freedom	Farmers	Literate	GNP	Doctors	Calories	AIDS	InfDeath	LifeExp
Nepal	3	Partly	81.0	27.5	200	5	2,339	0.8	98.0	54.7
Netherlands	3	Free	4.0	99.0	21,970	264	3,259	29.6	5.5	77.0
New Zealand	0	Free	9.8	99.0	13,190	210	3,405	17.1	7.0	75.8
Nicaragua	0	Free	31.0	65.7	330	82	2,328	3.6	49.0	65.0
Nigeria	50	Partly	54.0	57.1	280	21	2,609	14.4	87.0	56.3
Norway	0	Free	6.0	99.0	26,480	296	3,350	13.7	5.2	77.8
Pakistan	97	Partly	47.0	37.8	440	52	2,408	0.1	91.0	60.7
Panama	0	Free	26.8	90.8	2,670	119	2,556	52.5	17.7	72.9
Peru	0	Partly	17.0	88.7	1,890	73	2,310	24.5	60.0	66.0
Poland	0	Free	26.0	99.0	2,470	268	3,344	1.5	13.5	71.9
Portugal	0	Free	12.0	85.0	9,370	291	3,658	48	7.9	74.8
Romania	0	Free	36.4	97.0	1,230	176	2,943	22.8	23.9	69.7
Russia	50	Partly	20.0	98.0	2,650	380	2,720	0.2	17.5	64.8
Saudi Arabia	100	Not Free	5.0	62.8	7,240	166	2,735	1.7	24.0	69.9
Singapore	15	Partly	11.4	91.1	23,360	147	3,228	9.1	4.0	76.0
South Africa	2	Free	30.0	81.8	3,010	59	2,933	29.6	46.0	66.0
South Korea	0	Free	21.0	98.0	8,220	127	2,905	0.2	11.0	71.6
Spain	0	Free	8.0	96.0	13,280	400	3,295	123.3	7.2	77.2
Sri Lanka	8	Partly	37.0	90.2	640	23	2,263	0.4	18.4	72.5
Sudan	70	Not Free	80.0	46.1	290	10	2,391	5.9	80.0	54.3
Sweden	0	Free	3.2	99.0	23,630	299	3,160	17.6	4.4	78.2
Switzerland	0	Free	4.0	99.0	37,180	301	3,280	83.8	5.1	78.4
Syria	90	Not Free	40.0	70.8	1,120	109	3,339	0.3	44.0	66.1
Tajikistan	85	Not Free	52.0	98.0	350	210	2,129	0	47.0	68.3
Thailand	4	Free	54.0	93.8	2,210	24	2,334	101.1	34.5	70.0
Trin.& Tobago	6	Free	9.5	97.9	3,740	90	2,751	199.9	12.2	70.6
Tunisia	98	Not Free	22.0	66.7	1,800	67	3,250	3.6	43.0	67.8
Turkey	100	Partly	42.5	82.3	2,450	103	3,568	0.4	47.0	67.6
Ukraine	0	Partly	24.0	98.0	1,570	429	2,753	0.7	14.3	68.4
Un. Kingdom	2	Free	1.1	99.0	18,410	164	2,753	25.9	6.2	76.5
United States	0	Free	2.7	97.0	25,860	245	3,642	225.3	7.5	75.7
Uruguay	0	Free	11.0	97.3	4,650	309	2,830	28.7	20.1	72.6
Venezuela	0	Free	13.0	91.1	2,760	194	2,398	30.4	23.5	71.8
Vietnam	13	Not Free	65.0	93.7	190	135	2,502	1.3	42.0	65.2
Yemen	95	Partly	92.0	38.0	280	26	2,034	0.5	83.0	51.7
Yugoslavia*	30	Not Free	35.0	90.5	1,100	219	2,336	1.1	18.6	71.5
Zaire**	10	Not Free	65.0	77.3	110	1	1,815	80	108.0	47.6
Zimbabwe	1	Partly	74.0	85.0	490	14	2083	564.4	52.8	61.5

*Republic of Macedonia; **Republic of Congo

1. What kind of nation is most likely to suffer a high prevalence of AIDS (e.g, an Asian, high Muslim population, low GNP . . . with . . .)? Develop this profile by crosstabulating AIDS by each of the following:

> (a) Region
> (b) Muslims
> (c) Freedom
> (d) Literate
> (e) GNP
> (f) Doctors

(a) AIDS (Y) by Region (X):

CrossTab: AIDS / Region

(**Table**: Percent Down)

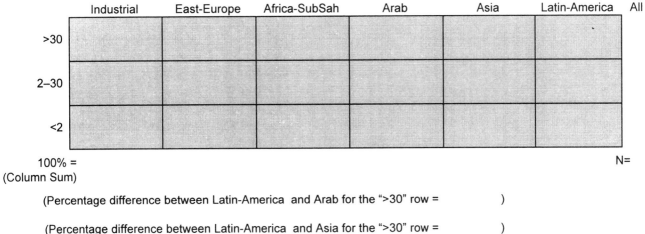

	Industrial	East-Europe	Africa-SubSah	Arab	Asia	Latin-America	All
>30							
2–30							
<2							

100% =
(Column Sum)   N=

(Percentage difference between Latin-America and Arab for the ">30" row =   )

(Percentage difference between Latin-America and Asia for the ">30" row =   )

Prediction:

Findings:

(b) AIDS (Y) by Muslims (X):

CrossTab: AIDS / Muslims

(**Table**: Percent Down)

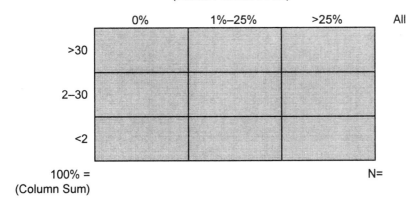

	0%	1%–25%	>25%	All
>30				
2–30				
<2				

100% =
(Column Sum)   N=

(Percentage difference between >25% and 0% for the ">30" row =   )

Prediction:

Finding:

(c) AIDS (Y) by Freedom (X):

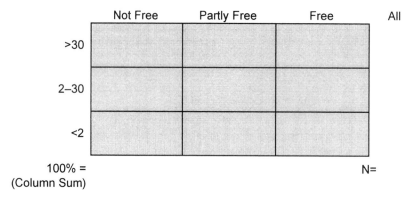

CrossTab: AIDS / Freedom
(**Table**: Percent Down)

	Not Free	Partly Free	Free	All
>30				
2–30				
<2				
100% = (Column Sum)				N=

(Percentage difference between Free and Not Free for the ">30" row =   )
Prediction:

Finding:

(d) AIDS (Y) by Literate (X):

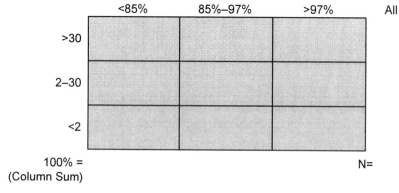

CrossTab: AIDS / Literate
(**Table**: Percent Down)

	<85%	85%–97%	>97%	All
>30				
2–30				
<2				
100% = (Column Sum)				N=

(Percentage difference between >97% and <85% for the ">30" row =   )
Prediction:

Finding:

(e) AIDS (Y) by GNP (X):

CrossTab: AIDS / GNP

(**Table**: Percent Down)

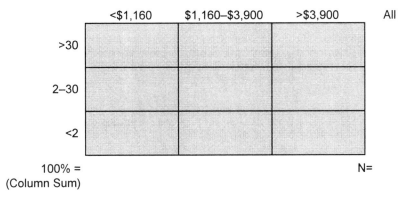

	<$1,160	$1,160–$3,900	>$3,900	All
>30				
2–30				
<2				
100% = (Column Sum)				N=

(Percentage difference >$3,900 and <$1,160 for the ">30" row =   )

(Percentage difference >$3,900 and <$1,160 for the "<2" row =   )

Prediction:

Findings:

(f) AIDS (Y) by Doctors (X):

CrossTab: AIDS / Doctors

(**Table**: Percent Down)

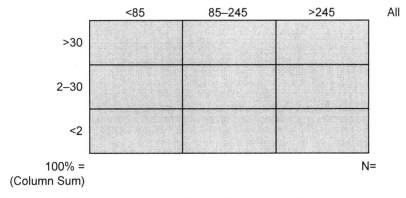

	<85	85–245	>245	All
>30				
2–30				
<2				
100% = (Column Sum)				N=

(Percentage difference between >245 and <85 for the ">30" row =   )

Prediction:

Finding:

Write your profile below (it must contain six characteristics); "the typical nation having a high AIDS prevalence is . . . . ."):

2. Based on your reading, class discussion, and/or your own intuition:

   (a) why do you think *Region* is related to *AIDS* in the way in which it is?

   (b) why do you think *Muslims* is related to *AIDS* in the way in which it is?

(c) why do you think *Freedom* is related to *AIDS* in the way in which it is?

(d) why do you think *Literate* is related to *AIDS* in the way in which it is?

(e) why do you think *GNP* is related to *AIDS* in the way in which it is?

(f) why do you think *Doctors* is related to *AIDS* in the way in which it is?

Suggestions for Further Study

Sam Mirmirani observes that the United States healthcare industry has witnessed major changes in its focus and structure since World War II. National policies have alternated demand and supply sides of the market to improve the health status of the nation and control rising costs. Still serious problems of cost, inflation, inefficiency, and equity dominate the industry, and Americans are generally not satisfied with their healthcare system. Mirmirani argues that the restructuring of the healthcare industry is a reflection of overall changes that are occurring in the economy. As in other industries, the main issue confronting the healthcare market is the declining competition among providers of services. This is prompted by the rapid growth of managed-care systems. He argues that the potential outcome of the managed-care market might be fewer choices for consumers and initially a slower growth of cost inflation due to economies of scale. Furthermore, he points out that the problem of "class division" in American society will be further exacerbated by the current restructuring whereby low-income individuals will have less access and perhaps receive lower quality services than their more prosperous counterparts. See his "Restructuring the Health-Care System and Its Broad Implications for the United States," pp. 339–345 in Gregg Lee Carter (ed.), *Perspectives on Current Social Problems* (Boston: Allyn & Bacon, 1997).

In another essay in *Perspectives on Current Social Problems* ("HIV/AIDS as a Social Problem," pp. 349–358), Joseph J. Lengermann and Roberta B. Hollander observe that HIV/AIDS is a significant social problem, one that forces us to reconsider what we know, what we believe and how we behave. They present a sociological understanding of HIV/AIDS, focusing on the cultural, legal, political and ethical issues surrounding the disease and its virus. In particular, they focus on the experiences of those infected in the workplaces, and the discrimination they face — both potential and actual.

Relevant World Wide Web Sites

The General Social Survey contains many items relevant to health, as well as individual attitudes and behaviors regarding AIDS (www.icpsr.umich.edu/gss); also see the other public opinion data repositories cited at the end of Chapter 1. The HIV/AIDS Treatment Information Service web site is another important source of data and reports on AIDS (www.hivatis.org), as is the Cable News Network (www.cnn.com/health/aids).

Both the U.S. government and the United Nations maintain a plethora of on-line reports and data files on U.S. and cross-national health matters, in general, and on AIDS, in particular. Most importantly, see:

Centers for Disease Control	**www.cdc.gov**
United Nations Programme on HIV/AIDS	**www.unaids.org**
World Health Organization	**www.who.org**

Exploratory exercises for the *Health95* and *AIDS98* data files have been included with those for Chapter 11; see p. 259.

Chapter 10. Education Issues

Predicting Minority Success in School—Individual and Contextual Factors

As demonstrated Chapter 4 of this workbook, African Americans and Latinos have, on average, significantly lower levels of educational attainment compared to their white counterparts. For example, more than 8 in 10 white adult Americans has a high school diploma, compared to 7 in 10 for black adults and about 5 in 10 for their Latino counterparts. Looking at the current generation of adolescents, the dropout rate for white, non-Hispanic students is 8 percent, while it is 13 percent for black students and 25 percent for Latinos.[1] Deficiencies in high school generate more of the same at the college level, where for the current generation of young adults (ages 25–29), we find 34 percent of whites with a college education, but only 17 percent of blacks, and only 16 percent of Latinos.

As you also discovered in Chapter 4, differences in educational attainment go a long way in explaining differences in the incomes of blacks, whites, Latinos, and Asians in contemporary American society. On the face of it, reducing educational differences among different race/ethnic groups seems a quicker route to solving the "race problem" (discrimination and the inequalities in material, social, and psychological well-being stemming from it) than trying to transform the minds of people (reduce their prejudices and willingness to discriminate). The question then becomes how is this best done? More particularly, how can we raise the educational attainment of the minority populations in American society to be at least on par with that of whites? Until recently, the strategy has been to try to reduce school segregation—that is, to try to get public schools to be more racially and ethnically integrated. Because of the pervasiveness of residential segregation, the basic strategy used in the 1970s, 80s, and 90s was to try to obtain this goal via busing. However, two sets of unintended consequences resulted: First, "white flight" thwarted the achievement of integrated schools—rather than accept integration and busing, many white families either moved to racially homogeneous (all-white) suburbs, or removed their children from public schools and enrolled them in private ones; and whether public or religious, these schools also tend to be more racially homogeneous. Secondly, many studies have found "that such factors as unequal socioeconomic status, widely divergent family backgrounds, racial tensions in the schools, and competitive classroom environments among academically mismatched students have worked against any significant gains" from desegregation.[2]

As a result, many frustrated minority parents now favor minority-only schools as offering a better atmosphere and role models to meet their children's needs. They contend that the money spent on desegregation would be better spent on increased funding of the traditionally under-financed minority schools."[3] Although this new mindset worries many educators—who see it as an updated version of the racist "separate but equal" doctrine, and as denying both white and minority students the opportunity to learn to "live together"—it is the wave of the future. Indeed, an even more radical version of this wave is not only to allow segregation by race/ethnicity, but also—simultaneously—by gender. In short, to promote the concept of single-sex, minority schools. Sociology of education specialist Cornelius Riordan contends that there are two strong rationales supporting this concept: First, the values underlying "youth culture" are diminished in single-sex schools. This subculture centers on athletics, social life, physical attractiveness, heterosexual popularity, soap operas, rock concerts, and negative attitudes toward schoolwork. "Black and Hispanic

---

[1] See *Digest of Education Statistics, 1998* (Washington, D.C.: National Center for Education Statistics, U. S. Department of Education, 1999),Table 105, p. 124. The World Wide Web site for the National Center for Education Statistics is the best single source of current and historical data on educational attainment, both for the U.S. and cross-nationally (www.nces.ed.gov).

[2] Vincent N. Parrillo, John Stimson, and Ardyth Stimson, *Contemporary Social Problems* 4th ed. (Boston: Allyn & Bacon, 1999), p. 169.

[3] *Ibid.*, p. 169.

youth in particular are subject to the most intense forms of anti-academic [youth] culture. In predominantly Black and Hispanic schools across the country, students who aspire to succeed academically are harassed by their peers and they come to experience the fear of 'acting white.'" Second, single-sex schools provide more successful same-sex role models. "In terms of academic outcomes, single-sex schools may be particularly advantageous for girls and minority males since the top students in all subjects and all extracurricular activities will be of their own gender."[4]

Whether single-sex, predominantly minority schools are better or worse for minority students is an empirical question. We need to examine the data and see where they lead us. The CHIP data file *HSB82a* will allow you to do such an examination.

File: **HSB82a** (High School & Beyond Study, 1982 Follow-up, Black sophomores only)[5]

Info: Region→Sex→SES→Family→RaceSchl→SexSchl→ReligSchl→DropoutSchl→Performance
(4)　　(2)　(3)　(2)　　(2)　　　(3)　　　(3)　　　　(3)　　　　(3)

Region	Northeast (CT, ME, MA, NH, NJ, NY, PA, RI, and VT)
	Midwest (IL, IN, IA, KS, MI, MN, MO, NE, ND, OH, SD, and WI)
	South (AL, AR, DE, FL, GA, KY, LS, MD, MS, NC, OK, SC, TN, TX, VA, and WV)
	West (AK, AZ, CA, CO, HI, ID, MT, NV, NM, OR, UT, WA, and WY)
Sex	Male, Female
SES	("Socio-Economic Status" — based on a composite measure of the student's parents' level of education, income, and occupational prestige) Low, Middle, High
Family	(Is the student's family intact? That is, are both his/her mother and father present in the household?) No, Yes
RaceSchl	(Racial composition of the student's school — based on what percentage of the student population is African American) <50%, 50%+
SexSchl	(Gender composition of the student's school) All-Boy, All-Girl, Coed
ReligSchl	(Religious composition of the student's school) Public, Catholic, Other
DropoutSchl	(Dropout rate of the student's school) <5%, 5–14%, 15%+
Performance	(Academic performance, as measured by the student's combined scores on standardized math and reading tests; divided into bottom, middle, and top one-thirds) Bottom1/3, Mid1/3, Top1/3

Basic

1. One reason why African American and Latino students tend to have lower academic achievement than their white and Asian counterparts is because of the correlations among race, ethnicity, and social class in the United States. More specifically, African American and Latino students are more likely to be poor, and students from poor families tend to perform less well in school. Test the fundamental notion that socioeconomic status and academic performance are positively correlated — regardless of racial or ethnic background — by crosstabulating Performance (Y) by SES (X); also examine the relationship graphically (after doing the **CrossTab**, select the **Line** alternative for the **Plot** option under the **Table** command and highlight the "Top1/3" category). Did you find the expected relationship?

---

[4]Cornelius Riordan, "Minority Success and Single-Gender Schools," pp. 175–193 in Gregg Lee Carter (ed.), *Perspectives on Current Social Problems* (Boston: Allyn & Bacon, 1997).

[5] The High School and Beyond 1982 Follow-up data set is one of the most important in the sociology of education field. It was gathered by the National Opinion Research Center on behalf of the National Center for Education Statistics: 36 seniors and 36 sophomores per school were randomly chosen from each of a probability sample of 1,122 high schools. Data on a large number of student and school variables were collected — representing a broad range of topics, e.g., family background, race, ethnicity, the kind of school being attended, and so on.

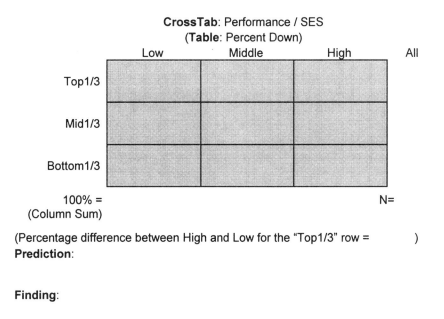

(Percentage difference between High and Low for the "Top1/3" row =)
Prediction:

Finding:

2. Another reason why African American and Latino students tend to have lower academic achievement than their white and Asian counterparts is because of the correlations among race, ethnicity, and family structure in the United States. More specifically, African American and Latino students are more likely to live in families that have been affected by divorce, separation, desertion, and widowhood. But students from intact families (both parents present) tend to perform better in school: Many single-parent families face challenges that make successful parenting more difficult—including quite often a scarcity of parental resources such as time, money, and the emotional strength to deal with psychological stress. Test the fundamental notion that family structure and academic performance are correlated by crosstabulating Performance (Y) by Family (X). Did you find the expected relationship?

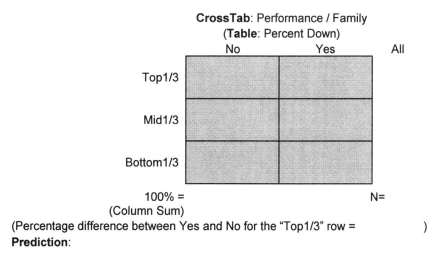

(Percentage difference between Yes and No for the "Top1/3" row =)
Prediction:

Finding:

3. A fundamental precept of the social sciences is that individuals with the same personal characteristics behave and think differently when exposed to different social situations; this precept is given the label "contextual effects." For students from low-income families, perhaps the degree to which their poor backgrounds influences their academic achievement depends upon the social context of the school that they are attending. Let's test this notion out by recalculating the percentages in #1 above, but this time taking into account whether the school is Catholic versus public. The important issue is not religion per se, but the assumption that Catholic schools are more likely to be socially organized in ways that encourage academic achievement—regardless of a student's social class origins. More specifically, Catholic high schools are much more likely to be college preparatory (versus being "vocational" or "general") and much more likely to have a high level of discipline. Thus, we are testing the notion that poorer students respond differently in different educational environments. When they are exposed to college-oriented, disciplined academic environments, their family backgrounds become less important in determining their academic achievement. Test this hypothesis by cross-tabulating Performance (Y) by SES (X), controlling for ReligSchl (Z)—focusing your attention on the "Public" and "Catholic" partial tables. Discuss what you actually found—is a "contextual effect" evident? Refer to the correct percentage-differences to support your answer.

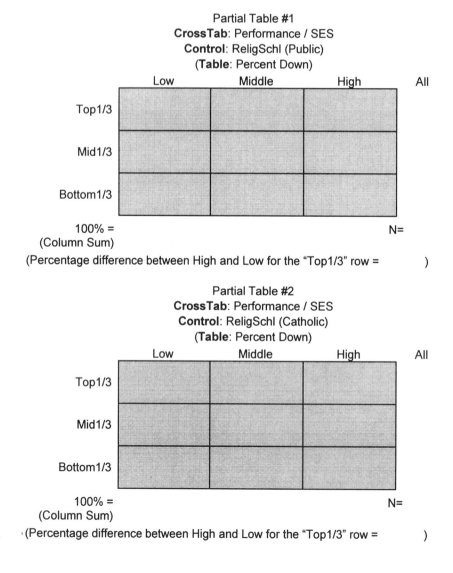

Partial Table #1
CrossTab: Performance / SES
Control: ReligSchl (Public)
(**Table**: Percent Down)

	Low	Middle	High	All
Top1/3				
Mid1/3				
Bottom1/3				
100% = (Column Sum)				N=

(Percentage difference between High and Low for the "Top1/3" row =   )

Partial Table #2
CrossTab: Performance / SES
Control: ReligSchl (Catholic)
(**Table**: Percent Down)

	Low	Middle	High	All
Top1/3				
Mid1/3				
Bottom1/3				
100% = (Column Sum)				N=

(Percentage difference between High and Low for the "Top1/3" row =   )

Answer/Discussion

4. Let us test the somewhat extreme idea developed in the introduction to this chapter that minority students perform better when they attend single-sex schools. Let's do the analysis first for boys, then repeat it for girls.

   (a) Use the **Modify** command to **Omit** the "Female" category of Sex; then to **Omit** the "All-Girl" category of SexSchl. Verify that you have done your modifications correctly by executing an **Info** command: you should see the number of categories for Sex having been reduced from 2 to 1; the number of categories for SexSchl from 3 to 2; and the new (reduced) sample size of 1,194.

   (b) Then crosstabulate Performance (Y) by SexSchl (X). What did you find?

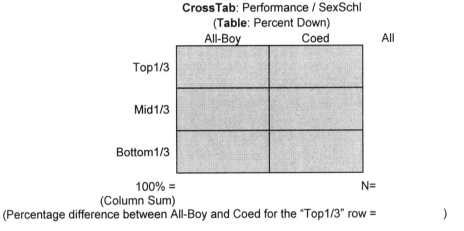

CrossTab: Performance / SexSchl
(Table: Percent Down)
(Percentage difference between All-Boy and Coed for the "Top1/3" row =)

   (c) Next, re-**Open** the *HSB82a* data file, and use the **Modify** command to **Omit** the "Male" category of Sex; then to **Omit** the "All-Boy" category of SexSchl. Verify that you have done your modifications correctly by executing an Info command: you should see the number of categories for Sex having been reduced from 2 to 1; the number of categories for SexSchl from 3 to 2; and the new (reduced) sample size of 1,570.

   (d) Then crosstabulate Performance (Y) by SexSchl (X). What did you find?

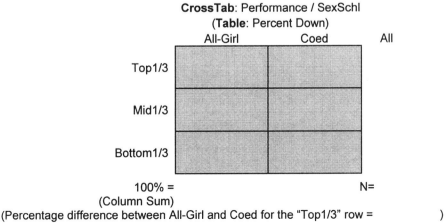

CrossTab: Performance / SexSchl
(Table: Percent Down)
(Percentage difference between All-Girl and Coed for the "Top1/3" row =)

Answer/Discussion

Suggestions for Further Study

Two important articles cited in this chapter are reprinted in Gregg Lee Carter (ed.), *Perspectives on Current Social Problems* (Boston: Allyn & Bacon, 1997). Michael Fraleigh's article on "Single-Parent Families, Blended Families, and the Academic Achievement of Adolescents"—which demonstrates that children in two-parent homes do better than their counterparts in single-parent homes—is summarized at the end of Chapter 8 in this workbook. The second article, Cornelius Riordan's "Minority Success and Single-Gender Schools" (pp. 175–193 in *Perspectives on Current Social Problems*), contains an extensive analysis of the High School and Beyond data set used in this chapter. Riordan finds that single-sex schools have mixed consequences, but that the preponderance of evidence favors the idea that minority students of both sexes—as well as white females—do better in single-sex environments. However, whether we should encourage such schools is still a hotly debated question: Proponents of single-sex schools for minority students argue that they provide needed discipline and adult role models. But critics respond that such schools are in violation of the law and smack of the racism of segregated schools in pre-1965 America.

Relevant World Wide Web Sites

The National Center for Education Statistics is the best single source for education-related data at all levels of analysis—the individual, school, city, state, U.S., and crossnational: www.nces.ed.gov. The United Nations maintains an important database on crossnational differences in educational attainment; see, especially, www.un.org/Depts/unsd/social/education.htm. Other organizations maintaining web sites with important reports and data files relating to education include:

National Education Association	www.nea.org
American Federation of Teachers	www.aft.org
National Parent Teachers Association	www.pta.org

Exploratory exercises for the *HSB82a* data file have been included with those for Chapter 11; see p. 259.

Chapter 11. Environmental Issues

The Correlates of Environmental Destruction: Crossnational Findings

Both developed and developing countries are currently contributing to the destruction of the natural environment—though in different ways. In their quest for development and to exploit their natural resources to sell in the world market and thereby acquire wealth, developing nations are destroying their forests. Indeed, the tropical rain forests of the Caribbean, West Africa, Southeast Asia, and Latin America "are being destroyed at the rate of one and a half acres a second, night and day, every day, all year round." This massive destruction is encouraged by lumber and mining companies in league with those in control of the national governments. Many of these companies are U.S.-based multinationals such as Georgia-Pacific, Weyerhaeuser, Alcoa, Amoco, Arco, Chevron, Exxon, Freeport McMoRan, Maxus Energy, Mobil, Occidental, Oryx, Texaco, Texas Crude, Unocal, Castle & Cooke, Chiquita, Kimberly-Clark and Hawaiian Electric—to list but a small portion. In general, the local populations support deforestation, as it provides cleared land for farming and ranching, as well as scrap timber for firewood used for cooking and heating.

A major environmental consequence of this deforestation is the changing of the climate. "The climate is affected in several related ways. As hundreds of thousands of forest acres are destroyed, rain patterns, change. Huge areas once covered with plants, which give off moisture, are replaced by exposed, sandy soils. Also, the massive burning required to clear the land creates clouds of smoke that block the sun and lead to weather change. Thus, lush, green areas often become near-deserts. The tropical forest in Brazil (the world's largest) has so much rainfall that it provides 20 percent of the earth's fresh water supply. What will be the long-range effects as this water supply dwindles? Just as important, forests absorb huge quantities of carbon dioxide through photosynthesis. Thus, as forests are diminished so, too, is the earth's capacity to absorb the gas most responsible for global warming. This diminished capacity to process carbon dioxide, changing it into oxygen, leads to changes in the climate and to desertification."

The automobiles and industrial plants in the semi- and fully-developed nations of the world create massive quantities of CO_2 (carbon dioxide) that, along with the destruction of the tropical forests, contributes to the "greenhouse effect." The phenomenon occurs when harmful gases—such as CO_2—"accumulate in the atmosphere and act like the glass roof of a green house. Sunlight reaches the earth's surface, and the gases trap the heat radiating from the ground." The results "are a warming of the earth, the melting of the polar ice caps, a significant changing of climate, mega-storms, and the rapid spread of tropical disease such as malaria, dengue fever, cholera, and encephalitis." The earth is now the warmest it has been the past 6,000 years.[1]

In short, two major environmental issues facing the world today are air pollution and deforestation. The CHIP data file *Pollut98* allows you to explore some of the predictors of these phenomena, using crossnational comparisons of economic development, urbanization, industrialization, and occupational structure.

---

[1]See D. Stanley Eitzen and Maxine Baca Zinn, *Social Problems* 8th ed. (Boston: Allyn & Bacon, 2000), pp. 87–91; compare Daniel J. Curran and Claire M. Renzetti, *Social Problems: Society in Crisis*, 5th ed. (Boston: Allyn & Bacon, 2000), pp. 365–366; and Vincent N. Parrillo, John Stimson, and Ardyth Stimson, *Contemporary Social Problems*, 4th ed. (Boston: Allyn & Bacon, 1999), pp. 432–434.

File: **Pollut98** (Cross-national data on the environment, late 1990s)[2]

Info: Region→Pop→Farmers→Births→GNP→Urban→Electric→CO2→Deforest
    (6)   (3)   (3)   (3)   (3)   (3)   (3)   (2)   (2)

(Note: Pop—Electric are divided into three categories: bottom, middle, and top third.)

Region	(United Nations regional designation) Industrial, East-Europe, Africa-SubSaharan, Arab, Asia, Latin-America
Pop	(Population size, in millions) <5.9m, 5.9–24m, >24m
Farmers	(Percentage of the workforce in agriculture) <15%, 15–40%, >40%
Births	(Birth rate—births per 1,000 population) <16, 16–29, >29
GNP	(Per capita GNP in 1997 U.S. dollars) <$1,000; $1,000–$3,200; >$3,200
Urban	(Percent urban) <50%, 50–73%, >73%
Electric	(Kilowatt hours per capita) <900kw; 900–3,200kw; >3,200kw
CO2	(Per capita carbon dioxide emissions, in metric tons; this is a key measure of air pollution) Low (<3.2), High (>3.2)
Deforest	(Serious deforestation occurring on a regular basis?) No, Yes

Country	Pop	Farmers	Birth Rate	GNP	Urban	Electric	CO2	Deforest*
Albania	3,282	49.5	23.1	360	37.9	1,801	0.6	0.0
Algeria	29,006	22.0	30.4	1,690	57.2	708	3.3	1.2
Angola	11,469	85.0	47.2	260	32.3	169	0.4	1.0
Argentina	34,684	12.0	19.8	8,060	88.6	2,076	3.7	0.3
Armenia	3,768	38.0	13.7	670	69.1	1,708	1.0	−2.7
Australia	18,342	5.0	14.4	17,980	84.6	9,820	17.0	0.0
Austria	8,077	8.1	11.0	24,950	64.4	6,882	7.3	0.0
Azerbaijan	7,559	32.0	21.4	500	56.3	2,308	4.0	0.0
Belarus	10,297	19.0	9.8	2,160	72.5	3,119	6.0	−1.0
Belize	215	30.0	38.1	2,550	46.4	808	1.6	0.3
Brazil	160,523	31.0	24.6	3,370	79.6	2,026	1.7	0.5
Cameroon	13,609	74.4	40.7	680	46.4	203	0.3	0.6
Canada	29,965	3.0	13.2	19,570	76.8	20,904	13.8	−0.1
Cen.Afr.Rep.	3,274	85.0	41.5	370	39.9	31	0.1	0.4
Chile	14,470	19.2	21.0	3,560	84.2	2,169	3.4	0.4
China	1,217,616	50.0	17.1	530	31.9	891	2.8	0.1
Colombia	37,999	30.0	26.8	1,620	73.6	1,228	1.8	0.5
Costa Rica	3,574	21.6	26.2	2,380	50.3	1,428	1.4	3.1
Cuba	11,007	20.0	14.0	2,000	76.7	1,201	2.8	1.2
Denmark	5,245	5.0	13.4	28,110	85.4	7,510	10.8	0.0
Domini. Rep.	8,089	50.0	28.6	1,320	63.3	860	1.6	1.6
Ecuador	11,662	29.0	28.9	1,310	60.4	792	2.1	1.6
Egypt	63,693	40.0	29.5	710	45.1	801	1.5	0.0
El Salvador	5,904	40.0	32.1	1,480	45.6	599	0.7	3.3
Estonia	1,470	11.0	9.5	2,820	73.5	5,604	11.2	−1.0
Fiji	811	67.0	25.1	2,320	41.2	684	1.0	0.4
Finland	5,127	8.6	12.7	18,850	63.9	15,515	11.6	0.1
France	58,426	5.0	12.2	23,470	75.0	7,508	6.2	−1.1

[2] *Sources*: Central Intelligence Agency, *The World Factbook 1999* (Dulles, VA.: Brassey's Inc., 1999); United Nations, *Human Development Report 1999* (NY: Oxford University Press, 1999).

Country	Pop	Farmers	Birth Rate	GNP	Urban	Electric	CO2	Deforest*
Georgia	5,376	25.0	10.7	580	59.3	1,344	0.6	0.0
Germany	81,694	2.7	9.3	25,580	86.9	6,605	10.5	0.0
Ghana	17,972	61.0	41.7	430	36.8	326	0.2	1.3
Greece	10,492	19.8	9.8	7,710	59.3	4,632	7.7	−2.3
Guatemala	9,858	58.0	36.0	1,190	39.4	320	0.6	2.0
Haiti	7,269	66.0	35.3	220	33.0	87	0.2	3.5
Honduras	5,605	37.0	33.8	580	45.0	485	0.7	2.3
Hungary	10,197	8.3	10.8	3,840	65.5	3,624	6.0	−0.5
Iceland	270	5.1	16.7	24,590	91.9	18,934	8.1	0.0
India	949,592	67.0	28.5	310	27.4	459	1.1	0.0
Indonesia	201,425	41.0	24.1	880	37.4	368	1.2	1.0
Iran	63,101	33.0	36.1	1,780	60.0	1,180	3.8	1.8
Iraq	21,422	30.0	44.1	1,940	75.5	1,439	4.4	0.0
Ireland	3,588	10.0	13.4	13,630	57.9	5,358	9.8	−2.6
Israel	5,819	2.6	21.1	14,410	90.9	5,678	9.3	0.0
Italy	57,339	7.0	9.3	19,270	66.7	4,870	7.1	−0.1
Jamaica	2,594	22.5	23.7	1,420	54.7	2,424	4.0	7.5
Japan	125,792	6.0	9.6	34,630	78.4	8,074	9.3	0.1
Jordan	4,232	7.4	32.0	1,390	72.6	1,085	2.5	2.5
Kazakhstan	16,460	23.0	18.0	1,110	60.4	3,894	10.4	−1.9
Kenya	28,176	80.0	40.4	260	30.4	141	0.3	0.3
Kyrgyzstan	4,579	40.0	24.6	610	39.2	2,551	1.4	0.0
Latvia	2,476	16.0	8.5	2,290	73.4	2,536	3.7	−0.9
Lebanon	3,776	7.0	25.2	3,350	88.5	1,879	4.6	8.1
Lithuania	3,708	20.0	11.5	1,350	73.1	3,120	3.7	−0.6
Mauritania	2,333	47.0	39.1	480	54.0	66	1.3	0.0
Mauritius	1,129	14.0	19.6	3,180	40.7	1,112	1.5	0.0
Mexico	94,843	21.8	27.1	4,010	73.8	1,754	3.7	0.9
Moldova	4,329	40.2	14.3	870	53.1	1,739	2.7	0.0
Morocco	27,563	50.0	28.6	1,150	53.3	490	1.0	0.3
Mozambique	16,537	80.0	45.2	80	36.5	66	0.1	0.7
Nepal	23,226	81.0	38.6	200	10.9	56	0.1	1.1
Netherlands	15,545	4.0	12.7	21,970	89.1	6,143	10.0	0.0
New Zealand	3,602	9.8	16.2	13,190	86.3	9,976	8.3	−0.6
Nicaragua	4,584	31.0	33.4	330	63.2	454	0.7	2.5
Nigeria	103,912	54.0	43.1	280	41.3	129	0.7	0.9
Norway	4,384	6.0	13.8	26,480	73.6	23,830	15.4	−0.3
Pakistan	133,516	47.0	39.0	440	35.4	407	0.7	2.9
Panama	2,655	26.8	21.7	2,670	56.5	1,486	2.5	2.2
Peru	24,041	17.0	28.5	1,890	71.6	837	1.1	0.3
Philippines	71,974	39.8	29.7	960	56.0	502	0.9	3.5
Poland	38,639	26.0	11.5	2,470	64.4	3,541	9.3	−0.1
Portugal	9,942	12.0	10.6	9,370	36.5	3,532	4.9	−0.9
Russia	147,700	20.0	9.3	2,650	76.6	5,588	10.7	0.0
Saudi Arabia	19,354	5.0	36.1	7,240	84.1	5,528	14.2	0.8
Seychelles	75	10.0	23.4	6,210	56.1	1,730	2.3	0.0
Singapore	3,045	11.4	16.0	23,360	100.0	6,932	19.5	0.0
South Africa	44,485	30.0	31.0	3,010	49.7	3,888	6.9	0.2
South Korea	45,253	21.0	15.2	8,220	83.5	5,022	9.0	0.2
Spain	39,250	8.0	9.2	13,280	76.9	4,368	5.9	0.0
Sri Lanka	18,396	37.0	19.9	640	22.6	241	0.4	3.2
Sudan	28,855	80.0	42.2	290	33.3	49	0.1	0.8

Country	Pop	Farmers	Birth Rate	GNP	Urban	Electric	CO2	Deforest*
Switzerland	7,101	4.0	11.9	37,180	61.6	7,734	6.1	0.0
Syria	15,609	40.0	43.9	1,120	53.1	1,186	3.1	2.2
Tajikistan	5,935	52.0	28.2	350	32.4	2,581	1.0	0.0
Thailand	60,657	54.0	20.2	2,210	20.6	1,570	3.5	2.6
Trin.& Tobago	1,272	9.5	18.3	3,740	72.7	3,501	17.2	1.6
Tunisia	9,163	22.0	22.5	1,800	63.4	857	1.8	0.5
Turkey	63,898	42.5	22.8	2,450	71.9	1,468	2.9	0.0
Turkmenistan	4,624	44.0	32.0	640	45.0	1,757	8.3	0.0
Ukraine	51,148	24.0	10.0	1,570	71.1	3,482	7.7	−0.1
Un. Kingdom	58,764	1.1	12.7	18,410	89.3	6,249	9.5	−0.5
United States	265,182	2.7	14.9	25,860	76.6	12,977	19.7	−0.3
Uruguay	3,186	11.0	17.9	4,650	90.7	2,041	1.8	0.0
Uzbekistan	23,188	44.0	29.4	950	41.6	2,004	4.1	−2.6
Venezuela	22,311	13.0	25.6	2,760	86.5	3,251	6.5	1.1
Vietnam	76,580	65.0	30.0	190	19.5	217	10.8	1.4
Yemen	14,661	92.0	52.6	280	35.3	70	1.1	0.0
Zimbabwe	11,515	74.0	34.5	490	33.2	961	1.6	0.6

*Annual rate of deforestation (%)

Basic

1. Test the fundamental notion that the developing and developed regions of the worlds both have serious problems of environmental pollution, but of different types:

(a) Crosstabulate CO2 (Y) by GNP (X); also examine the relationship graphically (after doing the Cross-Tab, select the **Line** alternative for the **Plot** option under the **Table** command and highlight the "High" category). Did you find the expected relationship?

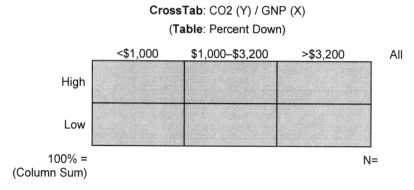

CrossTab: CO2 (Y) / GNP (X)
(**Table**: Percent Down)

(Percentage difference between >$3,200 and <$1,000 for the "High" row =   )
Prediction:

Finding:

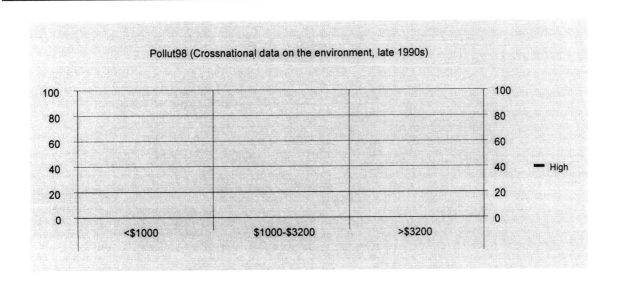

Pollut98 (Crossnational data on the environment, late 1990s)

(b) Crosstabulate Deforest (Y) by GNP (X); also examine the relationship graphically (after doing the **CrossTab**, select the **Line** alternative for the **Plot** option under the **Table** command and highlight the "Yes" category). Did you find the expected relationship?

CrossTab: Deforest (Y) / GNP (X)
(**Table**: Percent Down)

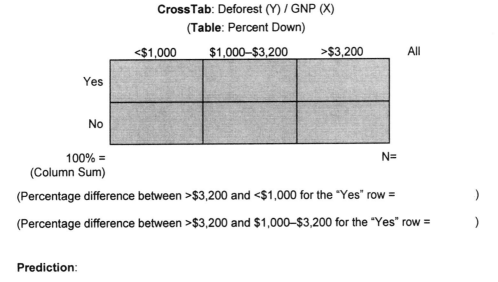

(Percentage difference between >$3,200 and <$1,000 for the "Yes" row =   )

(Percentage difference between >$3,200 and $1,000–$3,200 for the "Yes" row =   )

Prediction:

Findings:

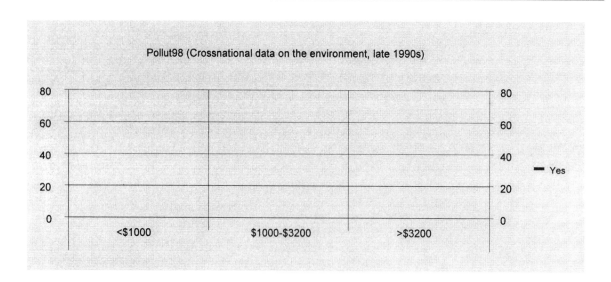

Pollut98 (Crossnational data on the environment, late 1990s)

2. In developing nations with large tracts of tropical rain forest, government policy encourages lumber and mining companies to "build roads to extract their products and transport them to market." Furthermore, governments encourage their "poor people to settle in these regions by building roads and offering land to settlers, who must clear it for farming."[3] Test the idea that nations with large proportions of their population involved in agriculture have strong tendencies toward deforestation by crosstabulating Deforest (Y) by Farmers (X); also examine the relationship graphically (after doing the **CrossTab**, select the **Line** alternative for the **Plot** option under the **Table** command and highlight the "Yes" category). What did you find?

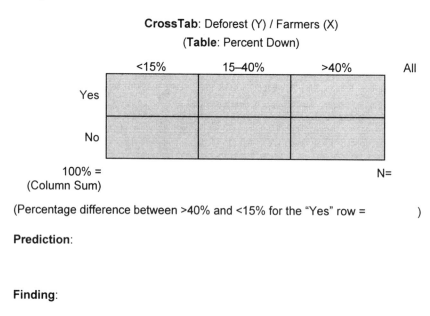

CrossTab: Deforest (Y) / Farmers (X)
(**Table**: Percent Down)

(Percentage difference between >40% and <15% for the "Yes" row =   )

Prediction:

Finding:

---

[3] Eitzen and Zinn, pp. 89–90.

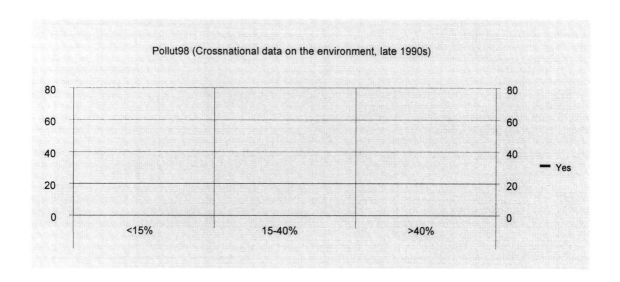

Pollut98 (Crossnational data on the environment, late 1990s)

3. In developed nations, carbon dioxide and other emissions from electrical and industrial plants are a major source of air pollution. Such plants release billions of pounds of pollutants annually, posing great risk to human health.[4] Test the idea that nations with large electrical/industrial output generate the heaviest amounts of air pollution by crosstabulating CO2 (Y) by Electric (X); also examine the relationship graphically (after doing the **CrossTab**, select the **Line** alternative for the **Plot** option under the **Table** command and highlight the "High" category). What did you find?

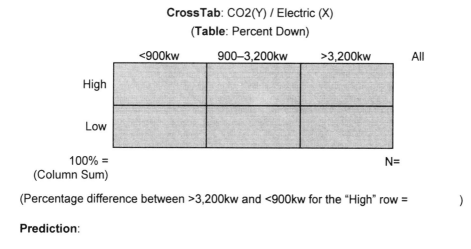

CrossTab: CO2(Y) / Electric (X)
(**Table**: Percent Down)

(Percentage difference between >3,200kw and <900kw for the "High" row =   )

Prediction:

Finding:

---

[4] Eitzen and Zinn, pp. 89–90.

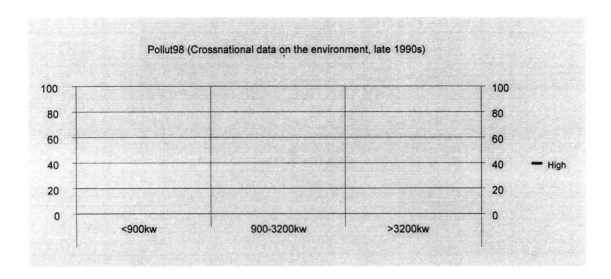

Suggestions for Further Study

"Hunger, Malnutrition and Food Supplies: The World Situation in the 1990s" is a United Nations report reprinted in Gregg Lee Carter (ed.), *Perspectives on Current Social Problems* (Boston: Allyn & Bacon, 1997, pp. 359–368). The report reveals that many millions of people in the world go hungry. In recent years, the nutritional situation has shown signs of improvement in Asia, long-term deterioration in Africa, and stagnation or some worsening in Latin America. In the face of such starvation, "saving the rain forest" — for whatever reasons — is an idea that many developing nations are presently slow to embrace.

Relevant World Wide Web Sites

The U.S. Environmental Protection Agency has a large number of studies and large amounts of U.S. and international data relevant to environmental destruction and pollution (www.epa.gov), as does the United Nations (www.un.org). Other important web sites containing such reports and data are those maintained by nature groups. Although you should be wary of their strong "environmentalism" — and how this can tint their presentation of findings — they still are well worth consulting. Most importantly, see:

The Sierra Club	www.sierraclub.org
The Audubon Society	www.audubon.org
Earth First!	www.enviroweb.org
The Nature Conservancy	www.tnc.org

Exploratory

I.   Using any of the CHIP data files for this or the preceding two chapters (*Health95*, *AIDS98*, *HSB82a*, or *Pollut98*), state a hypothesis relating an X and a Y variable that have not already been analyzed together.

II. Sketch the bivariate model.

III. Give a brief interpretation of your hypothesis — that is, describe what is going on in the world such that we would expect to find data patterned in the way in which you have predicted.

IV. (a) Test your hypothesis with a **CrossTab**, putting your Y variable on the rows. Was your hypothesis confirmed? (Note: you may need to delete three columns; the following 3x6 table shell is simply a starting point.)

Original Table

CrossTab: _____(Y) /_____ (X)

(**Table**: Percent Down)

All

100% =   N=
(Column Sum)

(Percentage difference between the highest and lowest values of X on the highest value of Y =   )

Prediction:

Finding:

(b) Use **Plot** under the **Table** option to display the above relationship graphically. Feel free to be creative—trying out each of the plot types (line, bar, pie, stacked). Print out and attach the plot that you think best captures the relationship between your X and Y.

> ### Do *either* parts V–VIII *or* parts IX–XII below.

V. Perhaps the relationship you uncovered in #IV is spurious; that is, perhaps a third variable is predictive of both X and Y; if this is so, then the relationship between X and Y would exist **not** because X is causing Y, but simply because of their covariation with this third variable. If this third variable is held constant, then the relationship between X and Y will weaken greatly or disappear. Choose a third variable that might possibly be generating a spurious relationship between X and Y. Sketch the model showing the relationship between this third variable and X, and between this third variable and Y, as well as the lack of causal relationship between X and Y. Hint: refer back to the discussion on page 25 in the introductory chapter entitled "Elementary Data Analysis Tools Needed to Study Social Issues."

VI. A good social scientist does not choose just any variable to test for spuriosity. Just as you were able to defend the hypothesized relationship between X and Y in #III, develop a brief interpretation to defend the hypothesized relationship between Z and X, then between Z and Y.

(a) Interpretation of the Z–X relationship:

(b) Interpretation of the Z–Y relationship:

VII. Test the alternative model sketched in #V by crosstabbing Y by X and controlling for Z—using the appended table shells. (Note: you may need only 3 columns in each of these shells; also, you may not need all 6 of the partial tables provided; of course, you will need one partial table for each value of Z.)

VIII. What are your conclusions? For example, is the original X–Y relationship spurious? Is it nonspurious (i.e., causal)? Is a multivariable model evident?

IX. Examining all the variables in your data set, which one do you think might be serving as a causal mechanism connecting your X with your Y? In other words, which variable would you choose as "Z" in the following sketch: X→Z→Y? Hint: refer back to the discussion on page 26 in the introductory chapter entitled "Elementary Data Analysis Tools Needed to Study Social Issues."

X. A good social scientist does not choose just any variable to test as a causal mechanism (intervening variable). Just as you were able to defend the hypothesized relationship between X and Y in #III, develop a brief interpretation to defend the hypothesized relationship between X and Z, then between Z and Y.

   (a) Interpretation of the X–Z relationship:

   (b) Interpretation of the Z–Y relationship:

XI. Test the alternative model sketched in #IX by crosstabbing X and Y and controlling for Z—using the appended table shells. (Note: you may need only 3 columns in each of these shells; also, you may not need all 6 of the partial tables provided; of course, you will need one partial table for each value of Z.)

XII. What are your conclusions? Most importantly, do your findings support the notion that your Z is acting as an intervening variable (causal mechanism) connecting your X and your Y?

Partial Table #1

Cross Tab: _____ (Y) / _____ (X)

Control: _____ (Z value)

(Table: Percent Down)

				All

N=

100% = _____
(Column Sum)
(Percentage difference between the highest and lowest values of X on the highest value of Y = _____)

Partial Table #2

Cross Tab: _____ (Y) / _____ (X)

Control: _____ (Z value)

(Table: Percent Down)

				All

N=

100% = _____
(Column Sum)
(Percentage difference between the highest and lowest values of X on the highest value of Y = _____)

Partial Table #3

Cross Tab: _____ (Y) / _____ (X)

Control: _____ (Z value)

(Table: Percent Down)

				All

N=

100% = _____
(Column Sum)
(Percentage difference between the highest and lowest values of X on the highest value of Y = _____)

Partial Table #4

Cross Tab: _____ (Y) / _____ (X)

Control: _____ (Z value)

(Table: Percent Down)

				All

N=

100% = _____
(Column Sum)
(Percentage difference between the highest and lowest values of X on the highest value of Y = _____)

Partial Table #5

Cross Tab: _____ (Y) / _____ (X)

Control: _____ (Z value)

(Table: Percent Down)

				All

N=

100% = _____
(Column Sum)
(Percentage difference between the highest and lowest values of X on the highest value of Y = _____)

Partial Table #6

Cross Tab: _____ (Y) / _____ (X)

Control: _____ (Z value)

(Table: Percent Down)

				All

N=

100% = _____
(Column Sum)
(Percentage difference between the highest and lowest values of X on the highest value of Y = _____)

About the Author

Gregg Lee Carter is Professor of Sociology at Bryant College in Smithfield, Rhode Island. He is a graduate of the University of Nevada at Las Vegas. He earned his M.A., M.Phil., and Ph.D. degrees at Columbia University in New York City. His research articles on contemporary social issues have appeared in more than a dozen scholarly journals. He is the author of *Doing Sociology with Student CHIP: Data Happy!* (Allyn & Bacon, 1995, 1998, 2001), *Empirical Approaches to Sociology* (Allyn &  Bacon, 1994, 1998, 2001), *How to Manage Conflict in the Organization* (with Joseph F. Byrnes; American Management Association, 1994), *Learning Research Methods with SPSS* (Harcourt Brace, 2001), *Perspectives on Current Social Problems* (Allyn & Bacon, 1997), *The Gun Control Movement* (Prentice Hall International and Twayne Publishers, 1997), and *Working Women in America: Split Dreams* (with Sharlene Hesse-Biber; Oxford University Press, 2000). Professor Carter is past President of the New England Sociological Association and a former associate editor of *Teaching Sociology*. His personal web page can be found at http://www.bryant.edu/~gcarter.